INDIA
IN THE
CARIBBEAN

G000126108

Edited: Dr David Dabydeen
Dr Brinsley Samaroo

A Hansib/University of Warwick, Centre for Caribbean Studies
Publication in cooperation with the London Strategic Policy Unit

India in the Caribbean is one of the six titles published by Hansib to commemorate the 150th anniversary of Indians in the Caribbean. Other titles are:

Benevolent Neutrality: Indian Government Policy and Labour Migration to British Guiana 1854-1884

Indo-Westindian Cricket

The Open Prison

The Second Shipwreck: Indo-Caribbean Literature

The Web of Tradition: Uses of Allusion in V.S. Naipaul's Fiction

© David Dabydeen, Brinsley Samaroo, 1987

First printed in September 1987, reprinted October 1987

Design and production by: Hansib Publishing Limited, 139/149 Fonthill Road, London N4 3HF, Tel: 01 281 1191
Printed in England by: Hansib Printing Limited, Unit 19, Caxton Hill Industrial Estate, Hertford, Hertfordshire, Tel: 0992 553592

The publication of this book was made possible by support from the London Strategic Policy Unit, Middlesex House, Room 602, 20 Vauxhall Bridge Road, London SW1V 2FB

Paperback ISBN 1 870518 00 4   Hardback   ISBN 1 870518 05 5

Photographs courtesy of: Anne Bolt   Royal Commonwealth Society

To Joan Samaroo,
and to Reya, Surya and Seta
of the Dabydeen family

"...those Indian hands – whether in British Guiana or Trinidad – have fed all of us. They are, perhaps, our only jewels of a true native thrift and industry. They have taught us by example the value of money; for they respect money as only people with a high sense of communal responsibility can."

George Lamming, 'The West Indian People' *(New World Quarterly,* Vol. 2, No. 1, 1966, p. 69)

A group of coolie immigrants – British Guiana

A Voyage of Discovery

On 5 January 1881 the sailing ship 'Ellora' arrived in Georgetown after a voyage of nearly six months from Calcutta. Its human cargo was indentured labourers for the sugar plantations of British Guiana. Among them was a widowed mother and her son of 9, bound for that same estate at Vreed-en-Hoop that the abolitionists had singled out for attack over forty years earlier and with which, under the then ownership of Sir John Gladstone, the whole system of Indian indenture to the Westindies had begun.

In 1983 at the end of the Commonwealth Prime Ministers' Meeting in New Delhi – the first ever held in India, and held (as we know now) just in time for us to have the privilege of Indira Gandhi's chairmanship. After that meeting, I travelled to Benares and the surrounding countryside from which that brave woman (a great-grandmother that I never knew) and her son (my grandfather, whom I did) crossed the 'seven seas' just over a hundred years ago. It was a return journey of a kind: one not conceived as an intensive search for 'roots' but from which came insistent reminders that they were not far away. The highlight of that pilgrimage was my being received by the pandas (or priests) of Gaya in Bihar as a true son of the region and admitted to the inner sanctum of the Vishnupad temple – still one of India's most sacred places.

My ancestral link with the Vishnupad Temple is still a matter of influence and surmise. But there were other links even in that place. At the entrance to the Temple is a bell bearing the following inscription: 'A gift to the Vishnupad by Mr Francis Gillanders, Gaya, 15 January 1790'. Francis Gillanders was a Collector in Gaya in the late years of the eighteenth century. What links were there between this man and 'Gillanders, Arbuthnot & Company' of Calcutta, to whom Sir John Gladstone had written that first letter in January 1836, the letter that, in a sense, 'brought' me to Guyana?

That visit to Bihar was inevitably a visit of many reflections, not least on the strange pathways that led my forbears to Guyana and now led me back to India through a modern Commonwealth that India's freedom had first made possible. Those pathways, in due course, took me from Guyana to London, to occupancy of the then official residence of the Commonwealth Secretary-General at 5

Carlton Gardens, St James's. One hundred and forty-two years earlier, to the month (July 1833), Sir John Gladstone, abandoning his nomadic existence in Demerara, had bought and moved to the address next door – 6 Carlton Gardens. July 1833 was just one month before the Emancipation Bill was passed and before Wilberforce himself passed away. In that same month John Gladstone and William Wilberforce breakfasted together in London: two old men at the end of their very different lives which, because of their incongruences, had come together to influence the lives of generations to come – and, rather specially, my own. The records do not reveal whether they breakfasted at Carlton Gardens; I like to think that Gladstone went to Wilberforce.

Sir Shridath (Sonny) Ramphal,
Commonwealth Secretary-General and former Minister of Foreign Affairs, Guyana, in *Caribbean Alternatives,* University of Warwick, 1984

CONTENTS

POEMS

PROSE

Preface

'Bred to sacrifice and to achieve'
(Rajkumari Singh)

This book of essays, poems and prose is published to commemorate the 150th anniversary of the arrival of Indian people ('East Indians') in the Caribbean.

The first boatload of indentured 'coolies' arrived in British Guiana in 1838 and from then on several thousand Indians crossed the 'black waters' *(kala-pani)* to the new lands.

Crossing the 'kala-pani' was an act of some consequence for the adventurers — it meant 'caste defilement and severe social ostracism. To be readmitted into his caste the returned emigrant had to spend a substantial part of his savings to feast his Guru (spiritual leader), relatives and friends. Beside caste dinners and gifts the emigrant was required to perform a purification ceremony'.[1]

Nevertheless, Indians undertook the hazardous physical and spiritual journey for a variety of reasons. Lower caste Indians, sometimes existing in a state of virtual slavery in India, were glad to flee their landlords and creditors for the prospect of a new beginning in new lands. Others were enticed by the fanciful tales of recruiters employed by the British, and deceived by false promises of plenty. Famine and civil war further swelled the numbers of emigrants. The British, short of labour in one part of the Empire, were only too happy to find supplies in another part.

The Indians occupied the old slave quarters and worked in the sugar plantations, inheriting many of the conditions of servitude of the previously enslaved Africans. The essays in this volume deal with their subsequent plantation experiences, their active and passive resistance to bondage and exploitation, and their efforts at self-betterment. Whilst their history is not a 'heroic' one (examples of failure, in-fighting, wrong-doing and self-destruction abound), it is nevertheless remarkable in many respects.

Indians have been able to make significant, sometimes unique, contributions at every level of Caribbean activity, in spite of the injustice and violence they endured. Their peasant agricultural skills for instance fed, and still feed, Guyana. In the realm of politics, leaders of Indian origin like Cheddi Jagan spearheaded the Caribbean movement towards independence and became world figures as a result of their agitation. In the arts, writers like the Naipauls and Sam Selvon were pioneers of Caribbean literary expression. In such a central Caribbean cultural activity as cricket, players like Rohan Babulal Kanhai and Sonny Ramadhin startled and excited the crowds by their genius.

These few instances of achievement can be multiplied endlessly by reference to the fields of medicine, law, business, and science. Nevertheless, in spite of their contributions to the making of Caribbean societies, and in spite of the fact that Indo-Caribbeans now comprise the majority populations of three major Caribbean countries — Trinidad, Guyana, Surinam — their history and culture have, until recently, received scant scholarly attention.

Scholarly research has been focussed overwhelmingly on the African dimension, and in the resulting Afro-centric view of the Caribbean, the Indo-Caribbean is relegated to a footnote. (The same can be said of Amerindian studies; the annihilation of the Amerindians has been both physical and intellectual). Such academic marginalisation of Indo-Caribbeans, which leads to a flawed conception of the region, has been paralleled, and perhaps reinforced, by the deliberate efforts to withhold economic and political power from them.

Guyana is particularly relevant in this respect. Under the régime of the People's National Congress (PNC) of Forbes Burnham Indo-Guyanese were systematically denied resources and opportunities through blatantly racist practices. The régime was able to perpetuate itself by the creation of an Afro-dominated military machine, and by the rigging of the local and national elections. Guyana inevitably suffered the self-afflicted economic consequences of moral and political corruption. Today, it is one of the poorest of Caribbean countries, and, in the scramble to survive or to emigrate, Guyanese have developed reputations in the rest of the Caribbean as 'hustlers', 'thieves' and 'illegal immigrants'. The killing of Walter Rodney in 1980 became for many symbolic of the final slide into degeneracy. Two decades earlier, Indians had been massacred at Wismar, Demerara, by Forbes Burnham's African supporters. Indian resentment of African domination in Guyana however must be accompanied by an appreciation of the motives of rulers like Forbes Burnham. For over three hundred years Africans have been coerced into labour under terrible conditions and with enormous losses of life. It was largely their labour which created profitable colonial enterprises, and they saw little of the rewards for themselves. Freedom from slavery saw a resolve never to be dominated again by other ethnic groups. From the very beginning of the indentureship period, Indians were perceived as a threat to African security, a threat to adequate wages and other material resources. The tensions between the Indian and African communities, exacerbated by the British policy of 'divide and rule', lasted throughout the nineteenth and into the present century. With full independence from Britain, the Africans naturally strove to acquire and maintain power, not wanting to be under the subjugation of Indian rule. The numerical supremacy of Indians in Guyana was an obvious threat to African political ambition, since voting in elections tended to be along racial lines. The electoral system therefore had to be tampered with, and once in power (with the assistance of the CIA) the African-dominated PNC party had to put its supporters into prominent social and economic positions so as to ensure future control of the society.

If the Indo-Guyanese have to learn to recognise and appreciate the history of African sacrifice, and therefore the rights to power of the Afro-Guyanese, then equally the Afro-Guyanese must be educated as to the Indo-Guyanese role in the making of the Caribbean. Historic suffering and sacrifice (from which modern claims of inheritance to power are made) were not the prerogative of any one ethnic group. The Amerindian peoples for instance, whose land we now occupy and squabble over, were nearly wiped out in two continents. African, and then Indian peoples, were subsequently exposed to European tyranny. An urgent priority in Guyana, and the rest of the Caribbean today, is the working out of sensible methods of power-sharing whereby all the ethnic communities are allowed to participate equally in the remaking of their societies. The alternative is ethnic tyranny, moral and economic backwardness and perpetual Third World status.

The academic essays in this book are selected from three Conferences on Indo-Caribbean History held at the University of the West Indies (UWI) between 1979 and 1984. They illustrate various aspects of Indian resistance, survival and triumph. Some of the finest writers from the Caribbean are of Indian origin, and a small selection to illustrate the creativity of such writing is included in the volume. The editors wish to thank all essayists and writers for their kind permission to publish their work. We offer this book as a small tribute to our Indian ancestors, and we hope that it will encourage Caribbean governments and academic institutions to sponsor further research and publications on their populations of Indian origin.

Dr David Dabydeen
University of Warwick, 1987

NOTES

1. Basdeo Mangru, *Benevolent Neutrality: Indian Government Policy and Labour Migration to British Guiana 1854-1884* (Hansib Publications, forthcoming).

Three Into One Can't Go – East Indian, Trinidadian, Westindian

Sam Selvon

(Opening Address to *East Indians in the Caribbean* Conference, University of the Westindies, Trinidad, 1979)

When I was a little boy growing up in San Fernando, there was a dark old Indian named Sammy who came around to our street selling fish. He was partly paralysed and walked with a limp, dragging one foot after the other, and when he sat down he could not get up without the aid of his walking stick. Customers had to help him lift the tray of fish off his head and back on again, and the scales shook in his hands as he weighed the fish. He was the butt of the neighbourhood and we teased and jeered at him whenever he came. One day he turned up with a white man toting the fish for him: I learnt afterwards that he was an escaped convict from Devil's Island whom Sammy had come across on the beach and took in hand to be his assistant. I was furious with the old Indian for putting the white man in such a humiliating position. My heart went out in a wave of sympathy and dismay for him in a way it never did for the poor crippled Indian struggling to earn an honest living.

When one talks of colonial indoctrination it is usually about oppression or subjugation, or waving little Union Jacks on Empire Day and singing God Save the King. But this gut feeling I had as a child, that the Indian was just a piece of cane trash while the white man was to be honoured and respected —— where had it come from? I don't consciously remember being brainwashed to hold this view either at home or at school. In fact there was a white boy in my class who came in for the same rough play and treatment as anybody else – if anything he got the worst of an argument or fight, being in the

minority. In school there was no significance in the fact that we were
of different colour and race. Fitz was a brownskin boy with curly hair,
but what I remember most was that he got licks all the time for bad
behaviour by the Headmaster of the Canadian Mission School in
Vista Bella – himself a short grey-haired East Indian. And I don't
remember Bunsee because he was an Indian but because he copied
from my exercise book and cuffed me regularly in the bargain, and
Peter was a black boy but the main thing was that he could pitch
marbles better than anyone else.

If I try to explain it I can only say it was some vague and undefined
concept which I accepted as unquestioningly as washing my face or
brushing my teeth in the morning when I got up. White people were
the rich ones and the bosses, living in big houses and driving motor
cars: they were the people in charge of everything. The Inspector
who came to school was white. My father's boss at work was white.
The Minister in the church I went to was white, and a mysterious awe
surrounded them all that I had not the slightest inclination or
curiosity to investigate.

Another concept, springing from just as mysterious a source, was
that Indians were 'better' than Negroes. I have the word 'better' in
quotes because I use it as we did as a limitless comparative adjective.
White people came first, then Indians and then the Blacks.

I accepted these concepts without question or motive: they were
not important, they had no meaning that directly influenced my
actions or behaviour, and even calling one another 'whitey cock-
roach' or 'nigger' or 'coolie' held less racial significance than the
transient anger or sarcastic reproach of the moment.

My mother's father was a Scotsman who married an East Indian,
and she spent her childhood and grew in an Indian village in Icacos
where he was the owner of a coconut plantation. She spoke fluent
Hindi and wanted me to learn it at school, but I was too busy going to
the cinema to see American films, or playing with an ethnic mixture
of friends to bother with any stupid 'kar-har-jar', though I did learn a
few phrases by listening to my playmates, like 'mai kay-chooday',
which I only knew much later on in my life meant cursing one's
mother, or 'paisa na ba', when a beggar asked for alms. My mother
spoke Hindi with the vendors who called at the house, but I never
heard my father, who was a Madrasee, speak anything but English,
nor any of the numerous Indian relatives who visited from time to
time. In our house we only ate curry once a week – the other days it
was creole food, souse and black pudding on Saturday night, and

stew beef or chicken and calaloo for Sunday lunch.

Apart from my mother's ill-fated efforts to make me learn the language, I remember little in those early days which caused me to think consciously of race. Of course there were the childish allusions to one's ancestry and colour, but I never stopped from being friendly with or playing with anyone in the neighbourhood because they were a different colour or race. We never observed any religious or cultural ceremonies, nor wore any national garments. To me, the Indian was relegated to the countryside. When I went to spend the holidays in Princes Town or Gasparillo, I saw workers in the canefields, or thatched huts along the roadside and brown children bathing under the standpipe, or else there was the occasional 'country bookie' who came to town, or the vendors and the beggars who migrated to the pavements in the high street.

By the time I was in my teens I was a product of my environment, as Trinidadian as anyone could claim to be, quite at ease with a cosmopolitan attitude, and I had no desire to isolate myself from the mixture of races that comprised the community. If I say that the ritual of a Hindu wedding meant nothing to me because I did not understand it, then I have to say in the same breath that a Shango ceremony was even more of a mystery. It was almost as if these two events, for example, were outside the day-to-day social rounds we led. I never had a friend who was bride or bridegroom at a wedding, nor did I know anyone who took part in a Shango ceremony. Someone would hear that one of these events was to take place and we would form a party and move out of our environment and go to see what it was all about.

At this time I was putting down the roots of the mixture of characteristics, attitudes and mannerisms which comprise the Trinidadian. I was one of the boys, doing my jump-up at Carnival time, giving and taking picong, liming for a freeness, drinking coconut water around the Savannah or eating a late-night roti down St. James.

You can call this another kind of indoctrination if you like, and it was as subtle and unconscious as my childhood racial experience. I think I can say without question that this creolising process was the experience of a great many others of my generation. It was so effective that one even felt a certain embarrassment and uneasiness on visiting a friend in whose household Indian habits and customs were maintained, as if it were a social stigma not to be westernised. The roti and goat-curry was welcome, but why did they have to play

Indian music instead of putting on a calypso or one of the American tunes from the hit parade?

It is important to point out that all the races in Trinidad were involved in this processing and coming under the influence of western culture, and there were as many Blacks ignorant or indifferent to the Shango cult, to stick to the example, as there were Indians to their own ritual.

Some of you may remember the late forties when the Indians in Trinidad were offered the chance to return to India when that country gained independence, or to take out or convert passports to Indian citizenship. Great political issue was made of the matter, but in the atmosphere that prevailed at the time, not many were attracted to the idea. The number that showed interest in the venture came mostly from the country districts where the majority were still adhering, or trying to adhere, to the traditions and customs brought from India. It is a measure of their racial loyalty and determination that they threatened to commit mass suicide unless the government took action to send them back. And what is perhaps more significant, they persisted in the face of a strong appeal from Pandit Nehru himself to remain where they were and help to build the country in which they had settled. I might mention that the return to India was not a great success for many of them, and some actually came back to Trinidad with stories of great hardships and inability to reorganise their lives in the mother country.

Apart from the sugarcane riots in the thirties, and the aftermath of the last general elections, I consider this to be one of the most important events in our history: certainly a milestone, relating back as it did to the terms of indentureship when the first Indians landed on these shores. The full story in all detail is worthy of record, setting out the facts and figures with an analysis and description of the times in which it occurred.

When I left Trinidad in 1950 and went to England, one of my first experiences was living in a hostel with people from Africa and India and all over the Caribbean. It is strange to think I had to cross the Atlantic and be thousands of miles away, in a different culture and environment, for it to come about that, for the first time in my life, I was living among Barbadians and Jamaicans and others from my part of the world. If I had remained in Trinidad I might never have had the opportunity to be at such close quarters to observe and try to understand the differences and prejudices that exist from islander to islander. Shortly before I left, the dream of Federation had evaporated because of those same differences and the failure to organise a unified body that would be representative of the Caribbean as a whole.

And up to this day, no matter where he is in this world, it remains a grievous flaw – one might almost say characteristic – in the composition of the Caribbean man. Some kind of communal defence was pressed upon us by necessity to rally against the discriminations and hardships of living in a white society, but pockets of various islanders persisted with a settling among their own countrymen by choice, and argument and dissension continued about who was the 'better' man, and which was the 'best' island.

As far as the English were concerned, we were all one kettle of fish and classified as Jamaicans. Their ignorance of the Caribbean was astonishing. You can imagine, after being brought up to believe that Britain was the fountainhead of knowledge and learning, how staggered I was to be asked if we lived in trees, or if there were lions and tigers in my part of the world. Their ignorance engendered a feeling of pride in my own country: I have always thought it would be a most interesting experiment to pit the most ignorant Trinidadian against the same Englishman and see who would win.

I wrote a story once which was based on fact, about a Trinidad Indian who couldn't get a room to live in because the English landlord didn't want people from the Westindies, only bona fide Indians from the banks of the Ganges. So my boy posed as a true-true Indian and got the room. And I understand that in the United States, the romantic Americans call people from the East 'Asians', and have strange notions about the mystery and magic of the Orient, and it is possible to put on a turban and pose as a maharajah or a prince and receive red carpet treatment.

But truth is even stranger than fiction, for when I applied to the Indian High Commission in London for a job, I was told that I was not an Indian because I came from Trinidad and was not born in India. We managed to circumvent that in the end, and I had the experience of working and getting acquainted with people from India. I was under suspicion to begin with, with my westernised attitudes. There were great differences in mentality and temperament between us. English was a second language for them, while it was my one and only, and they were cautious to establish any relationship. I was more at ease with the Anglo-Indians as we had a common familiarity with western culture, and it perked me up to find out that a lot of them didn't know any Hindi either. Differences extended even to the food they ate. In all my years in England, I never came across the kind of curry we ate in Trinidad, and I searched all over London for a dhall pourri, and never saw one until an enterprising Trinidadian started up a little cookshop.

When the Notting Hill riots flared up in London, it was only that the pot boiled over and drew attention to conditions that were existing all the time. What I found disconcerting, and alarming, was that the people from India living in London didn't identify themselves with the struggle. To them the trouble was between the Whites and the Blacks. Even the High Commission stuck its head in the sand and took no active part in trying to bring about a solution. I noticed that some people started to sport saris and turbans in case they were mistaken for Blacks. Ironically enough, when the scapegoat changed later on from the immigrant to Paki-bashing, some of them forsook their national garments in favour of collar and tie. But the greatest irony was that to the English, as long as you were not white you were black, and it did not matter if you came from Calcutta or Port-of-Spain.

Once the situation came into the open, the ignorant English blamed the poor Jamaican for everything, and something similar to the attitude of the Indians happened, for small-islanders were no longer shame-faced to say they were from St. Kitts or St. Vincent, and some suddenly remembered that they were not from an island at all but one of the Latin-American countries. With no tradition, no national pride or patriotism, lacking values but full of calypso and Carnival and what-happening-boy, it was as easy as kissing hand to deny their birthright. And there was the usual wrangling and hassle about who should be chairman or secretary of such groups as came into existence.

As for the Caribbean man of East Indian descent, he was something else. He wasn't accepted by those from India, and he wasn't wanted by the others because he wasn't a black man so he couldn't understand what was going on. If he could play cricket, he could join the team, but leave the politics alone.

Caribbean people carry their bad habits with them wherever they go, and as Federation collapsed in the islands, so constant disagreement kept them apart. When Black Power came into vogue, it widened the gulf and emphasized the displacement of the Indian . Black Power was never for the 'coloured' races as such. It was for the black man only. Like the White Bogey, we now had the Black Bogey to contend with. And once again, the strategy of keeping people apart, of creating division, came into operation. The wheel of history groans and squeaks as it repeats itself, but the process is everlasting, for the lesson is never learnt.

Whatever terms you choose to describe the white races – slave masters, colonists, Imperialists, Capitalists – the fact remains that we only augment their power and diminish ours when we allow ourselves to be divided. And the most hurtful part of it is when we ourselves become the protagonist who manipulates the division. The example is alive right here in this island. It would not take a great deal to bring about a state of civil war. Some of the most devastating wars in history have been triggered off by some ridiculous situation, and in Trinidad where life is so cheap, it might only lead the wrong person to call the wrong man a coolie or a nigger for some primitive to press the button.

After Black Power, as if he discontent with the first and only world that God make, Man decide to create a Third World. In his arrogance and rashness, he skip 'second' and shift right up to 'third'. And it came to pass that yet another division was made to harass we. This time the world divide up in the so-called developed countries and the so-called under-developed countries struggling for independence or learning what to do with it when they get it. And it seems to me a clear enough division of the white races from those that are not white. I will have to go back to school to learn geography, because it have so many new countries, and some old ones change their names, and boundaries and borders shifting all over the place. Look at what happen in Africa. I will take a bet here tonight that it ain't have three of you could name all the countries and states that exist in Africa today. They slice up the country like a shoemaker table.

In order to present its credentials this Third World is making an all-out effort to catch up with tradition and culture, and the advent of independence in many countries has started up a new occupation for the labour forces – the digging up of 'roots'. Suddenly every man and his neighbour want to trace his ancestry, and it is not enough to say that one's forebears came from Africa or India, we have to know the exact location, and which tribe. People are finding out that they been thinking the wrong thoughts, living in the wrong place, christened with the wrong name, following the wrong creed, and want to metamorphose themselves.

With all that, and in spite of the cultural growth in these islands since the last war, we are still being indentified on a level which does not seem to rise above cricket, calypso, steelband and limbo.

Although we have artists and writers, and participants in various fields of knowledge and technology who have achieved international renown, we are still a long way from being accepted as a contributing factor to World Culture. I mention two of the reasons I see for this: first, established cultural traditions belong to the white world and gatecrashers are not welcome. From the birth of history all 'coloured' races were considered savages and primitives, and it is inconceivable that they should rise above the war dance or beating music from a dustbin lid. Furthermore, there seems to be some insidious intention to keep this myth alive. In literature, for instance, there is a feeling that Third World writers can only produce novels and poetry of protest, or rattle the chains of slavery. We ourselves, not so long ago, were saying that you were headed for the madhouse if you wanted to be a writer.

This leads me to the second point, which is perhaps the more important one, that the population itself continues to be apathetic or indifferent towards those of us who try to elevate our values. It's still common enough to see the works of Caribbean authors gather dust in the bookshops while foreign books are sold out. Even when the books are free in the libraries they are not read. Recently in Toronto I met a Trinidad woman working in one of the public libraries who had fought to set up a Caribbean section, but the books are not being used and they may have to shut it down. In the same city I was taking part in a television programme, and discussing our aptitude for crying down anything cultural, when the selfsame thing happened, as if to prove the point – Caribbean viewers began to phone in to interrupt the discussion and demand reggae music instead. What was even more depressing was that as I was leaving the show, I heard a big argument going on with the technicians, who were all Caribbean men learning the job – one of them was beginning to act too bossy and he had to get out or everything would turn old mass.

Certain standards of cultural value and social behaviour have been allocated to us, and we behave and aspire accordingly. And what is most regrettable of all is that when we try to get out of the rut it is our own people who let us down. What our culture needs desperately is not support from the top. We need the foundation, and the push, of our people from below. You can't start to climb a ladder from the top.

To return to the digging of roots, a commess start from the very beginning of our history, when Columbus thought he was going to India, and call these islands the Westindies. We got discovered by mistake.

The term 'Indian' was used for more than a hundred years for the inhabitants of any newly-discovered country, and even Africans were so described. There are varieties and species of Indians all over the world, and while first and foremost the word means a native of India, even a white man living in that country for a long time was called an Indian. If you look in the dictionary – I use Chambers myself – the definition for an East Indian means an inhabitant of the *East* Indies. This starts to be bewildering, and gets even more so, for when we have East Indians born in Trinidad, we should have to call them East Indian Trinidadians. And the people living in these islands are called Westindians. So by definition, what we have here is really an *East Indian Trinidadian Westindian.*

Christopher Columbus must be killing himself with laugh, but he should wait until he hear the whole story. We find Columbus had a brother who was a tally clerk counting the first East Indians who ever came to Trinidad as they land off the ship. He can't understand them when they talk, so he spelling and writing down the names what he think he hear, and allocating groups to the sugarcane plantations regardless of skill or craft, caste or religion.

This theory isn't as farfetched as it sounds. A few weeks ago I saw a show on television in the United States which concerned a white receptionist greeting a party of African guests. The white hostess was telling her, as she poised with pencil and notebook, to be sure she got the names right as the guests arrived and introduced themselves. Needless to say there was confusion and perplexity as the receptionist tried to identify them afterwards, having hopelessly scribbled down the strange sounding names.

We also have here a mixture of various castes and religions. We have Hindus and Muslims, we have those of Christian belief, we have those of creolised stock. We have the sophisticated urban man and we have the peasant in the canefields. We have the rich and the poor. We also have Indians from other parts of the Caribbean who may voice opinion and feeling of their particular region which may or may not parallel the experience of the Trinidad Indian, and it might as well be said, even though it's apparent, that the two countries mainly concerned in this respect are Guyana and Trinidad.

Now, in defining the Trinidadian, we have got to remember that every one of us comes from the immigrant stock, unless we can claim ancestry with an indigenous Carib or Arawak. Our forefathers came from different lands to settle here, and in the mixture that makes up the population, it is easy to forget, as the Blacks and the Indians dominate the arena and cross swords, that there are white people, for instance, who were born and bred in these islands.

God alone knows what happening to *them*.

I went to a television studio one day in Toronto, and the door-keeper was a white man. Naturally I thought he was Canadian, until he came out with a 'what happening man, which island you from', in an unmistakable Trinidad accent. Another time I spoke with two Caribbean Whites at a Black Writers' Workshop in Winnipeg, and they told me how disappointed and frustrated they were, that because of the nature of things, the Whites had been left out completely from Caribbean affairs. Massa day may be done, but he left a string of white piccaninnies throughout the Caribbean who make an essential ingredient in the melting pot. Dip into it and pull out a race or a colour and you hold a little piece of these islands in your hands.

Events in the times we live in have re-awakened the Federation dream, and we have to broaden our concepts to include the whole Caribbean area. There is more traffic between the islands: it's no big deal now to spend a weekend in Barbados or Jamaica and jet back in time for work Monday morning. And I am sure that in the audience here tonight there is a fair sprinkling from the other territories. Even among the immigrants abroad, when they talk of returning home the concept has widened into the greater area rather than to any particular island. When the subject reaches into the realm of the calypso, as it does in Black Stalin's 'Caribbean Unity', it is surely a sign that the dream of a common nation is not only grass-rooted in the masses, but that it persists in manifesting itself at critical times in our history. This calypso also instances what I mean when I talk about us placing a limitation on our creativity, for granted the scope and range of the calypso, it conveys the sentiment of the people in their most popular and evocative means of expression. It is ambitiously beyond the jump-up and the bacchanal and tackles a subject which is the most important issue in these parts today. It transcends the parochial and becomes regional rather than insular.

Alas and alack, and inevitably, some Indian in the community springs up to protest that the calypso is racial, and once more we get on the treadmill of hassle and argument. Let me make it clear that I do not know Black Stalin from Adam before somebody take a lag in my arse for praising a black man calypso.

One would have thought that by now we would have ironed out our differences, but after thirty years or more the vision of a Caribbean nation still seems remote, and even more so now that several territories have gained independence. The question of identity has assumed greater importance, and in the context of the Third World the inhabitants seem to be thinking of themselves not as Trinidadians or Barbadians or Jamaicans, but as East Indian or African. I mention these two predominant races because like the Whites, God alone knows what is happening with the Chinese and the Portuguese and the other elements that are sandwiched between them.

Now these divisions have always existed in some shape or fashion, but today they are termed 'minority' or 'ethnic''or 'cultural' groups, as if putting on new clothes is going to change anything. But the quest for identity remains, and the right to live by one's own creed peacefully in a mixed society such as we have in Trinidad.

When I look at the scene here I find it all confusing. I see big new buildings, flashy cars, and many signs of material progress. Things look good. But under the surface of affluence there is resentment, bitterness, tension and dissatisfaction between the Blacks and the East Indians, and all the old handicaps standing in the way of a peaceful settlement. It is no wonder to me that some of our best citizens have fled and have nightmares about returning to a crippled and voiceless community. For which we have nobody but ourselves to blame, and let us not forget the great contribution they have made to bring the attention of the rest of the world to the conditions in these islands.

One good sign I see is the awareness of the new generation, but I could well imagine young East Indians growing up and being bewildered and frustrated and struggling with a feeling of inferiority because we of the older generation have failed to provide them with any foundation of confidence or assertiveness. The biggest insult to their pride is that up to today, the East Indian community is without a leader, without a voice. We have not had one person, or one party, rising with any degree of power or authority to instil some measure of dignity for them, even of mere basic representation. Indeed, what a state this island must be in when it has to recall a retiring leader because there is no one else to take his place. Though I make the point wholeheartedly and fearlessly that in my opinion, in my lifetime, he has done the greatest amount of good for Trinidad, and we might well be out of the frying pan if he wasn't stoking the fire.

What is one to make of the state of affairs these days? I do not know if I am East Indian, Trinidadian, or Westindian. I've spent a great many years abroad, and it would be presumptuous of me to attempt to analyse the situation without the facts and knowledge of what has been going on, or what has been done or is being done. But from all accounts, there is great unrest and dissension. I hear that the East Indians in Guyana are on the brink of a revolution. I hear that the hoardings in Trinidad exhort the citizens to 'rape coolie chicks'. Just before leaving Canada an East Indian told me, "Aye boy, you better watch your arse if you go down there and try to talk up for the Indians, you will land up in jail".

Another thing I heard – and I stand to be corrected – is that this Conference is keeping a 'low profile'. These new words and phrases don't baffle an old Trinidadian like myself. You could construe your own meaning, but what that means to me is that we best hads don't talk too loud before we antagonise the black people and cause further botheration.

If we feel that we are being oppressed and suppressed, all the more reason, I say, to blow our trumpet loud and fly our kite high.

It is easy for anyone to stir up the mud. I haven't added any new dimension to the situation, and I don't think I've said anything much which is news to anybody. But I do not want to leave you with the impression that I am one of those who live abroad and come home to make adverse criticism. This island is my shadow and I carry it with me wherever I go, and my roots are the same as a mango tree or an immortelle. I am fully aware that there are those among you who are gravely concerned and alarmed with the direction that things are taking, and are doing your level best to pull us out of the lurch. I myself have one or two ideas which I would hope to be discussing during the Conference, for what they are worth.

If I have sounded gloomy, it is not that I am in despair or without hope. Indeed, I think we should all look to this conference as a great opportunity to pool our resources and come up with a realistic approach, at least, to all problems, for it is high time to put a spoke in the wheel of our destiny.

I hope that this Conference will be more than a proclamation of what East Indians in the Caribbean have accomplished, though perhaps the time is ripe to remind ourselves and others of what we have contributed and sacrificed for the upliftment of the society in all spheres of life.

But I hope above all that it will be an inspiration to the new generation, and supply the impetus we sorely need in these times to put our house in order and work together for the benefit of the people of the Caribbean.

Two Abolitions:
African Slavery and East Indian Indentureship

Brinsley Samaroo

In 1840 the British Secretary of State, Lord John Russell, started a debate about the nature of East Indian indentureship.

> *I should be unwilling to adopt any measure to favour the transfer of labourers from British India to Guiana...I am not prepared to encounter the responsibility of a measure which may lead to a dreadful loss of life on the one hand, or on the other, to a new system of slavery.* [1]

It is the purpose of this essay to add to this debate by drawing further parallels between the systems of slavery and indentureship than those elaborated by Professor Tinker in the first chapter of his work. It hopes further, to indicate similar motivation and action among those who agitated against both systems and, finally, to dwell briefly on the Caribbean causes of the worldwide movement for the abolition of East Indian indentureship.

The two systems were similar in the first instance, in the pious pronouncements of officialdom regarding the welfare of the enslaved persons in both instances; pronouncements which were in stark contrast to the reality of this trade in human beings. Queen Elizabeth, for example, on hearing of the slave-trading activities of Sir John Hawkins was full of solicitude for the poor African:

> *If any African were carried away without his free consent it would be detestable and call down the vengeance of Heaven upon the undertaking.* [2]

Such a pronouncement, however, did nothing to mitigate forced capture of Africans, sale and kidnapping in West Africa, nor did it mean that the slaves were entitled to have any idea as to where they were being taken. As with the African, so with the Indian. Despite the pious pronouncement of Lord John Russell, the practice was quite different. At Negapatam, a recruiting station in South India, for example, the British subcollector for that region reported that recruiting there was conducted by 'a regularly organised system of kidnapping.'[3] Another government official in India noted, in 1875, that the recruiting men (*arkatis*) were 'for the most part unscrupulous scoundrels' who had no qualms about duping ignorant country folk in order to get them to offer themselves for indenture.[4] Planters in British Guiana were reluctant to take on reindentured Indians since these knew the ropes. It was much better, they argued, to have the 'newly-arrived simpleton [who] in his blissful ignorance, will have to grin and take what is given him.'[5] In the same manner that the African did not have a clue as to where he was going when he left Africa, and quite often harboured the mortal fear that he might even be eaten, so too was the Indian paralysed by a fear of the unknown. Many had the fear that

> *they will be converted into Christians both Hindoos and Mohamme-dans and the Hindoos will be fed with beef and the Mohammedans with pork, the thread of the Brahmins and the heads of the Hindoos will be taken off and they will not be able to keep their caste.*[6]

By the late nineteenth century, the citizens of the recruiting areas in India began to learn of the names of the colonies to which indentured labourers went: 'Damra' or 'Damraila' for Demerara, 'Sranam' for Surinam, 'Mirick' for Mauritius and 'Chinitat' for Trinidad.[7]. Even so they had no idea where these places were; they remained as no more than faraway places with strange-sounding names.

In continuing this comparison between slavery and indenturship we must look at the instruments of coercion used by the state. Whilst the whip and other brutal physical forms of punishment were mainly absent during the days of indentureship, a series of criminal laws were now enacted to keep the East Indian under control. An idea of the severity of these laws can be gleaned when we recall that for arson the immigrants could be sentenced for fifteen years; for burglary, eight years' hard labour in chains.[8] These laws served to keep the labourers immobile and insulated from the rest of the population. These conditions were deliberately arranged by the planters and 'were maintained in part at least by the failure of the Colonial office to exercise its vaunted role of trusteeship.'[9] So restrictive were these laws that an immigrant who came to Georgetown to give evidence against his master could be himself arrested and jailed for being absent from his estate.[10]. These severe restrictions often led to suicide in the same way that slaves took their own lives when they could hold the strain no longer:

> *If any coolie fails to work for a single day of the week, he is sent*

> *to jail for two or four days, where he is forced to work while day and night kept under chains. We are tortured very much. For this reason two to three persons died by swallowing opium and drowning themselves.*[11].

Very briefly, we can add to these considerations the fact that as it was with slaves, the prospective Indian immigrant was carefully, cosmetically prepared for examination before he was placed at the recruiter's desk and in the Caribbean, rested, like the slave before him, until he was ready for allocation to the highest bidder. Neither slave nor indentured labourer had a choice of master. The major difference lay in the time of servitude: for the slave it was a lifetime experience, for the East Indian it was, in the first instance, for five years.

East Indian resistance to indentureship, often expressed in fashion similar to the African resistance to slavery, took the form of riots, strikes, desertion and murder of offending managers and overseers. Such resistance was invariably, as in slave times, put down with exemplary harshness. Yet resistance persisted, as Indians were becoming increasingly better organized, producing strong leadership as the immigrants grew more accustomed to the new environment.[12] As in the abolition of slavery movement, such disturbances added to the burden of maintaining an already costly system, both financially and in human terms, and therefore contributed to this later abolition movement. Details in this regard will be discussed presently.

There are interesting similarities between the two abolition movements. In the same way that the Colonial Office and colonial planters saw nought but total bleakness in the prospect of the abolition of slavery, so too did their latter-day counterparts predict doom upon the end of indetureship. In 1901, for example, the Hon. E Cipriani warned a meeting of Trinidad planters that without Indian immigration 'the colony would be nowhere.'[13] Eleven years later the same fear was haunting the head of the West Indian department in the Colonial Office:

> *I am sure that the cessation of Indian emigration to the Westindies would bring these colonies to the verge of ruin, and in the end the movement of population would have to be started again.*[14]

The anti-indenture campaign produced its own Wilberforces and Clarksons in people like Baron Brougham (1778-1868) who, having participated in the movement for the abolition of slavery, now sought desperately for something else to abolish and whose agitation was to a degree responsible for the first, temporary ending of indentureship in 1838.[15] The movement for ending indentureship also attracted other Englishmen such as the Revs. C F Andrews and W Pearson who abandoned their evangelical missions in India to answer this new call. Finally, when in 1916 the Government of India under unrelenting pressure from the subcontinent, insisted on the cessation of indentureship, the Colonial Office, with a strong vested interest in the maintenance of a prosperous plantocracy, did its utmost to institute a variation of apprenticeship, a modified version of helotry suitably disguised under less offensive terms:

> *Get rid of 'Immigration' and 'Indenture', words which act like rags and substitute 'Colonization'. India lays stress on Indians becoming 'citizens' of Colonial Communities... As W.I. master and servant Ordinances are as a rule antiquated and harsh, the West Indian colonies to adopt the Indian law of master and servant as far as possible. It will be a great thing if we can say that the Indian will be under the same law as at home.*[16]

The system of indentured Indian labour stood on very shaky ground from its very inception. For one thing, British recruiters in India and planters in the colonies had undergone very little change of attitude regarding non-white workers since the days of slavery. For the initial (1838) experiment of recruiting labourers for Gladstone's Guianese estate his recruiters in India, Gillanders, Arbuthnot and Company, gave the assurance that the Indians being recruited 'have no religion, no education and in their present state, no wants beyond eating, drinking and sleeping.'[17] In dealing with such people, therefore, recruiters felt that it was perfectly in order to dupe prospective immigrants into signing contracts which they did not understand. In July 1838 a meeting of prominent citizens of Calcutta passed a resolution stating 'its deliberate conviction that the hill coolies and other natives of India do not understand and are not capable of understanding the terms of the contract which they are said to enter.'[18] This resolution was passed with respect to indentured emigration which had started to Mauritius in 1834 and extended to British Guiana in January 1838. The claim of the resolution was not without basis, for in February 1838 Gladstone was cheerily assured that the natives were 'perfectly ignorant of the place they agree to go to, or the length of the voyage they were undertaking.'[19] Throughout the period of indentureship recruiters thought nothing of telling an Indian labourer that he would be going to Chini-dad (land of sugar) or that Fiji was a place just beyond Calcutta.[20]

It was for reasons such as these that the system came under serious attack during the 1830s from groups in India as well as in England, and after a parliamentary enquiry in which the majority was in favour of total abandonment of the system, it was ended in 1838. Under pressure from the planting lobby the system was revived in 1842 when recruiting was resumed for Mauritius. Two years later it resumed for British Guiana and was simultaneously extended to Trinidad and Jamaica.[21] As the nineteenth century progressed, vigilance with regard to indentured conditions relaxed while the Anti-Slavery Society shifted its emphasis to Africa. Indian nationalists struggled to get their protest movements on firm footing, and Indians in the colonies were becoming seasoned to the new environment. With the opposition in temporary disarray the planters made significant extensions. Assam started recruiting indentured Indians in 1859, Natal followed in 1860, Dutch Guiana (Surinam) in 1872 and Fiji in 1879. During this period too the system was furthered into the smaller islands in the Caribbean: Grenada (1856), St Lucia (1856), St Vincent (1856), and St Kitts (1861). The French islands of Martinique and Guadeloupe recruited their first Indians in 1854.[22]

As the anti-indenture campaign picked up momentum once again from the late nineteenth century, the agitators were able with some research to compile as impressive a list of abuses as they had developed for just over thirty years. In addition there were contemporary pressing problems which needed attention. For one thing there was always considerable disparity betweeen the sexes. In March 1838 Gladstone was prepared to accept one woman for every nine or ten men; as the difficulty of procuring women increased, he intimated that one woman for every twenty-five men was good enough.[23] Although the Government of India, supported by the Colonial Office, stipulated that there should be forty women for every hundred men, ships often left India with less than this percentage.[24] In March 1914 the Colonial Office gave the following breakdown of the sexual ratio of the *total* Indian populations in four colonies:

COLONY	ADULT MALES	ADULT FEMALES	% OF WOMEN
Trinidad & Tobago	31,989	17,159	35%
British Guiana	53,083	34,799	40%
Jamaica	7,137	4,775	40%
Fiji	20,062	8,785	40%

The document from which this table has been drawn makes the significant point that 'this disproportion affects both indentured and unindentured labour, *the latter of course to a much less extent*'[25] (My emphases). Because of the unwillingness of Indians to marry or live with women of other races, this shortage of women led to all sorts of serious problems. In British Guiana, for example, it led to frequent wife murders:

> The disproportion of the sexes is the great exciting cause of the deplorable large number of wife murders which are perpetrated notwithstanding every precaution being taken to by removal or otherwise which can be taken to prevent them.[26]

By 1988 there was little change in the situation:

> I regret to have to report that there were during 1886 ten murders of women by their husbands or reputed husbands from motives of jealousy.[27]

C F Andrews and W Pearson, who visited Fiji in 1915, described how the law of the jungle operated with respect to the sharing of women. The strong men usually took one woman each, leaving the remaining women to be shared, one to four or five men. 'We heard of one estate where the overseer made the regular practice, in order to keep peace in the lines, of allotting so many men to each single woman. This amounted to legal prostitution.'[28] The abolitionists' appeal on behalf of indentured women was perhaps the most effective public issue used during the campaign.

Of equal if not greater importance to the movement was the increasing cost of Indian immigration, particularly when this is viewed against the background of the equalization of sugar duties from 1846, a problem compounded by the cane sugar depression which came in the wake of equalization. In British Guiana there were constant financial problems necessitating frequent borrowing from the London money market. As this borrowing became increasingly difficult, the planter-controlled legislature in British Guiana (as in the rest of the Westindies) began to extract, from the 1860s, the additional amounts required from the 'community as a whole.'[29] A former Indian immigration official reminisced in 1919 that a major reason for the reluctance of the Guianese planters in importing women and children was the expense involved therein; this was particularly so during the late stages of immigration when the recruiters in India were demanding £3-£5 for every man they obtained and £6 13 sh. for every woman.[30]

The fact that the rest of the community had to share immigration costs was in itself a major cause for abolition in that it stimulated a vigorous and sustained campaign in the Westindies from the 1880s until the termination of the system in 1917. The major arguments of the island agitators were that the non-Indian population was being forced to subsidize an immigration from which they gained nothing. Indeed, they argued, Indian indentureship was depriving easily available labourers from the other Westindian islands from employment in Trinidad and British Guiana. Indian immigration was depressing wages in the colonies and the planters were crying 'wolf' in claiming that there was scarcity of labour. In 1895, for example, H A Alkcazar, nominated member on the Trinidad legislature, protested strongly to the Secretary of State against the Council's decision to introduce two thousand immigrants during 1895-96.[31] The case against continued Indian immigration was taken up by black leaders in the islands and British Guiana using whatever platform that was available; colonial legislatures, the press, petitions to the Colonial Office followed by questions in parliament as well as in evidence before the Sanderson Commission in 1909.[32] It is significant that the arguments put forward by these leaders were cited in the Indian legislature during the 1912 debate on indentureship.[33] In British Guiana, James Rodway reported, the complaints were particularly bitter. People resented being taxed to 'keep up sugar' and the complaint was made that the 'coolie takes bread from the negro labourer and lowers the price of labour.'[34]

As the Indians became permanent settlers and purchasers of land from the late nineteenth century, their agricultural activities began to compete seriously with those of the plantations. This competition, the planters complained, was seriously cutting into their profits and decreasing their labour supply particularly when crop time on the Indians' holdings coincided with that of the estates. The planters used various devices to cut their losses. For one thing, they tried to keep the Indian as close as possible to the plantations even after his personal indentureship had ceased, in order that his labour could be tapped. To this end they supported the Canadian missionaries (to the Indians) who started work in the region in 1868; so successful was the initial mission in Trinidad that from this staging point the mission was extended to Grenada in 1884, St Lucia and British Guiana in 1885 and to Jamaica in 1894.[35] Planter support for the building of churches and schools in estate villages was liberal, and these instutitions were used to socialize the Indians into becoming a docile and tractable force. The siting of the schools in the villages served effectively to keep the education-hungry Indians near the plantations. It is hardly surprising, therefore, that he who defended indentureship before the Sanderson Commission was a Presbyterian Indian, who in 1912 became the first Indian to be nominated to the Trinidad legislature.[36] Another device of the planters was the use of their majorities in colonial legislatures and of their powerful lobby – the Westindia Committee in London – to cut costs of immigration and to reduce Indian competition. In 1875, and again in 1899, the Westindia Committee pressed the Colonial Office for the abolition of return passages for time-expired Indians.[37] To decrease competition by free Indians who were becoming successful cane farmers, the Trinidad Executive Council advised their Governor in 1913 to lease only rice lands to the Indians. The India Office, requested by the Colonial Office to comment on this proposal, stated that it had no objection thereto, provided that estate owners were prepared to provide long-overdue latrines on their estates.[38] In Jamaica, the Indians in the Westmoreland area complained to MacNeil and Chiman Lal, two Indian Government representatives sent on an inspection tour of the Caribbean in 1913, that the planters were making it very difficult for them to obtain lands to do their own cultivation.[39] From the late nineteenth century the competition from the rice industry in British Guiana and from gold prospecting and balata collecting increased considerably.[40] In fact, loss of labour to the Guianese plantations became such a problem that planters were increasingly being forced to adapt planting and reaping of their canes to periods of slack time in the rice industry.[41]

Adding considerably in terms of financial costs, administrative humbug and parliamentary embarrassment was the frequency of strikes and desertions on Caribbean estates. Indentured Indians deserted or caused unrest when, as the Trinidad Protector of Immigrants reported in 1910, 'young and overbearing overseers, unaccustomed to command and discipline' treated the immigrant 'harshly and without tact...' 'The majority of East Indians have much finer feelings than these young men imagine and are swift to appreciate kindness and forbearance.'[42] In addition to this lack of tact the Trinidad Protector felt that anti-Indian racism often caused dissatisfaction:

> *There are also on many estates coloured creole overseers and sirdars or 'drivers' as they are caller here, who look upon the immigrant as one of an inferior race, instead of the contrary, and treat them accordingly, causing them to rebel, refuse to work and*

eventually to abscond.

More fundamentally, however, the East Indians resisted, particularly from the 1880s, as they increasingly saw themselves as 'an integral part of the social and political landscape.'[43] Sir Henry Norman, one of the English commissioners sent to investigate the Hosea riots in Trinidad, noted that:

There is no doubt that the Coolies feel their power, or rather, I should say, have an exaggerated idea of that power... generally he does not behave as well as he used to.[44]

Now the East Indian felt that he was no longer a stranger; between 1882 and 1884 there were no fewer than twenty five strikes on sugar estates and in 1884 there was the 'grand finale' of East Indian resistance in the Hosea riots of that year, which resulted in the death of sixteen labourers and injury to no less than a hundred more:

The Hosea riots were a political proclamation which announced the movement of the Indian labourers away from an existence on the fringes of society to a more integral and full relationship.[45]

In Surinam and British Guiana there was also resort to violence as a final reply to the oppresiveness of indentureship. In Surinam there were five revolts between 1873 and 1916, in which the East Indians lost thirty eight of their number with only three Europeans killed.[46] The frequency of strikes and disturbances and the loss of man days resulting therefrom were noticed by Surgeon-Major Comins, Protector of Immigrants in Calcutta, who had been deputed to do an inspection tour of the Caribbean in 1893. Comins had commented on the seriousness of strikes in Trinidad during 1882, 1883 and 1884.[47] Adamson's chart of strikes in British Guiana between 1885 and 1903 indicates that there were, on average, a dozen strikes per year.[48] The 1912-13 season in British Guiana deserves special attention. At Ogle, indentured labourers beat their overseer and five men were convicted; at Lusignan one striking Indian was shot dead by a manager and sixteen 'ring-leaders' were transferred. In all there were twelve reported cases of assault and sixteen strikes. An overworked Immigration Agent General could find no good reason for this spate of unrest:

During 40 years experience in dealing with East Indians I have never known such a serious spirit of insubordination as has prevailed in recent years, I trust that the cause will soon be

> *definitely ascertained, so that there may be no ebb in the tide of*
> *that immigration from multitudinous Hindostan which has*
> *proved to be so useful to British Guiana.*[49]

On top of the financial losses due to desertion and labour unrest, Indian immigration came under increasing additional economic pressures in the early twentieth century. Commissions to the local recruiters (*arkatis*) had to be frequently increased because of competition from Assamese tea planters who were recruiting in the same catchment areas as the *arkatis* for Fiji, Mauritius and the Westindies; the British government's decision in 1911 to shift the Indian capital from Calcutta to Delhi siphoned a substantial number of labourers from north-central India; increasing administrative posts were forcing the amalgamation of colonial depots; especially during 1914-1916 and the closing of upcountry recruiting depots; planters' associations in India were calling on the government to end the export of Indian labourers since this was causing serious labour shortages in southern and western India.[50] Above all, the government of India was now insisting on the provision of better health and living conditions on the estates in the colonies and this was forcing unwilling planters into greater expense. By February 1916 at least one senior official in the Colonial Office had decided that as an economic prospect, immigration was no longer viable:

> *It is however, rather doubtful to my mind whether the colonies*
> *will wish to continue the system which tends to cost them more*
> *and more each year, and to give them rather less value for*
> *money. The latest unfavourable factor is that Nourse and*
> *Company, the contractors for the steamers which convey*
> *emigrants from India to the colonies are asking for a substantial*
> *increase (some 30 to 40 per cent) on present rates for a renewal of*
> *their contract with British Guiana and Jamaica which expires this*
> *year.*[51]

In addition to these substantial factors which were rendering immigration burdensome, there were other irritants which, cumulatively, did much to undermine the system. Comins reported that alcoholism was on the increase by citing the fact that as many as two hundred and five liquor shops had been opened by Indians in Trinidad in 1890.[52] So serious was the problem in this colony that one Canadian missionary dared disagreement with the Mission in declaring support for the Indian nationalists who were clamouring for an end to indentureship. To the young Rev William Green the situation was intolerable:

> *75% of our ex-pupils drink liquor, and drinking is on the increase. Every facility for drinking is given to our Indian people. No sooner does a prosperous little village of Indians spring up than some chinaman applies for a rum licence and before anyone knows what had happened a rum sign is hung out and the village debauched.*[53]

Green went on to point out that even the plantation owners were cashing in on this iniquitous trade:

> *It is bad enough that their [the Indians'] labour is taken cheaply but when estates set up rum shops and directly make money out of their benefactors' ruin, it is a great shame.*

There was also the problem of constant illness among the Indians. For one thing, many of those who were recruited in India were stricken with hookworm. When the Government of India cautioned the Calcutta immigration agent to send or at least offer medication to immigrants suffering from this disease, the agent Marsden protested strongly:

> *As 75% of the coolies are infected with this disease, and as the treatment is most obnoxious to the native, the effect on emigration will amount to a partial paralysis of Colonial Emigration work in India.*[54]

Marsden's colleague later reported that if the prospective emigrants were forced to take treatment for ankylostomiasis there would be a revolt 'en masse.'[55] Conditions in the Caribbean plantations did little to improve the health of the Indians, particularly during the nineteenth century. The labourers lived generally in swampy or improperly drained areas and the inadequacy of toilet facilities forced people to relieve themselves in fields, pastures or open drains. Since most Indians walked barefooted they fell easy victim to lurking hookworms. In Fiji 'these dispirited and exhausted people unknowingly suffering perhaps from hookworm infection, with nothing to show for their labour, were real victims of the system.'[56]

In Grenada, where indentureship lasted from 1856 to 1893, illness among the indentured Indians was so rampant that in 1866 a special commission had to be set up to enquire into the high incidence of death and disease.[57] In British Guiana, James Rodway reminded his readers of a picture of 'coolie beggars' in the *Illustrated London News* which, he claimed, points a moral. 'We (also) have the hospital records of the early forties as powerful lessons.'[58] Comins related in 1893 that unindentured Indians were denied access to estate hospitals although they lived nearby and often worked on the same estates.[59] Illness among the indentured Indians in Jamaica was no less serious than in British Guiana or Trinidad.[60]

Finally there was, in the Westindian colonies of indentureship, an active press campaign which veered from anti-indentureship to anti-Indian. In Jamaica, for example, the *Falmouth Post* of 20 July 1847 praised the Africans and plantation owners for being kindly disposed toward these 'poor and miserably degraded foreigners.' In Trinidad the Indians were advised to adopt 'the European standard of conduct and train of ideas' and were considered to be 'infesting our Christian civilization with a virus which it may be hereafter impossible to eradicate and which, if not checked in time will ultimately become fatal to us as a Christian people.'[61] In British Guiana, Indians were seen as people whose 'crude and indecent habits shocked the feelings of every virtuous family residing throughout the country districts.'[62]

One may well ask how these problems of sexual disparity, alcoholism, illness and newspaper vilification lead to the abolition of indentureship. They served to create an environment described fittingly, by the Indians in Fiji, as 'narak,' which is a Hindi word meaning 'hell.'[63] In this hell, as we have seen, murders were frequent and there was disorder quite often. The suicide rate was also high. During the period 1902 to 1912 the average rate of suicides in India as a whole was 51 per million of population; for Uttar Pradesh, from whence a large percentage of Indians came, it was 63 per million. For the colonies in the same period it was 100 per million for British Guiana, 396 for Jamaica, 400 for Trinidad and 926 for Fiji.[64] These factors caused the loss of workers and of working days; demoralization and homesickness decreased productivity and, as we shall presently see, this information was of much use in the campaign waged against indentureship in India.

Despite the general unpopularity of the system and its abuse-ridden nature, it enjoyed the support of the Colonial Office until late 1915 and among a number of planters in the colonies even after abolition. The Office, for example, could see no real reason for all the commotion that was going on. Indentureship saved Indians from the perils of famine ('such a thing as a coolie dying of starvation is unheard of') and of cholera; it gave them remunerative though light labour, they were protected by special laws and officers appointed to administer that law, and they were entitled to free or assisted return passages to India after the period of residence.[65] Four years later the justification was loftier:

> *All human systems are liable to abuses but I believe the world has been distinctly the gainer not merely in wealth but in civilization; as a direct consequence of this system for introducing a working race into lands half peopled by less progressive races.*[66]

Similarly, the planter and settler classes all over the world showed an amazing faith in the benefits which could be derived from indentured Indian labour. The Westindia Committee, for example, made frequent visits to the Colonial Office and wrote letters thereto, complaining that the Indian authorities were not supporting emigration sufficiently, that no Indians should be sent to Peru, that return passages be abolished.[67] From the 1870s until the onset of the First World War there were requests for Indians from Peru, Cuba, the French colonies in the Pacific as well as in the Caribbean, Hawaii, the Netherlands, and the East Indies, and for increasing amounts to Surinam. Indians were applied for by British Borneo, West Africa (to do agricultural work in the Niger Delta), Natal, German East Africa, Madagascar and Uganda, to which some nineteen thousand indentured Indians went to assist in railway building from 1896 to 1901.[68] It was against these powerful economic interests and the political influence which they wielded that the anti-indentureship campaign had to struggle. In the twentieth century, particularly from 1912, the struggle seesawed continuously whilst the agitators in India sought, by the mobilization of public opinion, to put an end to the actual recruiting in the areas where the *arkatis* worked.

The final and successful outcome of the campaign, from 1912 to 1918, was achieved because of the confluence of a number of important factors, which swung the battle in favour of the abolitionists. These were, firstly, the fact that the Indian National Congress (INC), founded in 1885, had now become the major representative pressure group in the nationalist struggle. By 1910 it had tightened its organizational structure and was exerting considerable pressure on the British administration for reform. One major area of this platform was the abolition campaign. It was taken up firstly in South Africa by Gandhi and Gokhale[69] and later brought to India. The second important consideration was the Viceroyalty of Lord Hardinge (1910-1916) at a crucial time in the abolition struggle. A liberal and very humanitarian administrator, Hardinge was prepared to put his Indian governorship on the line in his stand against indentureship. His denunciation of the system appears more suited to an Indian agitator than a British administrator:

> *Indentured labour really stinks in my nostrils as a form of slavery that we ought really to be ashamed of; there is no doubt that in a very large number of cases, there is a good deal of suffering entailed by it. Of course in Fiji the number of suicides is the most striking evidence of the viciousness of the system and nothing can explain this away.*[70]

It was during his regime that the decision was made to end immigration for the wartime.

The movement for the abolition of indentureship bore many resemblances to that for the abolition of slavery. In the first place the work of humanitarians in both movements was an important consideration. The humanitarians in both instances, through familiarity with actual conditions in the colonies, did much to raise public consciousness regarding these systems. In this way key decision makers were reached. But the economic considerations were of decisive influence in both situations. For one thing the cost of maintaining indentureship with all its attendant problems weighed heavily. In the same way, slavery had become increasingly unprofitable in the earlier era. British capitalism in that earlier period had also been pressing for the freeing of the slave so that a *purchasing* black population could be created in the Caribbean; slaves could not buy manufactured goods. Now in this later period this compulsion of the European capitalist continued, if the Africans could buy, why not the East Indian? In addition there was the hue and cry of the Indian capitalist in the Bengal jute industry, in the Assamese tea industry and in the manufacturing areas near India's great cities – that labour should not be exported abroad. It was needed at home. To these forces, which operated in both systems, we must add the clamour raised by the politicians who, for a vote, would support any cause! All these forces, in both abolitions, came together to end an era of slavery and of a new system of slavery as the Caribbean moved into the twentieth century.

NOTES

1. Hugh Tinker, *A New System of Slavery: The Export of Indian Labour Overseas 1880-1920*, (Oxford, 1974); frontispiece.

2. Cited in W Aykroyd, *Sweet Malefactor: Sugar, Slavery and Human Society* (London, 1967), p. 18.

3. R K Jain, 'South Indian Labour in Malaya 1840-1920', in K Saunders, ed., *Indentured Labour in the British Empire 1834-1920* (London, 1984), p. 25.

4. K L Gillion, *Fiji's Indian Immigrants* (Melbourne, 1973), p. 26.

5. A Adamson, 'The Impact of Indentured Immigration on the Political Economy of British Guiana', in Saunders, *op. cit.*, pp. 46-47.

6. Report from India, 1882. Cited by P C Emmer, 'The Importation of British Indians in Surinam 1873-1916', in S Marks and P Richardson, eds., *International Labour Migration* (London, 1984), p. 95.

7. G Grierson, *Report on Colonial Emigration from the Bengal Presidency* (Calcutta, 1883), p. 2ff.

8. Emmer, p. 108.

9. Adamson, p. 45.

10. Adamson, p. 46.

11. Complaint by a group of immigrants in Surinam, 1883. Cited by Emmer, p. 110.

12. For a useful sociological examination of this issue see K Haraksingh, 'Indian Leadership in the Indenture Period', in *Caribbean Issues* vol. I I , no. 3. Also, Haraksingh, 'Sugar Estates and Labour in Trinidad 1838-1845' Eleventh Conference of Caribbean Historians, Barbados, 1979.

13. CO 295/402. Enclosure in Trinidad despatch 256 of 17 June 1901, p. 5.

14. CO 323/602, no. 12861, minute by George Grindle, 25 June 1912.

15. J Geohagan, *Note on Emigration from India,* (Calcutta, 1873), p. 5ff.

16. CO 323/723, no 20011, minute by George Grindle, 5 May 1916.

17. Cited in I Dookhan, 'The Gladstone Experiment. The Experiences of the First Emigrants to Guyana 1838-1843', *East Indians in the Caribbean* (Trinidad, 1975), p. 4.

18. Cited in P. Saha, *The Emigration of Indian Labour 1834-1900* (Delhi, 1970), p. 87.

19. Dookhan, p. 3.

20. Accounts of such deception were frequently related to the author in Uttar Pradesh during 1964/65 as well as in Trinidad. See also K L Gillion, p. 34.

21. R Shiels, 'Indentured Immigration into Trinidad 1891-1916' B Litt. thesis (Oxford, 1967), p. 9.

22. G W Roberts and J Byrne, 'Summary Statistics on Indenture and Associated Migration Affecting the West Indies, 1834-1918', *Population Studies* vol. 20, no. 1, p. 128. Also, Singaravelou, *Les Indiens de Guadeloupe* (Guadeloupe, 1975), p. 14.

23. Dookhan, p. 5.

24. Geoghagan, p. 49.

25. CO 323/717, no. 41 of 1915, p. 4 for citation of 1914 figures.

26. *British Guiana Immigration Dept. Reports. 1875-1894,* Report of the Agent-General, 1875, p. 7.

27. *Ibid.,* report for 1888, p. 8.

28. C F Andrews & W Pearson, *Indentured Labour in Fiji: An Independent Enquiry* (Allahabad, 1916), pp. 45-48.

29.   A H Adamson, *Sugar without Slaves* (Yale, 1972), pp. 106-109.

30.   A H Hill, 'Emigration from India', *Timehri* vol. V1, 1919, pp. 45-48.

31.   Council Paper 82 of 1895, 8 April 1895.

32.   See, for examples, notice of question for House of Lords, 11 April 1916 in J. & P. 1425/1916 (India Office); *Hansard, Trinidad & Tobago 1904,* pp. 652-660; C P David, 'Ought not state-aided immigration to cease', *The Trinidad Magazine,* January 1902; CO 295/444 petition from Trinidad Workingmen's Association to Colonial Office, 21 March 1908. Also Cd. 5194, 1910, Part III.

33.   *Proceedings of the Governor General's Council in India,* 1912, p. 372. Hereafter referred to as *Proceedings.*

34.   'Labour and Emigration', *Timehri,* vol. VI, Sept. 1919, p. 36.

35.   K J Grant, *My Missionary Memories* (Halifax, 1923), pp. 161-166.

36.   Cd. 5192, 1910, p. 72 for citation of George Fitzpatrick's support of indentureship.

37.   Tinker, pp. 252 & 286.

38.   CO 885/21. Le Hunte to Harcourt Conf., 28 Oct. 1913. Also, No. 41670, India Office to Colonial Office, 2 Dec. 1913.

39.   *Report to the Government of India on the Conditions of Indian Immigrants in Four British Colonies and Surinam* Part II (London, 1915), p. 213.

40.   J Rodway, 'Labour and Colonisation', *Timehri* vol. VI, Sept. 1919, p. 34.

41.   T Ramnarine, 'The Growth of the East Indian Community in British Guiana, 1880-1920', D Phil. (Sussex, 1977), pp. 173ff.

42.   CO 323/597, no. 29708. Colonial Office to India Office, Encl. 2. dated 29 August 1910.

43.   This paragraph is based on a recent study by a researcher from the University of the West Indies, Ken Parmasad 'The Hosea Riots of 1884 (Trinidad)', MA history thesis (U.W.I. 1984).

44.   *Ibid.,* p. 48.

45.   *Ibid.,* p. 64.

46.   Emmer, p. 109.

47.   D W Comins, *Note on Emigration from India to Trinidad* (Calcutta, 1893), p. 42. Hereafter referred to as Comins's report.

48.   Adamson, p. 155.

49.   CO 114/143, report for 1912-13, p. 28.

50.   *Madras Mail,* Editorial, 23 July 1914.

51.   CO 323/717 no. 20735, minute by T C McNaughten, 12 Feb. 1916.

52.   Comins's report, p. 17.

53.   *Missionary Correspondence,* United Church archives, Toronto; William Green to Dr McKay, 26 April 1917.

54.   CO 885/21. H Marsden to Colonial Ofice, 13 Sept. 1911.

55.   *Ibid.,* R Gibbes (Emigration Agent for British Guiana) to Colonial Office, 9 Sept. 1913.

56.   Gillion, p. 107.

57.   *St George's Chronicle,* 14 June 1866, cited in G Brizan, 'The Indentured Immigration Scheme to Grenada 1835-1895', Typescript, (1976), p. 9.

58.   Rodway, *op.cit.*

59.   Comins's report, p. 48.

60.   L & M Mansingh, 'Indian Heritage in Jamaica', *Jamaica Journal* vol. 10, nos. 1-4, (1976), p. 10.

61. *Trinidad Chronicle* and *San Fernando Gazette* during the 1870s and 1880s, cited in G Tikasingh 'The Trinidad Press and the Issue of Immigration', Proceedings of the 9th Conference of Caribbean Historians, Barbados, 1977, p. 21.

62. *Argosy,* 26 March 1892, cited in Ramnarine, p. 202.

63. Gillion, p. 129.

64. CO 323/717, no. 41 of 1915, p. 3.

65. CO 884/9, West Indian, no. 152. Memorandum on East Indian Immigration to the West Indies, March 1906, pp. 3 & 4.

66. CO 323/571, no. 12518, p. 126, minute by C P Lucas.

67. Tinker, pp. 252, 259, 286, 292.

68. Tinker, pp. 259-292.

69. Gopal Krishna Gokhale (1866-1915) began his career as lecturer in economics and history at Fergusson College, Poona. He retired in 1902 to join the INC of which he became one of the recognized leaders. In 1902 he became a member of the Bombay Legislative Council and three years later was elected as a non-official in the viceregal legislature in Calcutta. Gokhale was a moderate in the nationalist struggle wanting self-government like Australia or Canada but not the ending of British rule in India. Of particular concern in this paper was his tireless campaign until his death in 1915, for the abolition of Indian indentureship.

70. Cited by Tinker, *op cit.*

The Indian Connection

The influence of Indian Thought and Ideas on East Indians in the Caribbean

Brinsley Samaroo

In 1912 Jaipal Chamar, then 25 years of age was indentured from his hometown in Basti District, Uttar Pradesh for five years' service in the Caribbean. Landed in Jamaica, he was first sent to Westmoreland where he re-indentured himself after the initial five-year period. After his indentureship, he worked in various parts of Jamaica as a paid labourer, finally settling down in Kingston where today he resides at the home of an adopted daughter. In his day Jaipal was a noted dancer and today treasures his old dancing costumes, brought from India, as dear as life itself.[1] In 1954 at age 66, Jaipal who had lost touch with his family in India was able to re-establish his Indian connection: he was able to trace and write to a son in Calcutta who was born some months after Jaipal's departure; born to a mother forcibly widowed by the vagaries of the system which Indians neither created nor desired. From Calcutta, Ayodhya Dass was equally happy to renew his connection. His letters to his father are as informative as they are poignant:

> *Respected father,*
> *You will be surprised to know that a son whom you might not have seen is replying from this side. I was about to born when you left this place. We were two brothers. Our mother looked after us anyhow and we came to Calcutta for service. Fifteen years ago my brother Dwarika passed away and left me alone, unlucky in this world.*[2]

As the correspondence developed, Jaipal's eagerness to find out about his wife and his village friends increased: 'Write me about your mother's welfare and the rest of the village. Respectful greetings to to all those who know me.' Ayodhya had a fervent wish to see his father. He begged him to return:

Whenever your letter comes I wish I had wings
And could fly away to see you.
Your destitute sister has no one and
I am looking after her
She has gone blind crying for you.
She now lives only with the hope of
seeing her brother's face.
And my mother after receiving your first letter
cried for ten days and died.[3]

Jaipal Chamar's search for his heritage has been re-enacted time
and time again by Indians settled abroad. The form of this quest has
not always been in direct correspondence with relations in the
ancestral place. During the century and a half that Indians have been
in the Caribbean they have constantly sought to maintain this contact
by seeking out, during indentureship, new immigrants who could tell
them of developments at home. This was a major means of contact
since indentured Indians were regarded and did regard themselves as
transients who were to return home after their indentureship.

The Indians therefore felt it necessary to keep abreast of
developments at home. Through these contacts indentured labourers
were able to renew their Indian connection. In this regard, there
developed a cadre of letter-writers drawn from among the more
literate of the immigrants. Babu Lal Behari, for example, who came
in 1867 from the village of Dumraon in Bihar became very popular in
his district because of years of free letter-writing performed for his
compatriots. When, therefore, the Presbyterian missionary K.J.
Grant went to the Cupar Grange area to win converts, all hands
pointed to the Babu as the man who could speak for them.

After indentureship ended the contact took other forms such as
visits by Hindu and Muslim missionaries, many of whom founded
new sects and schools of thought in the region. There was also the
posting to these colonies of Christian missionaries some of whom had
undergone training in India or in Indian religious thought in Canada.
As the Indian independence movement developed strength from the
twenties, Caribbean Indian journalists and politicians involved
themselves actively in supporting the agitation in India.[4] And from
the late thirties there was the introduction of Indian movies by Ranjit
Kumar, a London-trained engineer originally from Lahore. In 1935
Kumar introduced *Bala Joban* which was followed by others such as
Afzal, Chabukwali, Jungle Ka Chavan, Andaz and *Midnight Mail.*

These were shown to packed houses in Trinidad and British Guiana.[5] By 1945 these films had already started to make an impact: 'The Indian talkies have been responsible for a cultural re-awakening in Trinidad among Indians. Many are learning their own language with its help.'[6] As East Indian communities in the region increased in affluence from the forties they invited Indian artistes to perform particularly in Trinidad and British Guiana. Since this time too, an increasing number of Caribbean Indians were going to India; some on pilgrimage, others to visit ancestral places or to do business with Indian traders. By the late forties there was a clamour by Caribbean Indians for places in Indian universities. Many persons intending to study in India pleaded with former legislator and trade union leader A.C. Rienzi and he started negotiations with the Indian government. In a letter to the Department of Commonwealth Relations in Delhi, Rienzi pointed out that there was no facility in the Caribbean for the study of subjects such as Dentistry, Medicine, Engineering and Military Science, and that facilities in the United Kingdom and North America had become greatly reduced. Places for students from the Caribbean, Rienzi pointed out, should not be for East Indians alone. 'I would appreciate it if a percentage of the number suggested could be reserved for students of African descent.'[7] After much negotiation the Government of India agreed to Rienzi's proposals. University seats as well as scholarships were to be made available to students in Trinidad, British Guiana and the other smaller territories and were not to be restricted to East Indians.[8] By 1955 the facility was extended to Jamaica.[9] The scheme continues at the present time and students from the Caribbean go to India to study more widely than in the few areas initially opened.

It may be pertinent at this stage to look at some of the factors which have been responsible for this Indian connection. Many New World East Indians as well as persons of other races in their search for some philosophical baisis for life find Western values wanting in many respects. The emphasis on materialism, for example, offers no more than temporary palliatives for the many problems of life. They are therefore looking increasingly to old civilizations such as India to see how these societies coped with their dilemmas and this search has led increasingly to study and meditation inspired by Indian thought. And young East Indians, in their search for beauty in song and dance, are finding Indian musical and artistic forms highly satisfying. In this regard, the establishment of an Indian connection fulfils a profound emotional need.

There are other, equally compelling reasons why the East Indian in the Caribbean has always maintained a closeness with the ancestral culture. Migrant peoples throughout history have always felt the need to identify with their culture. It gives them a feeling of reassurance, security and comfort. The importance of Israel to members of the Jewish diaspora is a classic case and Irish Americans make frequent pilgrimage to the Emerald Isle. Indeed, their leaders seem to feel it necessary for them to make statements regarding major events in Northern Ireland. This sense of identification with an ancestral culture becomes all the more important when that culture is linked with significant works of art and literature. The majority of Indians who came to the Caribbean came from that very Gangetic plain which produced Indian religious heroes such as Lord Rama, Krishna, Buddha and Mahavira[10] and this very area was the scene for the enactment of great Indian epics like the Ramayana and the Mahabharata. Despite their illiteracy in English, they were able to recite with great pride verses from these epics and to set up, as ideals for their children, the qualities of these heroes. Indeed, East Indians have always chosen their children's names from among the characters in these epics, and allusions to the greatness of that culture and the need to keep up its good name appear again and again in their statements in the new homelands. In a farewell memorandum to departing Governor Chancellor for example the East Indian community in Trinidad pointed out that 'in keeping with the best traditions of our ancient race' their connection with Trinidad had been characterised by loyalty and patriotism to the British Empire.[11] Again in 1948 at the Jamaica celebration of the first anniversary of Indian independence the speakers recounted the great leaders which 'Mother India' possessed, all of whom were inspiring her 'to go forward in keeping her appointment with destiny.'[12]

Another factor which intensifies identification with the ancestral culture is a sense of persecution, either of the emigrant group or the ancestral race in the homeland. This consideration has been of considerable importance in solidifying the relationship between India and the Indians of the Caribbean. Indians in the Caribbean have always felt a sense of persecution. Ever since he was brought to the Caribbean in 1838 the East Indian was regarded as an interloper by the African population, as one who had come to depress wages in the colonies. In British Guiana the blacks felt that 'the coolie takes bread from the negro labourer and lowers the price of labour.'[13] An additional reason for anti-Indian feeling was the fact that East

Indians were culturally and physically quite different from the rest of of the population. And in a predominantly Eurocentric society, those who did not conform to socialization into a Western, Christian norm were regarded as strange, if not uncivilized. For example, the Trinidad paper *New Era* carried a number of articles during March and April of 1871 which described Indians as a dangerous element, standing as a menace to the whole society and responsible for crimes of violence. This view of the East Indian was not restricted to what one might term an irresponsible press. As high an official as Governor Byatt told a meeting of the Board of Agriculture in 1929 of 'a fairly large estate owned by an intelligent person, not the ordinary coolie.'[14] Additionally it was not until 1948 that recognition (for the purpose of state aid) was accorded to an East Indian primary school; this was the Islamia School at El Socorro in San Juan. This late recognition was certainly not for want of application by East Indian leaders. At a meeting of the East Indian Advisory Board of 7th June 1937 a request was made for the appointment of Hindus and Muslims on the colony's Board of Education.[15] And at the Board's meeting of 5th June 1939 Al Haj Moulir Ameer Ali moved that the Education Ordinance be amended to include all religious associations in the colony and not Christian denominations only.

In the face of these considerations, the Indians felt beleagured and therefore looked for some greater source of inspiration and protection. For this they looked toward India. Conversely when, from the 1880s, the Indian National Movement began in earnest, Indians abroad felt pride in associating themselves with that movement. From the 1930s their heroes became Gandhi and Nehru and their newspapers were filled with news of the agitation in India. Some Caribbean Indians domiciled away from the region regularly sent articles of magazines informing of the struggle;[16] others like the Indo-Trinidadian Adrian Cola Reinzi campaigned in Britain for Indian Independence.[17]

In the religious sphere the Indian connection has been strong and continuous. Between the Caribbean visits of Bhai Parmanand, an Indian mystic, in 1910 and that of Sant Keshav Dass in 1977, there has been a constant flow of Indian religious leaders to the Caribbean. But the movement has not been one-way; over the years a number of Hindus and Muslims have gone back to the sub-continent for training and inspiration. As early as 1888 Yacoob Ali of Princes Town went to India where he spent nearly a decade studying Islamic theology. He returned in 1898 as a Hafiz (i.e. one who has memorized the Holy

Quran) and as a Quari (one whose intonation of the verses thereof is deemed very correct).[18] And in 1976 Maulana Waffie Mohammed returned to Trinidad after years of religious study in Pakistan. Some of the many other visits of this two-way traffic will be discussed presently.

What have been the reasons for this intense religious contact? As mentioned before, the transience of Caribbean society and the consequent absence of thought therein created a void which had to be filled by imported ideology. For the East Indian the source of this ideology was India. More significantly there was what the Indians saw as the threat of Christianity and the prospect therein of the erosion of Indian values. From 1868 the Scottish Canadian Presbyterians of Nova Scotia started a mission of proselytism and education among East Indians in the Caribbean. Starting in Trinidad they moved to Grenada in 1884, St. Lucia and British Guiana in 1885 and Jamaica in 1894.[19] The Presbyterians paid close attention to the activities of the Indians, the better to understand them. Yacoob Ali's departure for India in 1888, for example, was carefully noted by Kenneth Grant, pioneer/missionary:

> *Their zeal is commendable. A devoted Muslim of considerable wealth and living not far from our house sent his son to be educated as a mullah or priest. He returned after an absence of five or six years bearing the title of 'Hafiz' which was given to one who had committed to memory the whole Koran in its original Arabic.* [20]

The Presbyterians often conducted campaigns against and debates with Muslims and Hindus and this was reciprocated by the East Indians. In 1906, for example, some Muslims in British Guiana published a pamphlet pointing out the hollowness of Christianity as compared with Islam.[21]

The trend of this paper might suggest that the contact between India and the Caribbean was only a contact between India and Indians in the Caribbean. This is not so. An indirect Indian connection had been established even before indentureship. African slaves destined for the Caribbean were often purchased with the currency of Indian fabrics; indeed the 'piece de Inde' became a standard measurement on the West African coast and 'Indiennage' (the manufacture of printed cloths to be used in the African trade) became an accepted part of the iniquitous dealing in human cargo.[22] Furthermore in the development of Caribbean education, India was the experimental soil in which the 'monitorial system', (which has played so important a role in the training of Caribbean peoples) was first introduced.[23] For Dr Andrew Bell, a British educator, developed the system in Madras from whence it came to British Guiana and to the rest of the Caribbean during the 1830s.[24] This Christian Indian connection was of course furthered during and after the period of indentureship by the Canadian Presbyterians. Despite the anti-Hindu/Muslim attitude of many of the Presbyterians, it is amazing to notice the degree to which these Presbyterians relied on India for the conduct of their work in the Caribbean. In 1854 the Canadians had sent a missionary to India to study its philosophy; before Canadians were sent to work in the Caribbean they had to undergo training in Indian thought; there was the constant importation of Christian Indian literature by the Presbyterians in the Caribbean, and the transfer of missionaries who had had experience in India, to stations in the Caribbean.[25] Indeed, Indian religious philosophy appears to have permeated so deeply into Caribbean Presbyterianism that when Trinidad's premier church was being built during the 1870s – Susamachar or Church of Glad Tidings – a sacred pipal tree brought from India was planted next to the church.[26] When, finally, the Presbyterians were finding difficulty in meeting the challenge of a reviving Hindu and Muslim consciousness from the late twenties, they invited a Christian Indian from India to seek to restrain Trinidad Indians from returning to their native faiths.[27]

Let us now look briefly at one aspect of the Indian connection that has received very little attention by researchers on East Indians. This is the contact between Caribbean Muslims and the Indian sub-continent. There has been a marked closeness between Muslims in this part of the world and India up to 1947 and with Pakistan since that time. In fact it would be no exaggeration to say that leadership of the local Muslim community up to the forties came largely from India-born Muslims or from Trinidadian Indians who had studied there.[28] The case of Hafiz Yacoob Ali has already been mentioned. An even more illustrious figure was Sayyad Abdul Aziz Meah. The latter came from Afghanistan in 1883 and worked out his indentureship in the Princes Town area. He then settled at Lere Village where John Morton the Presbyterian pioneer had started his work of evangelization. Aziz was very learned in Islamic theology and his ability to see himself not merely as a Muslim but also as part of a larger East Indian community endeared him to a wide cross-section of Indians to whom he provided leadership. In 1898 he joined with a

number of Hindus and Presbyterians to form the first organized
Indian pressure group in the colony – the East India National
Association with headquarters in Princes Town. Around the same
time he took a leading role in creating the Islamic Guardian
Association, and by 1907 he was appointed the first Kazi (or chief
religious leader) of Muslims in Trinidad. As a public leader his name
appears frequently on delegations to official quarters. For example,
in 1904 he led a group which saw Governor Henry Jackson on the
question of the recognition of Muslim marriages. Of course, such
recognition, when it did come, was due in large measure to agitation
conducted during his lifetime. Moreover, before he died, the Kazi
was able to see the fruition of another of his cherished dreams. By
1926 he was able to unite most of the colony's Muslims in the
Tackveeyatul Islamic Association (Society for the strength of Islam)
which was incorporated by Ordinance 39 of 1931. It was at TIA
school that the aforemention Islamia was recognized in 1948.

Whilst Aziz laboured in the South, another former indentured
labourer organized the early Muslim community in North Trinidad.
Haji Ruknudeen Sahib came to Trinidad from the Punjab in 1893 at
the age of 18; he was learned in Arabic, Urdu and Hindi which he
perfected by constant reading and recitation in Trinidad. After the
completion of his indentureship he settled in Tunapuna and acquired
sufficient affluence to be enabled to go on the Hajj pilgrimage in
Mecca. Under his leadership a number of jamaats were established in
North Trinidad and small schools set up in villages. In 1927 Haji
Ruknudeen was appointed Kazi in succession to Aziz Meah.

After these two leaders there came a succession of missionaries
from India; only the more significant ones will be mentioned here.
Moulvie Haji Sufi Shah Mohammed Hassan Hanafi Quadri came to
the colony in 1914. According to reports of those who knew him, his
was an Orthodoxy in Islam similar to that of Iran's leading present-
day Ayatollah. This rigidity was opposed by many including Haji
Ruknudeen and he left the colony in 1918. In 1920 there was the
arrival, at the invitation of local Muslims, of an Ahmaadiya
missionary from the Punjab, Moulir Fazal Karim Khan Durrani.
During his two-year stay here, Durrani opened the first major schism
in local Islam by his advocacy of the view that Mirza Ghulam Ahmed
came as a prophet after Mohammed (u.w.b.p.) whom most Muslims
regard as the last of the prophets. What was worse in the eyes of his
antagonists, was that Durrani arranged for the Indian/Islamic training
of Ameer Ali, a youth from Siparia in South Trinidad.[29]

Ali was educated at the Anjuman Ishaat-I-Islam in Lahore and made the Hajj to Mecca before his return home in 1930. From Trinidad he spent some time in Surinam as a Muslim missionary where controversy again raged between the newly organized Ahmaadiyas and the traditional Sunnis over questions such as the crucifixion of Jesus and the prophethood of Mirza Ghulam Ahmed.[30]

As a result of this schism new Muslim organizations were formed both in Trinidad and in Surinam. In the former colony a substantial number of Muslims withdrew to form the Anjuman Sunaatul Jamaat Association (ASJA) which was incorporated by Ordinance 24 of 1935. In Surinam, the Surinamese Islamic Organization was initiated. To counter the influence of Ameer Ali, the ASJA obtained the services of Mouvi Nazeer Ahmad Seemab of Lahore in 1936 but this visit was the cause of further division among the Muslims, resulting in Seemab's return to Lahore in 1938. One year later, he was invited to Trinidad and he founded yet another organization, the Tabligh-ul-Islam ('for the propagation of Islam through education'). Upon his death in 1943 his small group of followers merged with the TIA.[31] In the meantime further schism had developed in the TIA and in 1947 Moulvi Ameer Ali and a group of his followers left the Association and formed the Trinidad Muslim League (TML). This organization was incorporated in 1950.

The formation of Pakistan in 1947 did not by any means see the diminution of this connection. Indeed the TML was founded precisely on Pakistan Day, that is 15th August, 1947, to underline this connection with the sub-continent.[32] From this time not only did religious visits continue, but there was great rejoicing when civil or political personalities from Pakistan visited the Caribbean. In November 1948, for example, Mr M. A. Ispahani, Pakistan's envoy to the United States spent a few days in Trinidad. The island's Muslim community persuaded him to lay foundation stones for the proposed Jinnah Memorial Mosque and the Jinnah Memorial College, both institutions to be named after Mohammed Ali Jinnah, one of Pakistan's founders and its first Governor-General. Ispahani's visit was an occasion for celebration by Trinidad Muslims who held a number of functions in his honour.[33] In 1950 there was the extended stay of two of contemporary Islam's leading exponents: His Exalted Eminence Maulana Abdul Aleem Siddiqui and his Secretary Hafiz Dr Fazl-Ur-Rahaman Ansari. Among those who formed the reception committee was the ageing Haji Ruknudeen who must have been very pleased to see such eminent persons in the land of his adoption.

The visiting missionaries were on a world mission 'to unite the forces of religion against irreligiousness.'[34] They had toured the East Indies, Africa, Mauritius and Europe and were now in Trinidad which would be used as a base for visits to British Guiana, Surinam and the rest of the Caribbean. Indeed two delegates from the Guianese Anjuman came to Trinidad to meet the visitors and to arrange for their visit there.[35] The Maulana and the Hafiz were given a civic reception in Port of Spain and a ceremonial tour of San Fernando, they gave lectures and participated in prayers throughout the colony and at one meeting at the Queen's Park Savannah in Port of Spain they drew as many as 7,000 people.[36] This visit had an effect on the local Muslim population which no visit before or since has had. At important discussion relating to their faith, Muslims never fail to recount the event and as recently as June 1979 one Muslim organization used the taped voice of Dr Ansari in support of their efforts to obtain a teacher of Arabic.[37] And a masjid in Caroni was named Siddiqui Masjid.

In like manner, Hindu religious leaders, politicians and academics have made frequent trips to the region. Again, the treatment in this essay will be brief. The first missionary to the region appears to have been Bhai Parmanand an Indian leader of the Arya Samaj movement who went to British Guiana where he spent some months doing religious work.[38] It was from there that disciples of Parmanand went to Surinam and Trinidad extending the teaching and social work programme of this late nineteenth century reform movement. In 1914 Pandit Dimanath Tiwary came from British Guiana to Trinidad and he was followed shortly thereafter by Pandit Hari Persad whose work was concentrated in the Marabella/Gasparillo area. After the First World War other Hindu leaders from India followed. In 1928 Jaimini Mehta, a Vedic missionary and scholar, spent a few months in Trinidad where he was most enthusiastically received. One newspaper estimated that Mehta gave as many as 400 lectures [39] and older Trinidadians distinctly recall Mehta as a charismatic speaker who held audiences spellbound for hours. Under his patronage a Vedic mission was begun in Trinidad and a Vedic school opened.[40] From Trinidad Mehta went to British Guiana where he had an equally busy schedule and where he also started a school.[41]

In May 1929 there was the visit of C.F. Andrews, close associate of Mahatma Gandhi whom Indians re-named 'Deenabhandu': friend of the poor. Andrews had played a major role in the movement for the abolition of Indian indentureship for which he was publicly thanked by the Indian National Congress.[42] In 1929 he was deputed by a number of persons and non-governmental organizations in India to visit the Caribbean and report on the conditions of Indians who had made their permanent homes here. In a letter to Dr J.B. Singh of Georgetown, one of the organizers of Andrews' trip stated the reasons for their choice of Andrews:

> *Leaving out Mahatma Gandhi, he is the only man in India whose words carry the greatest weight with the Inidan public on the question of Indians abroad...He is one Englishman in India who completely identified himself with us.*[43]

Andrews arrived in Georgetown in mid-May 1929 and spent the rest of May, June and July touring extensively in the hinterlands where the Indians lived. He spoke at meetings almost daily on questions such as repatriation of Indians to India, re-settlement of labourers from the Indian sub-continent in British Guiana, race problems, alcoholism, Hindu ideals, the development of Islam and on a host of other matters.[44] Andrews' final report on British Guiana was lengthy and detailed and contains much prophetic analysis relating to that territory.[45] Whilst he was in British Guiana he also visited Surinam. In July 1929 he arrived in Trinidad where he stayed for just over a month doing similar work as he had done on the mainland.[46]

In the meantime, the Arya Samajists were busily organizing themselves and in the process, were inviting a number of theologians from India. In 1929 local Samajists invited Ayodhya Persad who had just attended the Parliament of Religions in the United States.[47] Persad appears to have spent a few years in the Caribbean, travelling and setting up well-organized branches of the Arya Samaj. By January 1935 the Trinidad branch was able to erect its own temple in Chaguanas. They were also able to invite two additional missionaries: Satya Charan Shastri in 1935 and Pandit Bhaskaranand in 1936. The latter was a native of Bihar in India, High Court advocate at Patna and son of one of the leaders of the Arya Samaj movement in India. He appears to have been on his way to Surinam as Vedic missionary to the Arya Samaj Association there.[48] In any event he gave a number of lectures in Trinidad, at the India Club and at the new Arya Mandir in Chaguanas.

The presence of Aryan missionaries stimulated the exponents of Sanatan Dharma (literally 'Eternal Religion' or the traditional, orthodox forms of Hinduism) to bestir themselves. In Trinidad the Sanatan Dharma Association was founded as early as 1881.[49] In 1930 local Sanatanists invited Pandit N. K. Banerji, a Sanatanist Hindu who spent a few years here, married locally and did much organizational work. He advocated the establishment of Hindu and Muslim schools, the teaching of Hindi in schools and spoke generally of religious developments in India.[50] With the aid of persons such as Banerji the Association became a legally recognized religious organization in 1932. Side by side with the Association there grew up a rival Sanatanist body, the Sanatan Dharma Board of Control located in Tunapuna (whereas the Association was located in Couva). The Board was also legally incorporated in 1932.

As early as 1933 the Sanatan Dharma Board of Control was in contact with the Sanatan Dharma Pratinidhi Sabha of the Punjab. One of the officers of this Lahore-based organization wrote a letter to the Secretary of State for the Colonies arguing that the Couva-based Sanatan Dharma Association had no claim to represent the Hindus of Trinidad since its President the Hon. Michael Sarran Teelucksingh was an Anglican.[51] Two years later the Board became affiliated to the Sabha at Lahore and in 1937 it delegated its President, Pandit Dimanath Tiwari to proceed to Lahore, there to seek that organization's assistance in tackling some of the problems affecting local Hindus and to obtain, if possible, the assistance of a missionary therefrom.

It was in this context that Dr Parashuram Sharma arrived in the colony in 1938 and stayed for a year. Dr Sharma was an extremely energetic person and made tours to British Guiana and Surinam advocating the formation of a Sanatan Dharma Federation of the West Indies. He led delegations to government officials seeking legal permission to enable Hindus to cremate their dead by the pyre system, advocating the teaching of Hindi in schools and the legalizing of Hindu marriages.[52] Above all, Dr Sharma did his utmost to unite the Hindus under the umbrella of one organization. In this he was not successful and, writing from Lahore in 1940, he claimed that one of the reasons for this was the 'mutual jealousy' of the organizers of the various Hindu groups. He added:

> *The standard of organization in Western countries , of which so much is said, is one which is based mostly on selfish ends to exploit weaker nations. As I attach importance to the higher feelings and ideas, I find people wanting in following higher objects. I should hope that the Hindu Maha Sabha in Trinidad will not lose sight of this ideal and will not sacrifice quality and character at the altar of quantity, intolerance and favouritism.[53]*

It was not until 1952 that some semblance of unity among Sanatanists was achieved with the formation of the Sanatan Dharam Maha Sabha.

In this quest for identification with a larger and more recognized centre of Indian resurgence, particularly in the twentieth century, Caribbean Indians have accepted ideas and institutions which have given them a sense of pride and dignity. Whenever learned secular-minded Indians visited the region this sense of achievement was high. For example when Dr D.P Pandia (member of the Indian National Congress and itinerant champion of Indian causes in the United States, Jamaica, Central America and Trinidad) visited in 1941 he became a focus of attention for East Indians who were more interested in the culture rather than in the propagation of religion. In this way such visits formed a brake of the incipient communalism that was ever-present in the society in that it brought together East Indians of varying religious backgrounds. Pandia provided leadership for such people during the year he spent in Trinidad and he was instrumental in the building (physical and organizational) of India Club, opened in 1942. Educated East Indians also felt proud to be able to present one of their race to their non-Indian peers.[54] The same pride was felt by Jamaican Indians when A.K. Kalekar, Indian parliamentarian, visited that colony in 1958.[55]

On the other hand the encouragement of religious leaders from the sub-continent denied Caribbean East Indians the necessary opportunity of struggling to find solutions to their problems in the new and very different environment. Instead, these religious leaders brought with them many of the prejudices and irrational conflicts which had divided India over the centuries. When the Presbyterians brought Rev Netram in 1930 to stem the tide of a resurgent Hinduism and Islam, he indulged in the senseless condemnation of 'heathens' which many Christians in India and Europe were engaged in. This was the cause of serious divisions in the colony and angry letters and meetings demanded his withdrawal from Trinidad.[56] Similarly, Hindu and Mulsim missionaries by their constant and intense debate divided their own faiths and fed conflict between Hinduism and Islam. Such conflicts persist today and go a long way in maintaining a divided society.[57] This religious conflict has at times manifested itself in political form. In 1946, for example, the local newspapers published stories about communal violence in India during the turbulent days of partition.[58] Such news conspired with the growing feeling of communalism in the Chaguanas/Bejucal area to produce a good deal of tension leading to violence. By November of that year the situation had deteriorated so much that Muslim, Hindu and Christian Indian leaders joined with other civil personnel and toured the area in an attempt to quell the uprising. At one meeting Hindus and Muslims were advised to 'bury the hatchet'.[59] This development of conflict, coinciding with the increasing presence of missionaries from the 1920s stood in marked contrast to the previous years. During the years 1897 to 1921, Professor Jha points out, there was a good deal of cooperation among Indians of all persuasions who were seeking to organize themselves into pressure-groups geared to solving their problems.[60]

A major dilemma of the East Indian in the Caribbean, particularly at this time when Afro-Caribbeans are also actively seeking their roots, is the clarification of his relationship with India. The India implied here is not necessarily the physical land mass but a whole complex of attitudes, thought-processes and beliefs which come as a part of the inheritance of that civilization. And these have to be viewed in relation to their relevance in the New World. For an Indian like Jaipal Chamar, India is physically and culturally very real and so he has no problems in identifying with it. For second and third generation East Indians, torn between East and West, this attempt at clarification can be tortuous, even traumatic. V.S. Naipaul, for example, for whom India in 1964 was an area of darkness, returns to it in 1977 but with a chastened perspective. India is now a wounded civilization:

> *India is for me a difficult country. It isn't my home; and yet I cannot reject it or be indifferent to it; I cannot travel only for the sights. I am at once too close and too far...An enquiry about India – even an inquiry about the Emergency – has quickly to go beyond the political. It has to be an enquiry about the Indian attitudes; it has to be an enquiry about the civilization itself.*[61]

The Westindian East Indians will be neither Westindian nor East Indian until they first of all come to terms with themselves; and this process certainly involves an understanding of their Indian connection.

NOTES

1. Interview with Jaipal Chamar. Kingston 15 July 1979. The author is grateful to Dr Ajay Mansingh for arranging this meeting and for providing access to Jaipal Chamar's letters.

2. Ayodhya Dass to Jaipal Chamar, 29 December 1954.

3. *Ibid.* 15 May 1955.

4. See, for examples, *Trinidad Guardian,* 15 March 1921, p. 5. for article on Gandhi. Also, *The Beacon* (Trinidad) which ran an 'India Section' from March 1932 to November 1933 when the magazine ended. For similar reactions in Jamaica see *The Indian,* Vol. 1, No. 1, September 1940.

5. Interviews with Mr Ranjit Kumar in June and July 1979. The author is grateful to Mr Kumar for allowing access to his private papers.

6. M.J. Kirplani et al, *Indian Centenary review,* 1945, p. 70.

7. A.C. Rienzi to N.C. Sen, 28 November 1946, *Rienzi's Personal papers.*

8. *Evening News,* Trinidad 17 April 1947; Also *Trinidad Guardian,* 19 April 1947.

9. *Daily Gleaner,* 14 November 1955.

10. L. Mansingh, 'Cultural survivals among East Indians in Jamaica'. Paper presented at Second Conference on East Indians in the Caribbean, Trinidad 1979, p. 6.

11. Chancellor Papers, 4(1) Trinidad. Rhodes House Library. Oxford.

12. *Daily Gleaner,* 16 August 1948. For a similar sentiment on the occasion of a subsequent Indian Independence celebration, see the *Gleaner,* 27 January 1953.

13. James Rodway, 'Labour and Emigration', *Timehri,* Vol. VI, September 1919, p. 36.

14. *Trinidad Guardian,* 10 April, 1929, p. 9.

15. Minutes of East Indian Advisory Board, 1937.

16. See, for example, the articles sent in from New York by George Madho Singh to *The East Indian Weekly,* 3 & 24 January 1931. In Jamaica the scrapbook of Mr J.G. Thakur contains magazines such as *Asia and the Americas,* New York, 1945, and *India News,* Los Angeles, 1943.

17. In London Rienzi met and was inspired by Gandhi. He was also one of the joint secretaries who convened the Third Indian Political Conference in London in 1933.

18. *Tribute to Hafiz Yacoob Ali,* ASJA Inc., (Trinidad, 1972)

19. K.J. Grant, *My missionary memories,* (Halifax, 1923), pp. 101-6.

20. *Ibid.,* pp. 67-8.

21. *Proof of the prophet Mohammed from the Holy Bible,* (Georgetown, 1906.)

22. Robert Stein. 'The Nantes Slave Traders, 1783-1815' Ph.D. History thesis, York Univ., 1975, pp. 37-64.

23. The Monitorial System was one in which the brighter students in the upper classes of primary schools were chosen to teach their juniors under the supervision of the head teacher or a senior teacher. It enabled large numbers of children to learn basic reading, writing and arithmetic at little extra cost to the system.

24. James Azeez, 'The Apprenticeship System in British Guiana'. M.A. History Thesis, Univ. of Guyana, 1979, p. 142.

25. This aspect of the connection is only summarized here. For a more detailed study see the author's 'Missionary methods and local responses: The Canadian Presbyterians and East Indians in the Caribbean'. Paper presented at First Conference on East Indians in the Caribbean, Trinidad, 1975.

26. The pipal or asvattha is often mentioned in Indian scriptures as a plant to be venerated; it has its roots in heaven and its branches on earth. To stand in its shade is to receive blessings; its leaves have a curative effect and these are often given in offerings at pujas.

27. *United Church of Canada Yearbook*, 1931, p. 80. The visitor was Rev J.W. Netram, son of one of the very early Presbyterian converts Balaram who had returned to India after his indentureship.

28. Information regarding the development of Islam in the Caribbean is scarce and scattered. For this section of the paper the author has attempted to reconstruct a tentative history mainly from the following sources:
(a) *Kirplani et al, op cit.*
(b) *The East Indian Weekly*, 1928-1932.
(c) Robert J. Smith, 'Muslim East Indians in Trinidad: retention of ethnic identity under acculturative conditions.' Ph. D. thesis (Anthropology), Univ. of Pennsylvania, 1963.

29. *East Indian Weekly*, 19 July 1930, p. 11.

30. T. Tjoe Nij, 'The East Indians of Suriname'. Paper presented at 11th Conference of Caribbean Historians, Curacao, 1979, p. 26.

31. M. Rafeeq, 'History of Islam and Muslims in Trinidad'. *Souvenir Brochure of the Jinnah Memorial Mosque*, (Trinidad, 1954), p. 33.

32. *Ibid.*, p. 34.

33. See *Port of Spain Gazette*, 10, 12, & 14 November 1948.

34. *Trinidad Guardian*, 5 March 1950, p. 1.

35. *Ibid.*, 12 & 22 March 1950.

36. *Ibid.*, 14, 17, & 22 March 1950.

37. 'Islamic Hour': Radio Trinidad, 15 June 1979. This recording was of a speech given in 1963 when Dr Ansari paid a second visit to Trinidad.

38. T. Ramnarine, 'The growth of the East Indian community in British Guiana, 1880-1920'. D. Phil Thesis, Sussex Univ., 1977, p. 204.

39. *East Indian Weekly*, 12 April 1930.

40. *Ibid.*, 7 September 1929.

41. *Ramnarine*, p.215.

42. N.V. Rajkumar, *Indians outside India*, (New Delhi, 1951), p. 56.

43. Letter from B.D. Chaturvedi cited in *Daily Chronicle*, Georgetown, 10 March 1929.

44. *Daily Chronicle*, 19, 24 & 29 May 1929. Also 21, 25 & 29 June 1929.

45. CO 111/689/1930: 'Impressions of British Guiana'.

46. For details see *The East Indian Weekly*, 3 & 31 August 1929; 14 September 1929.

47. *Kirpalani et al*, p.66.

48. *Trinidad Guardian*, 5 July 1936, p. 26.

49. *Kirpalani et al*, p.61. Also letter heads of the Association.

50. *East Indian Weekly*, 4 & 25 January, 1930; 22 August, 1931.

51. Dr Parashuram Sharma to Secretary of State, 11 January 1933.

52. Proceedings of the general meeting of the Sanatan Dharmic public of Trinidad, 13th November 1938, Couva, Trinidad.

53. Dr P. Sharma to President Hindu Maha Sabha of Trinidad 24 October 1940. Courtesy Mr Ranjit Kumar.

54. Dennis Mahabir et al: *A souvenir of Dr Pandia's visit to Trinidad*, (Trinidad, 1942). Also *The Observer*, Trinidad, December 1941 & February 1942.

55. *Daily Gleaner*, 5 May 1958. Also 3, 5, 7 & 8 July 1958.

56. *East Indian Weekly, 9, 16, & 23 August 1930. Also 4 October 1930.*

57. See 'A Hindu Protest', *Trinidad Guardian*, 28 September 1979, p. 12.

58. *Trinidad Guardian,* 22 October & 13 November 1946.

59. *Ibid.,* 17 November 1946.

60. 'East Indians Pressure Groups in Trinidad 1897-1921' *Political protest and political organization in the Caribbean from the late 19th century,* Vol. 1, St. Augustine, 1976, p. 75f.

61. V.S. Naipaul, *India: a wounded civilization,* (New York, 1977).

Control and Resistance among Indian Workers

A Study of Labour on the Sugar Plantations of Trinidad 1875 – 1917

Kusha Haraksingh

The sugar plantations of the Caribbean have been the location of much of the history of the region, and especially in relation to the period of slavery, a recurring theme in that history has been the ways in which the labour force was controlled and the means by which it sought to resist. Thus, a great deal of attention has been directed not only to the slave codes imposed by the different European nations with possessions in the area but also to their modification by local assemblies and councils, as well as to the actual practice of slavery itself. In terms of resistance, investigations have been undertaken both on passive and active manifestations, with the events in St Domingue in the 1790s being regarded as something of a zenith.[1] However, following the emancipation of slaves in 1838 attention in the British colonies at any rate is switched to the emergent peasantry, which is seen as constituting the more progressive sector of the economy, contributing directly to indigenous development as opposed to the plantations which supposedly continue primarily to promote metropolitan economic growth. The historians now explore the hardships and obstacles faced by the upcoming peasants, and for a time, as though with emancipation the battle had been won, tend not to be too concerned with the trials of free labour on the plantations.

Part of the reason for this shift in the focus of concern is the impression, unfortunately now almost axiomatic, that emancipation was accompanied in the larger territories by a general exodus of freedmen from the plantations. This picture was based on a number of considerations, including the feeling that any freed man worth his salt, and with the opportunity, would naturally have left the estates on which he had suffered so much as a slave. In truth, however, historians have been more eager to follow the freed men out of the estates than they themselves had been to leave. In Trinidad in particular, the evidence would seem to suggest that far from withdrawing from plantation labour, freedmen (especially women, children and those males past their prime) were being systematically pushed out by planters making way for contract workers from the smaller Caribbean islands and to a more limited extent from the United States.[2] At the same time, a vigorous campaign of planter propaganda about the extent of arable land in the island and the shortage of labour was laying the groundwork for a more elaborate system of contractual arrangements to replace slavery. For the planters had never been reconciled to the loss of servile labour; schooled in that tradition, they were convinced to a man that a tractable and dependable labour force was absolutely indispensable. By 1845 they had successfully persuaded the imperial authorities to sanction a scheme of Indian indentureship, and in May that year the first shipload of indentured immigrants from India arrived in Trinidad. By the time indentureship was abolished in 1917, owing largely to nationalist pressure in India, some 143,000 Indians had come to Trinidad. Less than one in four returned to their homeland, claiming the return passage to which they were entitled under the terms of their contract. The remainder exchanged their passage home for a grant of land and cash, and continued for the most part to work on the estates. The steady influx of immigrants, averaging 2,328 per year for the last three decades of the nineteenth century,[3] enabled the planters to stick to their policy of displacing free black labour. By the mid 1870s when the traffic in indentured Indians was well established and the rules governing the system firmly entrenched, Indians constituted 90% of the sugar estate labour force.[4]

The Indian workers can be divided into three distinct groups which each transcended barriers of age and sex. The first category comprised indentured workers, that is, those still under contract; these lived on the estates in barracks provided by their employers. The second group was composed of workers who had served out their contract but who still continued to live with their employers' permission in the barracks. The third category of workers had also completed their contracts; however, they lived not on the estates but in freehold or rented plots in surrounding villages. Each estate had its complement of indentured, free residential, and free non-residential workers. Generally, over the period the proportion of free non-residential to the other two groups combined remained fairly stable, while there was a close inverse relationship between indentured and free residential labour.

The preference for Indians over Blacks (though not for all types of work) has sometimes been summarised in one word: docility. But this general stereotyping is wide off the mark, as the frequent outbreak of strikes, riots and violence at the workplace would attest. The real explanation was that the system rendered the Indians controllable – to varying degrees obviously, for it was easier to control those still under indenture than those who had completed their contracts. The aim of this paper is to explore the means by which that control was accomplished, and the ways in which the process was made difficult.

In defining the context of control, one has to view the labour force as being held 'captive' at several different but connected levels. First of all, where the indentureds were involved there was a legal framework; they were obliged to work or in default to face penal sanctions. Then, for all workers, there was a spatial ambit; the planters, through their influence in the Legislature, were able to champion and secure policies which confined the workers either to or in the vicinity of the estates in the countryside. The promotion of indebtedness among the workers kept them imprisoned in economic terms, and consequently under compulsion to perform at the workplace. The ablest among them were often co-opted to serve as 'drivers' or foremen in the managerial system; ostensibly, they were required to perform the functions of a go-between, but in reality they simply concentrated on executing the wishes of their masters.[5] Thus, the workers were kept in check by their institutional leaders; the very agency which ought to have been the avenue for registering complaints and protest was subverted to other ends. In psychological terms, the prison walls were clearly discernible, for even the ordinary run of plantation life fostered a general feeling of helplessness; few, if any of the workers could have believed that man was the master of his destiny. Added to all of this, recurrent and wasting diseases, malnutrition, poor housing conditions and the low standard of amenities, as well as the low life expectancy, which together should have induced an inclination to escape, served only to create an oppressive sense of inertia. For those who did try to escape, it was often discovered that to slip off one of the bonds was simply to tighten those that remained. It was in essence a model of 'interlocking incarceration'. The avenue of escape was either total revolt – in which all the bonds would be removed at a stroke – or a slow painful struggle for economic independence by working hard and trying to save, during which the labourer would actually be fulfilling the purposes of his employer. The very presentation of these alternatives was itself a measure of control.

Immigrant labour is generally easier to control than local labour, for it is less secure, less confident and in instances of confrontation finds itself facing the weight, if not the wrath, of other social groups. This is even so where the immigrant comes from a society which in overall cultural terms is not dissimilar to the host environment. The less pronounced the similarity the more effective is the physical uprooting itself as a weapon in the arsenal of control. In the case of immigrant Indians in the Caribbean, the degree of similarity was minimal. The North Indian villages from which most of them came were quite literally on the other side of the globe. Deep distinctions in language, religion, social customs and world view separated the Indians from the creole society into which they were being introduced. Nor could it be expected that the differences would be transcended with ease, for the Indians were possessors of an elaborate and sophisticated cultural baggage which historically had demonstrated, even under sustained attack, a most formidable resilience.

In one area, however, the Indians could discern a certain continuity: this was in the metropolitan presence. In India the countryside had been able to ward off some of the social and cultural effects of foreign rule but had been less successful in resisting its economic impact. The penetrative tentacles of the land revenue administration stretched deep into the villages, and generally the disruption wrought by imperial policies which promoted the growth of non-food crops and the weakening of village craft industries was too formidable to be resisted. The ordinary villager who knew of the ultimate power of the British Government and its representatives in the countryside had developed, over generations of foreign control, a marked deference towards the *hukm* or government. In the case of the élite that deference was sometimes no more than a cultivated air, to mask an elaborate ploy to retain in Indian hands the substance of control, but the villager was usually genuine in his awe of the government. Growing rural population, increasing pressure on the land, recurring floods and famines, as well as in the individual case unfortunate personal circumstances, induced many to listen to and to believe the suitably embellished tales of the *arkatis* or recruiters. Those most willing to listen and to be convinced were in the nature of things generally among the least enterprising and successful of their

Old slave quarters on the outskirts of the capital, Georgetown. Sugar workers used to live in these

fellows. Thus, when in 1883 an Indian Government official investigated a group of 1,200 emigrants, he found that almost all of them were illiterate and that almost none had any experience outside the narrow limits of their village. Further, he discovered that one of the things which really united the group was their common experience of personal misfortune – they had lost their land, or antagonised a village big-wig, or had run foul of the authorities.[6] It was not so much that the system deliberately sought out the weak, though deliberate efforts were made to exclude some groups who were regarded as potential troublemakers, such as disbanded soldiers, members of the higher castes, or second-time emigrants. But the entire operation like a whirlpool in the ocean of life, had a way of turning up the flotsam and the jetsam, those most susceptible to push factors, and those most unlikely to resist.

The intending emigrant's first brush with restlessness would come before he left his native land, in the emigration depot while waiting to embark. Here, he would encounter people whom he ordinarily would not have met – from different regions, and speaking unfamiliar dialects and whom he normally would have avoided – members of another religion, and of other castes. The strange world of the depot would follow him on board ship, where the regulation clothing and the identity disc would proclaim him and his fellows as 'coolies', a designation which would confuse customary reference points and threaten established concepts of status and rank. Unsympathetic and sometimes cruel treatment at the hands of the ship's officers, as well as the physical discomfort of the long voyage, often marked by storms at sea or serious outbreaks of disease, would serve to heighten the sense of disorientation. And as one day slowly merged into the next, some would begin to have an inkling of the recruiter's forked tongue, and would come to realize that unlike what they had been led to expect, Trinidad was not a simple short journey away.

Those who were finally 'landed alive', as the ship's papers would describe them, had gone through a formidable experience; ahead lay another, not any less trying.[7] The daily routine of plantation life – long and arduous hours of physical work, punctuated by brief periods of rest in cramped and uncomfortable conditions – generated its own crippling yet steady momentum. Disease hung heavily over the estates, and early death often removed those on the verge of acquiring, in traditional terms, a 'suitable' age to impart direction and guidance to their uprooted countrymen. There was little scope for diversion or recreation, and the overwhelming presence of males in the recruiter's bag meant that many were denied the solace and support of female companionship. Again, it was not that these conditions were deliberately engineered to sap will and intitiative and to keep the workers responsive to authority, though one could justify the claim that plantation owners or managers did not go out of their way to make improvements. The truth was that neither the plantation nor the life which it dictated was in practice an easily malleable institution. The general sense of defeatism which most workers must have felt was matched only by the ponderousness with which the plantation, for so long accustomed to slavery, had responded to the changed circumstances of indentureship.

Indeed, throughout the indenture period, the assumptions and premises of slavery continued to inform management attitudes. The need to keep the workers under the strictest control was never questioned. In this context there was established an elaborate system of coercion, which included laws curtailing freedom of movement outside the estate. Thus, the worker who was legally entitled to refer complaints against his employers to the Protector of Immigrants whose office was located in the capital, had firstly to obtain his employer's permission to leave the estate in order to make the complaint at all. In addition, of course, worker mobilization beyond individual estates was rendered almost impossible. In any case, the magistrates who were empowered to investigate charges of maltreatment or violations of contractual obligations generally shared the class interests of the plantocracy. Frequently while making their rounds in the countryside they would be entertained or even hosted for the night by a manager who had a case to answer in court the following morning. No wonder then, that the regulations notwithstanding, the plantocracy hardly hesitated to impose upon the workers an array of punitive devices – floggings and beatings on some estates, arbitrary fines, and court sanctioned imprisonment which had the effect of lengthening the time under indenture, for periods spent in jail were not discounted. In addition, the planters devised a 'trust week', whereby one week's wage was withheld as a guarantee of satisfactory performance in the next. Those who were not cowed by these stratagems and were regarded as potential trouble makers were either co-opted into the system of control and made 'drivers' or leaders of work gangs, or neutralised by the threat of banishment to estates where they had no contacts and were unknown. The dominant quality of the overall arrangements justified the label of a 'new system of slavery'; though the regulations were supposed to act as a bulwark against the return of the bad old days, the rules were seldom in line with the reality on the ground.

The attitude of resignation which characterised the psychological profile of many of the workers could be linked in several instances also to provisions in the indenture contract which assured them of a return trip to India at the end of the stipulated term – by the 1870s five years of indentureship plus a further five years of 'industrial residence'. Without that guarantee, it is doubtful whether many Indians would have been induced to leave their native land. Once in the colony some took the view that they must act so as not to jeopardise or unduly delay their homeward passage. Thus, unexpected and unsuitable conditions would be tolerated in the same way in which a man, coming to the end of a long prison term, might decide to risk nothing which would delay the day of freedom. The nearer one came to qualify to return, the more decisive was this consideration. Thus the most vulnerable workers were precisely those who had almost travelled the distance.

As a group the indentured Indians were institutionally subject to more controls than time-expired workers. Therefore the planters insisted on replenishing their stock of indentureds by securing new arrivals. These were often provided with rations at deliberately inflated cost, and so commenced their working career in the colony saddled with debt. Of course the planters could justify the provisions of rations to their workers by reference to nutritional requirements and similar considerations, but what seemed on the surface a helpful gesture had sinister implications. The indebted worker was not only more vulnerable in that he was under greater pressure to perform at the work place, but also he would find it difficult to accumulate the money which might enable him to buy out the final years of his contract. Thus in 1889 the workers actually implored the Protector to put an end to the practice of rationing.[8]

The right to redeem through purchase up to the last two years of the five-year term of indenture had been stipulated in the early ordinances. But the planters naturally wished to make the most of their indentureds. So they began to argue that redemption was not in the interest of the sugar industry, since it allowed the more experienced hands to withdraw their services. Nor was it in the interest of the Indians themselves, they claimed, for many workers were tempted to borrow money at exorbitant rates of interest in order to exercise that option. The planters gained some ground with their argument, so that in 1876 redemption as a right was cancelled;

thereafter, the employer's consent had to be obtained. At the same time, the planters sought to induce time-expired Indians to reindenture themselves for further periods of one year at a time. The carrot was a cash bounty. The heyday of this scheme was the 1880s but by the mid 1890s the planters had little use for it.

In terms of control a pivotal role was played by the driver. The person appointed to that position (and on the typical estate there would be a number of them, each in charge of a group of about twenty-five workers) was generally hand-picked by the planter or his overseer. Selection was based on criteria which were sometimes at variance with the qualities which Indians expected in their leaders. This could lead to trouble, as when a low caste individual was appointed to head a gang of higher caste workers. The driver, by virtue of his office, was separated from the ordinary workers and the distinction was sealed by the higher remuneration and by certain modest fringe benefits which he enjoyed. These the driver would do his best not to lose, and so he strove to secure the approbation of his masters. However, merit and worth were gauged merely in terms of his efficiency in driving the workers to execute their tasks. Towards that end, some drivers surrounded themselves with henchmen who threatened and beat the workers, and who were least restrained precisely on those estates where the managers were inclined to be the most exploitative. But there were other ways apart from physical assault through which the workers were rendered compliant. One such avenue was provided by the method of paying the wages of the workers through their gang leader who simply pocketed a share for himself. Another arose from the existing lines of communication: the workers knew that the driver had the manager's ear, and could finger individuals as poor performers, in which case their pay might be withheld. But the most widely used method concerned the assignment of work. The driver could steer easier jobs to favoured or tractable workers who would then be able to complete more units of work which would enhance their earnings.[9] For the impoverished indentureds, financial reward was a prime mover; in ordinary circumstances they were inclined to calculate long and hard before engaging in any activity or behaviour which could result in a reduction in earnings.

The methods used to control free workers naturally required some additional ingenuity as compared to those unemployed in the case of the indentureds. The efforts of the plantocracy in four main areas can be isolated. Firstly, time-expired Indians were encouraged to continue to reside on the estates or to settle in neighbouring plots. Secondly, earning potential was cleverly manipulated as in the case of contract workers. Thirdly, seasonal unemployment and as the population grew, general underemployment rendered the labourers only too ready to turn out when work was offered. And fourthly, the maintenance of a stock of indentured workers served to undermine the bargaining position of free workers.

The planters correctly calculated that if the free workers were kept close to the estates in residential terms then they would have little option but to win their livelihood in the sugar industry. As a matter of fact, those who stayed in the estate barracks would have no other choice. But it was not a one-way street. The time-expired Indian who was already decided about returning to India and who therefore merely wished to complete his five years' industrial residence in order to claim his passage might have deliberately elected to remain in the barracks and so avoid the expense of having to set himself up in a plot of his own. Those who were as yet undecided about returning could keep their options open by living on the estates. Some single males undoubtedly preferred the communal atmosphere of barrack life to a lonely village hut, while other workers elected to remain on the estates to be near relatives or friends who were still indentured. For a significant number the decision to stay was imposed by the fact that they could not meet the expense of doing otherwise. In addition, the force of habit as well as uncertainty about the world outside the estates must have played a part. But whatever might have been the reasons for their continuing to live on the estate, those who did so opened themselves to planter pressure. In the daily run of things the distinction between them and the indentureds was often obscured. Also, the threat of eviction hung over their heads, and doubtless was used as a lever to enforce labour demands.

The free workers residing in the villages surrounding the plantations had more independence than other categories of estate workers but the planters could still remain reasonably certain, once alternatives were minimised, that they would work on the estates. It was for this reason that they themselves rented or sold portions of their lands to the workers, and also used their influence to have adjacent Crown Lands opened for settlement. But the planters were not comfortable unless they could be assured that the workers were rendered tractable and that they would perform reliably. Their inherited experience of sugar cultivation led them to believe that there could be no other way of doing business. They could point to the limitations imposed by the climate which restricted harvest to the first six months of the year and to the need to be able at short notice to take advantage of favourable weather conditions; to the need to orchestrate activities and to be able to deploy the labour force to advantage; to the need to keep as short as possible the time between cutting and crushing the canes, and to be able to harvest quickly a field which was accidentally burnt.[10] All of this necessitated a certain degree of responsiveness on the part of the workers and planter strategy was to set the situation so that that could be achieved.

The technique they chose was based on a perception which they had also inherited and accepted: the more the workers earned, the less reliably they would work. Or, to put it another way, the quicker their requirements were satisfied the less would be their total output at the work place. Hence, while stressing in reports and speeches cases of individual workers who had managed to accumulate comparatively tidy sums, the planters proceeded to manipulate the earning potential of the workers – not indeed to discourage the labourers altogether but simply to ensure that they would have to work more hours in order to maintain their overall earnings level.

Beginning in 1875 considerable efforts were made to reduce the wage rates of non-residential workers. By 1885 planter expectations were substantially fulfilled. They no longer needed to offer inducements for reindentureship, and the bounty system was accordingly phased out. Not only that, but with the reduced rate of pay to non-residential workers they were still able that year to turn out 'the largest crop of sugar the island [had] ever produced' up to that time.[11] However the planters apparently continued to reduce wage rates still further; by 1896 non-resident free workers were readily accepting and seeking work 'at all times' at indentured rates; and debate on an amendment to the Immigration Ordinance in 1897 revealed that they were prepared to do overtime at even lower rates.[12] In explanation, one manager offered that the coolie was showing 'a greater love of money' than heretofore.[13] But the real reason lay elsewhere: not in an increased thirst for wealth, but in the constantly increasing pressure to work.

Lowering wages was one simple way of reducing the earnings of the workers; another method was through an increase in the size of the tasks. This was a recurring planter strategy which the nature of the task system itself conveniently accommodated. For, though there were guidelines, there could be no standard task, especially in the fields where ground conditions varied from place to place and from time to time. Even a short downpour could make a big difference in the work of digging trenches, for example. The general effect of larger tasks was to increase the ratio of time and effort to money earned. But another result was a reduction in the units of work offered, and that paved the way for a policy of underemployment.

Over the years, as the level of earnings fell, the normal cycle of family development was leading at the same time to growing dependency burdens. One contributing factor was an improvement in the proportion of females to males stemming from both recruitment policy and local births. More children survived as infant mortality declined; and as more Indians settled in Trinidad, the age pyramid structure of the population whose livelihood was based on the sugar industry was altered. The accustomed bulge around the years 15 to 30 (which was the age group favoured by the recruiters) showed a tendency to flatten out, as the age composition of the population assumed a more normal mix. The pattern of family development increased the general compulsion of the labourer, especially as he was underemployed, to perform, and assured the estates also of a corps of child labourers at their command.

Within this general context, some workers were rendered more controllable than others by individual circumstances, such as indebtedness. This might have arisen from borrowing to meet the expense of initial settlement in the villages, or from events like the performance of life cycle rites or other religious observances. Or from expensive habits, like alcoholism. But the most serious cause of indebtedness, then as now, was underemployment in the rainy season, which forced the worker to rely on the credit facilities of the village shopkeepers (not unusually an ex-driver) through the period July to December. The heavier this reliance the greater was the compulsion to work during the harvest season, which was exactly what the planter wanted.

Those in peculiar circumstances, whether of debt or anything else, as well as the general population of free workers, had to reckon with the continuing presence of the indentureds. It was not only that the standards applicable to the coercive regimen of indentureship were transferred to free workers, and that over the years wage rates showed a tendency to move down from free rates to low contract rates.[14] More importantly, the presence of a group of workers who were legally bound to work undermined the bargaining power of free workers and reduced the pressure which a strike could exert on the planters. When the free workers contemplated withholding their services, they had to consider that the critical work might continue to be done by the indentureds. Thus, there was in operation a process of 'expansive control' whereby the planters, having a part of the labour force 'captive', could use it to capture another part. They were well aware of the value of their contract workers in this regard, so that even though by 1900 there was a surfeit of labour they continued to press for the retention of indentured immigration. Their arguments and the counter-claims of opposing groups dominate the literature on indentureship in Trinidad in the closing years of the system.

Data on resistance among sugar workers of all categories are not easy to come by. In the case of indentureds the local authorities, conscious of the watchful eye of the India Office and anxious to prevent any questioning of the system, consistently tried to convey the impression that all was smooth sailing. If there was any trouble it was because, as everybody knew, the workers were both indolent and grasping. As for the free workers, the records do not deal with them in any depth for they were strictly speaking no longer the responsibility of the Protector of Immigrants. However, it is possible to identify behaviour patterns which fall within the scope of resistance, from those which may be classified as active on the one hand to those which may be deemed as passive on the other.

The Indians demonstrated the capacity, not unknown to disadvantaged groups, to isolate from vicissitude elements of strength. In this connection the experience of the ocean passage stands out. Those who made that trip discovered in themselves resources of fortitude which they perhaps never knew they possessed. Emigrants on the same ship also developed the enduring ties of *jahaji bhai* or brotherhood of the boat. This new bond was also an example of cultural versatility, for it transcended the ordinary divisions of caste and religion, thereby demonstrating that Indians were prepared to devise new approaches for new circumstances.

Cultural resilience and adaptation might indeed be regarded as the most outstanding as well as the most persistent form of resistance among Indian workers. It permitted a definition of otherness which amounted to defiance, both in the insulation and consequent feelings of solidarity which that engendered, as well as in the divergent concepts of status and rank which were implied. Culture defined an area to which Indians, after defeats at the work place, could retreat to heal and bind the wounds, before sallying forth again. The self, derided and degraded, could be refreshed and injected with new esteem. For within the safety of the cultural boundaries, the idea of caste allowed notions of status to be overturned so that the white planter, for example, who had no caste, was accorded a place beyond the pale.

The culture of the Indians in Trinidad was to some extent a mix and match of various local practices and beliefs brought from India, but before long the Bhojpur tradition became dominant. This was derived from a cultural area in north-east India which was characterised in language by the Hindi dialect Bhojpuri and in religion by the great epics, the Mahabharata and the Ramayana. Those two religious works, but more especially the latter, provided the basis for folk songs and stories and defined ideals and values. Without instigating an attitude of dogmatism, they nevertheless allowed Indians to feel that those who did not share their ideals were the poorer for having yet to discover what life was all about. The performance of life cycle rites and ceremonies of a private kind set the seal on all of this. The public celebrations and festivals served to reinforce the point.

Public festivals could also become undisguised demonstrations against the established order. The most famous incident of this type occured during the *Muharram* of 1884 when grievances over the size of tasks as well as misgivings about new regulations concerning the conduct of the celebrations led Indians to defy the authorities. When the storm cleared, thirteen Indians, mostly in their late twenties, had been killed by police bullets and several others maimed and wounded.[15]

The odds were heavily stacked against achieving much by open defiance but that did not prevent Indians from trying and occasionally succeeding. Even on board ship, as during the voyage of the *Hesperides* in 1882, violence could break out. In the fields violence was never far below the surface, though it was usually directed against the driver rather than the planter. Such acts of violence were usually spontaneous and uncoordinated, but often managed to achieve the desired effect. In fact, the vulnerability of the drivers to a sudden assault in a deserted cane piece by an aggrieved worker wielding the tool of his trade – a cutlass – did force many of them to moderate their demands on the workers.

As one would expect the indentureship period was not a happy time for labour relations; there were too many avenues for conflict to develop. In a general sense, one could say that both indentureds and free workers were constantly engaged in a struggle to repossess the definition of the task. Sometimes the struggle took the form of starting work late or of staying away altogether and pretending, in the case of indentureds, to be ill. At other times, it took the form of an attack on the plant, that is, burning the canes or mistreating the draught animals. It often developed into a local strike, especially in the 1880s and 1890s, but it was not long before that was broken by pressure to earn in the case of free workers or police action in the case of indentureds.

The planters might describe burning the canes as a mischievous and wilful destruction of property but the Indians knew what they were about. It was one way of gaining some initiative in their dealings with the plantocracy. For one thing, there was little risk of being caught; the Indians in fact developed simple but crude incendiary devices, such as a lighted candle set in a bundle of straw. By the time the straw was set alight and the wind doing the rest, the worker would be far away. Burnt canes had to be quickly reaped and crushed, and with time then on the side of the workers, they could attempt to hold out for better conditions.

For many of the Indians resistance has to be seen in terms of who would have the last laugh. They would be compliant and would work hard, which undoubtedly kept the planters happy, but at the same time they were trying to lay the basis for their eventual escape from plantation life. Towards that end, they also resurrected caste-affiliated skills – such as that of the jeweller, or the potter – and engaged in their own private agricultural pursuits. A not inconsiderable number even became sugar cane farmers. They also rediscovered the economic usefulness of traditional institutions, such as the *bhaiacharaya* or cooperative brotherhood, which proved especially helpful in the cultivation of rice, and the box money arrangement – a kind of pool to which all would contribute at stated times and from which each in turn would draw a lump sum. The longing for economic independence earned some Indians the reputation of being tight-fisted, and the sacrifices which they were prepared to make even tempted the planters to lower their inducements to them. The argument was that the Indians would be satisfied with less, but it missed the point that the whole idea was to create a situation where more might be achieved.

Of course not every Indian had the singlemindedness of purpose to pursue the above strategy, and the resistance patterns into which some fell were essentially less positive. Taking to drink was one such pattern, and by the 1880s that had become a serious problem.[16] In the same vein may be considered the attitude of resignation and long-suffering which some developed – resistance by turning off. Others resisted by turning off altogether and taking their own lives. A small number took a less final and more positive gamble and absconded to neighbouring Venezuela. Again, individual circumstances – knowledge, elements of character, family connections and so on – would make one option more feasible than another and so determine how workers would respond.

The major consequences of the entire network of control and resistance as far as the Indian population as a whole was concerned could be traced to facilities which were provided for the development of schismatic tendencies. Thus, the dominance of the Bhojpur tradition resulted in a situation in which the Madrassis – workers who originated from South India and admittedly small in number – had some grounds for feeling awkward. And the heavy religious quality in that tradition meant that Muslims, even though they might have come from North India, would be set a little distance from the main body of Indians. So too would those who had begun to repsond to the ministrations of the Presbyterian missionaries. In addition groups like drivers and shopkeepers who did have some community of interest with the workers nevertheless stood somewhat apart. The contradictions which began to emerge, basically of religion and class, would achieve great significance when constitutional politics entered the system and the Indians began to extend their presence beyond the confines of the plantations.

NOTES

1. See C.L.R James, *The Black Jacobins: Toussaint L'Ouverture and the San Domingo Revolution* (Random House, 1963).

2. I have argued this in 'Sugar Estates and Labour in Trinidad 1838-1845' (11th Conference of Caribbean Historians, Curacao 1979). See also at the same Conference, D. Hall, 'Fort George Penn, Jamaica: Slaves, Tenants and Labourers, 1832-1843' and W. Marshall, 'The Ex-slaves as Wage Labourers on the Sugar Estates in the British Leeward Islands 1838-1846'. See also, D. Hall, 'The Flight from the Estates Reconsidered: The British West Indies 1838-42.' *Journal of Caribbean History*, Vol. 10 and 11, 1978.

3. Compiled from reports of the Protector of Immigrants printed in *Council papers* of the Trinidad Government.

4. See K. Haraksingh, 'Estates, Labour and Population in Trinidad 1870-1900' (10th Conference of Caribbean Historians, U.S. Virgin Islands 1978).

5. See K. Haraksingh, 'Indian Leadership in the Indenture Period', *Caribbean Issues*, Vol. 2, No. 3, December 1976.

6. For a profile of the emigrants, see H. Tinker, *A New System of Slavery: the Export of Indian Labour Overseas 1830-1920* (O.U.P., 1974).

7. See Tinker, Chapter 6.

8. Protector of Immigrants' Report for 1889, *Council Paper* 29/1890.

9. For a fuller description of the role of drivers see K. Haraksingh, 'Indian Leadership in the Indenture Period', *op. cit.*

10. See evidence of several planters to the West India *Royal Commission* 1897 (cmd. 8657).

11. Protector of Immigrant's Report for 1885, *Council Paper* 33/1886.

12. *Council Paper* 157/1898.

13. *Cmd. 8657*, p.239.

14. Argued in K. Haraksingh, 'Estates, Labour and Population in Trinidad 1870-1900', *op. cit.*

15. 'Correspondence Relating to the Coolie Disturbances in Trinidad 1884-5', *cmd. 4366.*

16. *Protector of Immigrant's Report for 1881, Council Paper 35/1882.*

Sugar cane being reaped by cutlass in Guyana

These large iron barges are used to transport sugar cane

The 'Caribbean Man'

A Study of the Psychology of Perception and the Media

Ramesh Deosaran

Introduction

This study looks at the most animated and pervasive calypso controversy in Trinidad and Tobago's [1] history. The controversy is used as a basis for clarifying race relations as well as establishing a theoretical framework to understand inter-group conflict in this multi-racial society. The focus is on the calypso 'Caribbean Unity'[2] sung by calypsonian Black Stalin during the 1979 calypso season. The calypso, popularly called 'Caribbean Man', won first prize in the island-wide Calypso Monarch Competition [3] but subsequently caused a nation-wide controversy over the question as to whether or not the lyrics describing the 'Caribbean Man' were confined only to those of African descent, thus excluding other ethnic groups in Trinidad.

The emotional impact and widespread interest generated by the controversy is evidenced by the fact that it occupied a total of 660 column inches and involved six of the seven national newspapers across the country. The controversy drew in strident contributions from major opinion leaders; among them prominent community leaders, reporters and columnists from the two major ethnic groups – Indians and Africans. As far as responses to the newspapers were concerned, the public debate lasted for two and a half months – February 28 1979 to May 12, 1979. It provided an exciting snap-shot of the social psychology of race relations in the country. The 'national conditions' under which the data was generated should add to the validity of the results in this study. The controversy also raised serious questions for social perception and inter-personal relation-ships among different ethnic groups in a mixed community.

Background to Controversy

Widely known as the Land of Calypso and Steelband, Trinidad has been putting increased emphasis on the calypso through financial support and popular patronage at the many calypso tents during the carnival season. This is also reflected in the increased tendency to play calypsoes on the radio stations during the entire year. There is also a widening call for the calypso to be taught in schools. The calypso therefore has a very significant place in Trinidad's culture.

Calypsonians here have as a rule been of African descent.[4] During the 1979 calypso season for instance, out of the eighty five calpsonians counted in the six tents[5] in Port of Spain, only two were of East Indian descent (Rajah and Prince who was formerly Indian Prince).

Calypsonians have also increased the emphasis on themes of African identity and culture, political satire and revolution. Of course, there was always a wide variety of themes in the calypso (Elder, 1966; Rohlehr, 1972; Hill, 1967), but this recent emphasis on black identity and radical change during the 1979 calypso season has secured the title of 'left-wing' calypsonians for Valentino, Black Stalin, and Mighty Explainer.[6]

There were, of course, many more calypsoes and reggae hits on the theme of black identity and African 'roots'. Bert Lynch's 'Black Man's Prayer', Merchant's 'Um-Ba-Yao', and Mighty Explainer's 'Mr. African' are examples. In fact during the 1979 calypso season a count at the city's six major calypso tents revealed a total of at least 21 songs on the theme of black identity and African 'roots'.

Early in the 1979 calypso season, the country's major Hindu organisation[7] publicly objected to Lord Shorty's 'Om Shanti'. 'Om Shanti', according to Lord Shorty, carried a 'message' for racial harmony in Trinidad. However the Hindu organisation commended the lyrics but objected to the calypso being played on the streets or in 'fêtes' since, they felt, the sacred words 'Om Shanti' would be desecrated. Such controversies over the calypso, carnival, or even Better Village Cultural Shows are not unusual.

In addition to Hindus, members of the Baptist and Shango faiths have regularly and publicly protested against alleged desecration of their rituals in calypsoes, or in other local cultural shows. For example, on August 11, 1979, Baptists publicly protested against the 'mockery of their religious beliefs and practices' in the Prime Minister's Best Village Trophy Competition.[8] Three years previously, Baptists in Tobago made a similar protest.[9]

The Pandits Parishad (a body of Hindu priests) also protested against 'mockery' by calypsoes. Citing a number of calypsoes, the organisation wrote: 'Over the years calypsonians mocked and heaped scorn on the Hindu religion and their priests by poking fun at them'

(Trinidad Express, March 9, 1979).

The religious and ethnic diversity of Trinidad though often hailed 'as an example to the world', also presents a source of social tension, especially at election time. Tables 1 and 2 reveal the religious and ethnic diversity of Trinidad.[10] The proportion of Africans and East Indians are almost the same. However, while the overall Trinidad population in 1970 increased by 12.4 percent from 1960, the proportion of Africans and Indians increased by 11.2 and 23.7 percent respectively. At this rate, it is quite likely that the 1980 census would reveal a greater proportion of Indians in Trinidad. On this basis, the matter of excluding Indians or other ethnic groups in the calypso 'Caribbean Man' is indeed notable. At the same time, the number of persons of African descent in those islands that attempted the West Indian Federation exceeds five million. As will be discussed later, the perception of the calypso is also implicated by which *number* provides the frame of reference, the Trinidad one or the Caribbean one.

Table 1
Ethnic Background of Trinidad and Tobago Population (1970)

Ethnicity	Number	Percentage
Negro	398,765	42.8
East Indian	373,538	40.1
White	11,383	1.2
Chinese	7,962	0.8
Mixed	131,904	14.2
Syrian Lebanese	993	0.1
Others	5,141	0.1
Not Stated	1,385	0.1
Total	931,071	99.8

Table 2
Religious Background of Trinidad and Tobago Population (1970)

Religion	Number	Percentage
Roman Catholic	331,733	35.6
Hindu	230,209	24.7
Anglican	168,521	18.1
Muslim	58,271	6.3
Presbyterian	16,673	4.2
Adventist	15,507	1.8
Methodist	39,363	1.7
Baptist	6,774	0.7
Moravian	6,527	0.7
Church of God	5,050	0.5
Others/Not Stated	52,443	5.6
Total	931,071	100.0

The role, theme, and social appeal of the calypso, as well as the ethnic background of the calypsonian in Trinidad become relevant alongside the distributions shown in Tables 1 and 2. This is especially so when matters of 'national culture' and social integration are discussed.

The 'Caribbean Man' controversy, because of its political and ethnic flavour eventually attracted arguments over socio-economic and political status between the different ethnic groups in Trinidad and Tobago.[11]

Generally, Indo-Trinidadians have found themselves the lowest income group, residing in the rural districts, and, as a group, effectively excluded from political power for the last twenty three years. Furthermore, they have always provided the base of the parliamentary opposition.

Afro-Trinidadians, as a group, are not much better off economically, but through the African-dominated People's National Movement, they have occupied political power since 1956.[12]

For the last twenty years, Indo-Trinidadians have been protesting against political patronage and job discrimination in the government services and public-projects. The psychological implications of such socio-economic and political imbalances were expressed in two hypotheses (Deosaran, 1978):

(1)   The further removed a cultural (or ethnic) group is from the source of socio-economic rewards, the greater the stress factors in the group's attempts to compete and gain access to such rewards.

(2)   The further removed a cultural (or ethnic) group is from the source of socio-economic rewards, the greater the pressure for deculturalisation and the greater likelihood that negative stereotyping would be used by the dominant group to justify the minority group's exclusion from socio-economic rewards. (pp. 14–15).

It was further explained (Deosaran, 1978) that the first hypothesis reveals the 'inherent injustice in a political system framed along functionalist notions of political bargaining' (p. 15). The second hypothesis reflects William Ryan's (1972) notion of how socio-economic victims are blamed so as to reduce or detract from any emphasis on the source of the socio-economic hardships. Both propositions have been features of Trinidad's heritage of multiracialism, capitalism, and an adversary system of politics. They also suggest the stress and outgroup status experienced by Indians. it is on this powerful socio-political basis that the psychology of social perception becomes extremely relevant within the different ethnic groups in Trinidad.

The socio-economic and political structures have thus helped throughout the years to harden suspicions between the two major ethnic groups, Indians and Africans.[13] It is within such an unsettling socio-political climate that such a controversy as the 'Caribbean Man' gained its ascendancy. Racial attitudes between East Indians and Africans here have been built up over the years, and hardened by periods of stress and electoral confrontation. These attitudes today provide differing perspectives, sensitive perspectives, through which issues of race and culture are viewed.

The Calypso

The other major factor in the controversy was the status of calypso itself. Is it a 'serious' art form? Is it 'merely' a lower-class attempt at social and political commentary? Should one attempt to define the artistic status or social role of the calypso at all? Or should one view calypsoes as other cultural forms, that is, calypsoes vary in status and function from one to the other?[14] Local commentators and resear-

chers on the calypso agree it is a serious art form (Rohlehr, 1969,
1979; James, 1962; Braithwaite, 1954; Deosaran, 1977; Elder, 1966).
Some have used it quite extensively as an object for serious study and
capable of dealing with serious social and political issues (Austin,
1976; Elder, 1968; Rohlehr, 1972.)

Whatever the view about calypsoes generally, the fact is that Black
Stalin's 'Caribbean Man' was widely acclaimed on the radio stations
and in the newspapers as being quite serious, and with a 'heavy'
message on Caribbean togetherness. (e.g. *Sun,* January 12, 1979)

But whether or not the calypso was viewed as 'serious' or not is not
really critical for this study. What is important here is the fact that a
major controversy emerged which appeared to mirror the underlying
social tensions in the country. It provided an opportunity for the
nation to talk to itself. Further, that calypso, being a prize-winning
one, peformed a social function in terms of its recognition and
widespread delivery.

In this sense, the calypso 'Caribbean Man' functioned as a viable
social stimulus which was perceived differently by persons of
different ethnic backgrounds. Whether the calypso in itself was
serious or not is helpful to know. But as a projective stimulus,[15] it is
similar to the ink-blot or thematic tests used for personality testing by
psychoanalysts. As such, the calypso 'Caribbean Man' became an
important and useful psychological instrument in this study of social
perception.

Specific Objectives of Study

(1)   To study the relationship between the social background
      of the respondents and their perceptions of the calypso in
      the controversy.

(2)   To apply a socio-psychological framework in under-
      standing the motivations for the different responses in the
      controversy.

(3)   To note the role of and implications for the media in such
      a controversy.

This study is also a response to the serious lack of research on the
psychological aspects of the calypso and the role of the media in a
multiracial society.

The Controversy

Throughout January and February 1979, 'Caribbean Unity' popularly known as 'Caribbean Man', gained increased popularity. It was

among the leading tunes in the popularity charts on the radio stations.

Before the controversy began in early March, the calypso was hailed by Blacks as bearing 'an important and moving message' for unity in the Caribbean. One reviewer (*Sun,* January 12, 1979) described it as the best move for Caribbean integration in the last ten years. At the 1979 (January) graduation ceremony of the St Augustine campus of the University of the West Indies, the song was sung by the university choir as a symbol of 'Caribbean togetherness'.

However, during that same period, many non-Blacks grumbled that the lyrics applied only to people of African descent and it implied that people of other races were left out in this 'message' for Caribbean unity.

The lines in the calypso which apparently offended were:

> *Dem is one race, De Caribbean Man*
> *From de same place, De Caribbean Man*
> *That make the same trip, De Caribbean Man*
> *On the same ship, De Caribbean Man...* (See Appendix A).

Hearing these lines, Reverend Dr. Idris Hamid (of East Indian descent), Director of the Caribbean Ecumenical Programme, on February 28, 1979, wrote the Editor of the *Trinidad Express,* when he complained: 'Stalin either does not respect facts or has no place for a significant number of Caribbean people'.[16]

Apparently Reverend Hamid perceived the calypso differently from the way the *Sun* reviewer and the university choir perceived it. In any case Dr. Hamid's letter was never published. And the subdued complaints continued, especially among East Indians.

Soon after, on March 1, 1979, calypsonian Black Stalin appeared on a television interview (*Panorama News Programme)* and said that his calypso was really confined to men of African descent, that his 'Caribbean Man' was of African descent, that Africans here were the ones who developed the Caribbean, and that they were the only ones concerned with Caribbean unity.

Hence, Stalin's views on television helped to confirm the perceived racial exclusiveness of his calypso. Hearing such views I criticised the calypso in the *Express* newspaper on March 5, 1979 by stating it was 'nothing less than an insult to the vast number of people of other races here who have come in different ships and from different places and who are also struggling to make this unity thing work'. I added:

*It should be said in no uncertain terms that we – Africans,
Indians, Chinese, Syrians, Whites, are all now in the same ship
together. And recognition of that fact is the Caribbean spirit.*

I called the calypso 'racist and sexist' and said:

*Whatever ambiguities there might have been about Stalin's lyrics
have been cleared up in the TV interview last Thursday* (March
1)[17]

In other words, I interpreted the calypso on the basis of Stalin's
television clarification. However, as the full release in Appendix C
will show, this part of the release did not appear in the newspaper's
story. But from this point, the public controversy warmed up.

On March 6, the day after my public comments in the *Trinidad
Express,* that same newspaper carried an editorial headlined: 'We
Find Black Stalin Not Guilty'. The editorial, without making
reference to Stalin's interview,[18] perceived the calypso differently. It
said:

*We believe Dr. Deosaran is really reading too much into this
calypso. We must remember, in the first place, that a calypsonian
has far wider licence than the ordinary person. Call it poetic
licence, if you wish.*

On March 7, the day after the *Express* editorial, a teacher, Paul
Walker (of African descent) in a letter to the *Express* editor,
criticised Stalin's television views as well as the calypso. The
published letter was headlined: 'Stalin, the Negro Race is not the
Only One in The Caribbean.' Walker said: 'Our Calypso Monarch
(Stalin) is definitely a segregationist'. He concluded: 'Sing on, Black
Stalin, but please give a pluralistic, yet unifying interpretation of your
beautiful verses.'

On that same day, the Sanatan Dharma Mahasabha, (SDMS) the
largest Hindu organisation in Trinidad,[19] had its protest against the
calypso published in the *Trinidad Express*. The SDMS perceived the
calypso as 'racist and anti-female' and further strongly condemned
the *Express* editorial (March 6) support for Stalin.

Without referring to Stalin's television interview, the SDMS wrote:

*When the Hindu community complained that Lord Shorty's 'Om
Shanti' (calypso) was desecrating their sacred religion, no news-
paper commented. Yet within 24 hours of Dr Deosaran's release the*
Express *Editor came out to find Black Stalin not guilty.*[20]

Interestingly enough, the SDMS added:

> *Let us work to provide equal media exposure to the various cultures in our midst and put an end to racial prejudices that exist at all levels in our society.*

The SDMS release was headlined: 'Now Hindus Condemn the "Caribbean Man"'.

On that same day, March 7, a representative of the 'newly formed non-political' People's Representative Organisation had its release published in the *Express*. This organisation was reported as asking Caribbean people to forget about 'racial segregation and inferiority complexes in the region and, as Stalin said, became Caribbean Men'.

The controversy raged through the months of March, April and May 1979. The newspapers and numerous public forums across the country became live with charges and counter-charges on the issue.[21]

It must be emphasised that the major issue at the beginning of the controversy was: were the lyrics in Stalin's calypso 'The Caribbean Man' confined only to those of African descent?

Whatever one's perceptions of the lyrics might be, it must also be noted that at least on two occasions, Black Stalin clearly said yes, his song, the 'Caribbean Man' was confined in this way. (Television interview on March 1; *Trinidad Guardian* interview May 6, 1979).

Again, this racial exclusion may or may not be perceived as 'segregationist, racist, or offensive', depending, as English and English (1958) explained, on one's 'personal interests, desires, fears, or expectations'.

Without Stalin's clarifications, the calypso itself had a reasonable chance of being ambigious enough to imply, for instance, inclusion of all races.

With Stalin's clarification, however, one expected the ambiguity in the calypso to be reduced. However as the results will show, Stalin's clarification did not make much difference in the perception of the calypso by the two major ethnic groups, Indians and Africans.

Method

Newspaper clippings of published comments with background of chief authors and organisations were collected between February 28, 1979 and May 12, 1979. These were categorised and analysed. The space allocated to such comments in the different newspapers was measured in column inches. Also collected were releases which were submitted to the newspaper but were not published. All these people responded *voluntarily* to the controversy.

Perceptual Categories

Three perceptual categories[22] were developed from all the responses in the controversy over that calypso, 'Caribbean Man'. (February 28, 1979 to May 12, 1979):

1. Those indicating yes or strongly implying that the calypso was either segregationist, racist, or offensive to East Indians or any other ethnic group: (YES).

2. Those indicating no, or strongly implying that the calypso was not segregationist, racist or offensive to East Indians or any other ethnic group: (NO).

3. Those that merely described, or commented on the controversy without taking either of the above two positions: (INDIFFERENT).

Social Background

Two social background factors of the respondents were measured: ethnicity and social class.

Ethnicity was quite easy to classify since all those who actively participated in the controversy (except one)[23] were already well known by ethnic background and name. Three ethnic categories were developed: Africans, East Indians and White/Uncertain.

Social Class was based on the coding scheme used by Graham and Beckles (1968) and modified by Miller (1973) for use in his study on the self evaluation of Jamaican adolescents. This classification of occupations[24] was divided into six groups, ranging from 1 (higher professional and managerial) to 6 (unskilled workers). For this study the two highest occupational groups were further classified as upper class; the middle two groups were classified as middle class; and the last two groups as lower class.

Analysis and Results

There was a total of 31 respondents in the controversy, six on behalf of organisations.[25] Twelve respondents were of African background, 17 were of East Indian, 1 was White, while 1 could not be ascertained. All the identifiable respondents (30) were either middle or upper class, and similarly distributed across the two major ethnic groups. In other words, the entire sample was fairly homogeneous with respect to their social class background. It is also quite interesting to note that only 1 of the 31 respondents was female — a sub-editor with the *Trinidad Express*. Appendix E provides background information on the organisations and/or chief author of the responses. This Appendix also shows the date and name of publication concerned.

Of the 31 respondents only 6 connected the television interview with the calypso (4 Indians, 2 Africans). Except for Paul Walker, hearing Stalin's television views or not appeared to make no difference in perception between Indians and Africans.

Table 3 reveals the strong relationships between the ethnicity of the respondents and their perception of the calpyso.

TABLE 3
Ethnicity and Perception of Calypso

Ethnicity	Whether Calypso Segregationist, Racist or Offensive			Total
	YES	NO	INDIFFERENT	
African	1	11	—	12
Indian	13	2	2	17
White/Uncertain	—	1	1	2
Total	14	14	3	31

The X^2 obtained from Table 3 confirms the significant relationship ($X^2 = 9.7$, d.f $= 6$, $p < .05$).

The proportion of 'Yes' and 'No' responses was similar within the sample (45.2% respectively). However, while 76.5% of the Indian respondents perceived the calypso as either 'segregationist, racist or offensive', 91.7% of the African said no. While 2 of the 17 Indians were non-committal, none of the Africans were.

This result was a clear indication that the perception of the calypso varied according to the ethnic background of respondents. In this sense ethnicity provided a frame of reference through which the calypso, as a social stimulus, was perceived. This result also provides some psychological support for the sociological concept of cultural pluralism in Trinidad. The pervasive and single ground for protest by East Indians was the perception of being excluded from the 'Caribbean Man' concept.

Further scrutiny of the data revealed that of the 14 persons who did *not* perceive the calypso as segregationist (10 were Africans), 11 *did admit* racial exclusiveness. However, these went on to justify racial exclusiveness on reasons ranging from priority for black identity to Caribbean unity among those of African descent as the majority group in the Caribbean. Of the 14 (3 did not admit racial exclusiveness), some forwarded more than one reason. Hence the total reasons (23) exceeded the number of such respondents (14) in Table 4.

TABLE 4
Frequency of Supportive Sentiments for the Calypso

Supportive Sentiment	Frequency
Priority for black unity in Caribbean	7
Should not take calypso/calypsonian seriously	4
Critics of the calypso/calypsonian were 'racist'	4
The Calypso/calypsonian really included all racial groups	2
Critics were reading too much into calypso	6
Total	23

In other words, the basic and early issue of racial exclusion or not was no longer in much contention for Africans. Most of the Africans responding admitted racial exclusions of other groups, but yet did not perceive the calypso as 'segregationist, racist, or offensive'. The above range of reasons was apparently used to justify this perception of non-segregation or at least non-offensiveness. These reasons help clarify the different frames of reference through which the calypso was perceived by the two ethnic groups and raise the issue of rationalisation for cognitive consistency. Even among the Africans who advanced the above reasons, there were notable differences and even inconsistencies. For example, two said the calypso or calypsonian was taken too seriously by critics, yet these two in the same response hailed the calypso's 'message' as being extremely important to Africans.

Social Psychological Framework

Two social psychological theories are relevant for understanding the different responses in the controversy. The first is symbolic interactionism; the second is cognitive dissonance. Together, these two theories help clarify why perceptions of the calypso differed so widely. And further, how the 'objective' dimensions of the situation clashed with 'subjective' ones. A look will also be taken at the psychological processes used to resolve apparent discrepancies between these two dimensions.

Symbolic Interaction

The methodology of symbolic interactionism assumes that the social world has no real meaning apart from the various meanings attributed to it by individuals (Blumer, 1966; Cooley, 1956; Garfinkel, 1967; Mead, 1974; Secord and Backman, 1974). The early perspective has been succintly summarised in W.I. Thomas' (1931) words: 'If mean define their situations as real, they are real in their consequences'.

This theory proposes that the social self is shaped through actual interaction, and further that one's actions as well as psychological dispositions become controlled to some degree by one's perceptions of how others expect one to behave (Mead, 1934). Both Blumer (1966) and Mead (1934) emphasise how persons actually behave in ways that mutually confirm each others' expectations. This psychological process lays the basis for stereotyping and the 'expectation' phenomenon whereby, for instance, bright but lower class students tend to behave in ways consistent with their teacher's low expectations of them (through the teacher's stereotyped low expectations for lower class students). Cooley (1956) suggested 'the looking-glass self', that is the 'self' we see reflected in the reactions of others to us.

Shott (1979) recently summarised four tenets of symbolic interactionism which are useful for understanding emotional responses as displayed in the controversy.

1. Study of the actor's definitions and interpretations is essential for an understanding of human conduct.

2. Human behaviour is emergent, continually constructed during its execution.

3. The actions of individuals are influenced by their internal states and impulses in addition to external events and stimuli, for actors' perceptions and interpretations are shaped by the former as well as the latter.

4.   Social structures and normative regulation are the framework of human action rather than its determinant, shaping
behaviour without dictating it.

This theoretical perspective appears useful for studying group
relations in a community where status and power have been so closely
related to race and colour. The stereotypes and behavioural
expectations from such history could be explicated and even
'corrected' by an application of the principles of symbolic interaction.
For example, inter-group conflict could be reduced by effective
communication between groups. But such communication could only
be facilitated if the groups are made to share a common frame of
reference. Racial stereotyping has been a barrier here (Brereton,
1974).

This perspective, in clarifying the critical mediating role of one's
psychological frame of reference, also identifies socio-economic and
normative institutions as essential for understanding human behaviour. Symbolic interactionism is thus clearly social-psychological.

It is clear from the data in the controversy that the two different
groups (Indians and Africans) were responding to the situation on the
basis of different perceptions of national identity. In this sense, the
controversy revealed a psychological struggle for power over a socio-
political norm. This led to much misunderstanding and controversy.
Quite relevant here is Cooley's (1956) explanation that 'the imagina-
tions people have of one another are the solid facts of society'
(p. 154).

Communication research has shown that news stories are interpreted quite differently by people of different ages and cultural
background (Weiss, 1969). Weiss explained:

> *The importance of discriminating between real and unreal events
> and reacting to them differently is a matter of learning and an
> aspect of socialisation; and the ability to make correct discrimi-
> nations is likely to depend on the background of relevant
> knowledge and experience* (p.95).

Weiss, like Secord and Backman (1974), was explaining how one's
perception of a situation does vary according to one's social
background and experiences. Apart from the perception of calypso
content, Caribbean and Trinidad research has documented the
relationship between different socio-political responses and differences in social and cultural background. (Bahadoorsingh, 1968;
Brereton, 1974; Braithwaite, 1974; Greene, 1973; Landau, 1974;

Lowenthal, 1974; Nettleford, 1978; Rubin and Zavalloni, 1969; Ryan, 1979; Stone, 1973).

The calypso is a form of communication, the psychology of which is comparable to that of a news story. Hence we consider Weiss' (1969) analysis:

> *Even when presented objectively news events are not 'raw facts' devoid of wider meaning of implications. They are oftentimes and for many people neutral or ambiguous in significances, capable of diverse and even contradictory interpretations.* (p. 103)

The general point at this stage is that as a social stimulus, the calypso especially without the television clarification was 'for many people ... capable of diverse and even contradictory interpretations'. And such diversity of perception was clearly linked to the diversity of the ethnic backgrounds of those who interpreted the calypso.

The distinction here is between psychological (or perceived) reality and the 'objective' reality. And the arousal which emerged from the psychological reality is what really motivated the voluntary responses in the calypso controversy. It is like saying that beauty lies in the eyes of the beholder. While acknowledging Stalin's television explanation, the *Express* editor (writing as Holden Caulfield) gave the interpretation that Black Stalin's explanation 'did not have much meaning and did not convey what everybody else seems to believe he was trying to put over in the calypso' (*Express*, March 8). Maybe it was hyperbole, but the claim of 'everybody else' at that stage was clearly not accurate.

It was also ironic that one of the extensive commentaries carried a bold headline: 'The Truth About "Caribbean Man"' (*Sunday Guardian,* March 11, 1979) in which the writer, a black sociologist claimed — contrary to what Stalin himself said — that the calypso included both Indians and Africans. The fact was that Stalin, rightly or wrongly, said the calypso included only those of African descent. There was therefore no 'truth' in that headline.

Sometimes actors in a social situation, as a matter of psychological convenience, redefine or distort the situation so as to make it consistent with their own expectations or attitudes. The calypso is a social sign, and as communication expert Wilbur Schramm[26] explains, 'signs can have only such meanings as an individual's experience permits him to read into them' (p.5). Schramm makes the essential point:

> *We can only decode a message in terms of the signs we know,*

and the meanings we have learned from them. We call this
collection of experiences and meanings a frame of reference, *and*
we say that a person can communicate only in terms of his own
frame of reference (p.5).

Frame of reference is the social psychological construct which leads
to differences in the psychology of social perception. This has been
quite evident in the controversy. An outstanding example was seen in
the *Express* editorial of March 6. The editorial chastised one critic of
the calypso for 'really reading too much into this calypso'. Yet, a few
paragraphs lower, the *same* editorial, in supporting the calypso's
orientation, stated: 'While we do not want to put words in Stalin's
mouth, we believe that he is trying to erase petty prejudices among
the people of his ethnic origin in the region'. So while the editorial is
against one person for 'reading too much' into the calypso, the
editorial itself takes the liberty of reading what it wanted into the
calypso.

This psychological process was again exemplified by a columnist[27]
who actually gave the longest commentary in the controversy (80
column inches). He accused critics of the calypso 'for making a
political mountain out of an artistic molehill', but he himself went on
to justify the calypso's orientation with an elaborate analysis of
Indian insularity, the Federation break-up and black identity. Such
an underlying justification surely does not make the calypso 'a
molehill'. Cohen (1955) explained:

> *Our beliefs about what is, what is possible and what consequ-*
> *ences flow from what actions do not necessarily correspond to*
> *what is 'objectively' true. The 'facts' never stare us in the face. We*
> *see them always through a glass... This glass is our frame of*
> *reference* (pp.52-53).

It seemed then that the frame of reference through which Indians
apparently perceived the calypso was related to the notion of
'equality among all races' within Trinidad and Tobago. On the other
hand, the frame of reference through which Africans apparently
perceived the calypso was the need for Caribbean unity among those
of African descent. Africans thus felt that the Indian response was an
unnecessary irritation.

However, Trinidad Indians may have a further psychological
investment in their frame of reference; that is, Caribbean unity
among those of African descent in the region could threaten the
numerical strength[28] of the Indians in Trinidad. At the same time,

Afro-Trinidadians may have a vested psychological interest in lifting the frame of reference beyond Trinidad, because in so doing a challenge by Indo-Trinidadians for a greater share in political power in Trinidad becomes either reduced or irrelevant to Afro-Trinidadians.

This issue was also put another way: (Deosaran, 1978):

> *Recently through visits by representatives from 'liberator groups' from abroad (e.g. Africa), and the stress on the international economic order as determinants of black oppression, many Trinidad blacks are increasingly moving towards a 'universal brotherhood of blacks'. There is thus a budding sense of enlarged destiny in this, and obviously an issue like multiculturalism for democratic living in Trinidad would take a subordinate place in what is considered by those blacks to be a 'higher mission' at the international level.* (p.54).

The boundaries of statehood and political power were thus indirectly implicated in this issue of national and Caribbean identity. In other words, the two ethnic groups in the controversy defined the situation according to their perceived socio-political position.[29] And their responses differed to the extent that the calypso and its various interpretations evoked some form of dissonance.

Cognitive Dissonance

This section will use the theory of cognitive dissonance to explain some of the specific conditions which led many participants in the controversy to experience dissonance. It will also discuss the relationship between perceptions of the calypso and the methods used to reduce dissonance.

The theory (Cohen, 1964; Festinger, 1957, 1967) states that:

1. Psychological inconsistency[30] between two or more cognitive elements[31] leads to a state of cognitive dissonance.

2. Cognitive dissonance creates psychological stress.

3. Such psychological stress gives rise to pressures to reduce the dissonance (i.e. a motivational state is created).

4. Reduction in such dissonance may occur through:
   a. A change in one's attitude or behaviour.
   b. By adding a new cognitive element.
   c. By distorting, redefining, or changing one's frame of reference (i.e. to fit within the consistent cognitive elements already existing).

This theory is useful for understanding a variety of conflict situations. In one of the rare occasions when the theory was used to understand social tension in the Caribbean, Greene (1971) explained how the anti-Williams campaign in 1970 created cognitive dissonance. Greene implied that the lack of concerted action against Williams was partly due to the differences in dissonance reduction by the different political groups. The theory is also useful in understanding the dynamics of attitude change and resistance to change, scapegoating, and social perception generally (Harding et al, 1969).

In the context of sensitive issues, a new point of view could lead to dissonance for the listener. In such a state, s/he could attempt to apply one or more of the techniques specified above to reduce dissonance. S/he could also attempt to discredit the source of information (Cohen, 1964). These techniques serve to maintain or restore psychological equilibrium, that is, cognitive consistency.

However, people do 'change their minds', but the dissonance is averted or easily reduced by making them feel it is 'worth their while' to do so.

In other words, people usually attempt to justify their behaviour, and actually do so at least to themselves. Hence, as was evident in the calypso controversy, what might appear as 'irrational' behaviour to an observer could actually be 'rational' to the actor, for after all, the actor has redefined, in some way, the context of his action to sustain psychological consistency (Elms, 1967; Festinger & Carlsmith, 1959; Janis and King, 1954).

Four statements linking symbolic interactionism to cognitive dissonance now seem plausible:

1. Differences in social background and experiences help create differences in frame of reference.

2. A person's frame of reference is likely to determine his perception of social events.

3. A person's perception of social events is such that it helps maintain or restore cognitive consistency.

4. Hence, persons who differ in social background and experiences would be likely to perceive social situations differently.

This, of course, does not mean that persons of different backgrounds *always* perceive the *same* situation differently. What is being argued here is that at least the perceived potential[32] for cognitive dissonance from the same social situation could vary from one person to the other. And it is this difference that is likely to result in their different perceptions, and hence different techniques of dissonance reduction.

At this stage, the case for analysis becomes

  1. specifying the 'facts'[33] of the situation as far as possible,

then 2. determining the extent to which the different perceptions of the situation have departed from those facts.

This is necessary, because as explained earlier people differ but not in everything, and when they do differ it is usually through interpretation of the situation. We are therefore going to identify two possible stages in the controversy.

  1. At first Black Stalin's calypso in itself was ambiguous, in that one could say he either included all races in the Caribbean or he confined it to only those of African descent.

  2. Black Stalin's subsequent explanation on television removed that ambiguity and made it clear that he confined his calypso only to those of African descent.

Personality psychologists (Sarason, 1967; Semeonoff, 1976) have indicated that the more ambiguous a social stimulus is, the more likely would an observer interpret it according to his predispositions (or existing attitudes and traits). In fact, this is typical of projective testing. Semeonoff (1976) explained that the person 'puts something of himself' into the situation. This is a psychological necessity, because it is often the easiest way for the person to 'make meaning' of an ambiguous situation. As indicated earlier, English and English (1958) describes such projection as 'the process of perceiving objective stimuli in line with personal interests, desires, fears, or expectations'. Hence Indians protested and Africans defended and counter-protested.

The early issue in the controversy, as stated previously, was whether or not the calypsonian confined his 'Caribbean Man' concept to Africans at the exclusion of other ethnic groups. Whatever the other issues raised, and whatever the various interpretations were, the fact was that the calypsonian himself said yes, he did confine his concept to only those of African descent.

Hence such expressed ethnic exclusiveness would possibly be dissonant even to those who initially supported the calypso, and some means would have to be adopted to reduce the dissonance or further justify their continued support for the calypso. Table 4 indicates the different rationalisations that were used, possibly to reduce the dissonance.

It is possible however, that the Afro-Trinidadians who supported the calypso, both before and after the television explanation, did not actually experience much dissonance, their 'Afro-Caribbean' frame of reference already being so entrenched.

In spite of this, Table 4 raises some interesting questions. For instance, some black supporters felt that the calypso was serious social commentary in calling for black unity. Yet when faced with the criticism of ethnic segregation in the calypso they said that the calypso and/or the calypsonian should not be taken too seriously.

Implications for the Media

During the controversy one newspaper columnist[34] noted:

> *It's one of the more baffling features of the media scene, here and away, that while print routinely reviews television, ... there is no serious monitoring of the impact of print, of the content of the press and the method of its display.*

He added:

> *The print media are surely going to be on weak ground if they resent comment and criticism of their own performance and priorities.*

Research into the local media is surely lacking. In his study on the role of the media in election campaigns, Nancoo (1978) recently wrote:

> *This research gap is extremely difficult to justify in light of repeated complaints that the mass media are not necessarily neutral but may deliberately favour certain parties, ideas and interest groups* (p.118).

This section takes a look at how the 'print' media performed in the social controversy and is an attempt to help fill the research gap. This is especially justified when one considers that of the 31 responses in the controversy, 22 (71%) were actually from people in the newspaper business, either reporters, regular columnists, editors or managers of newspapers. Of this 22, 11 protested that the calypso was segregationist, eight said no, and three were indifferent. It is also important to note that 8 of this 22 had some form of control in either the final content or presentation of the news to the public.

Apart from the few columnists involved, this preponderance of newspaper people who took positions in the controversy naturally opens up the issue of news bias. Could reporters or editors who openly take strong positions on sensitive issues subsequently accommodate differing viewpoints properly in the pages under their charge? The evidence (Weiss, 1969; Cirino, 1967) indicates that once editors or editorials take open positions on controversial issues, the news pages show a subsequent trend in the editor's or editorial's direction.

The point here is not that senior newsmen or editors should not take public positions on sensitive social issues as the one under discussion. What is advanced here is (1) that such positions should be taken without jeopardizing the newspaper's perceived ability to report fairly, accurately, and responsibly; and (2) that the right to reply by citizens be a standard practice within the limitations of space and the law.

Anything less in both cases could only lead to undermining public confidence in editors, editorials, and the newspaper itself. This is critical since a newspaper's moral authority lies in its credibility. Without this, it is really of little or no service to its readers.

In two important instances, releases on the controversy to the *Trinidad Express* from responsible sources were never published by the *Express*. One came from Reverend Dr. Idris Hamid (February 28), and the other came from the All Trinidad Sugar Estate and General Workers Union (March 10). These two releases[35] found the calypso 'segregationist'.

When this exclusion is considered alongside the strong *Express* editorial (March 6) in favour of the calypso, the serious question of bias is raised. The exclusion of these two views is even more serious when one recognises that 65.4% of the space in the *Express* taken up in the controversy went to those saying that the calypso was 'not segregationist, racist, or offensive'. Furthermore, checking only those who said 'yes' or 'no' across all newspapers, the proportion of space taken up by those saying that the calypso was 'not segregationist' was 61% as against only 39% for those saying 'yes'. In this context non-publication of views submitted on the 'yes' side becomes of some concern. One could even get the wrong view of 'public opinion' by looking at the 61% vs 39% comparison.

The *Sunday Guardian* carried two lengthy commentaries (March

11,18), a total of 117 inches.   Both commentaries made some inaccurate comments on my earlier view on the calypso. For example, one said I should have responded to the Stalin interview and not only to the calypso. This was a critical point. The fact is, as substantiated in the release in Appendix C, it was on that interview that I based my response. Yet the *Sunday Guardian* editor refused to publish my subsequent correction.

Mass Communication expert Charles Steinberg (1970) reflects this concern and adds:

> *In a democratic, pluralistic society, the objective should be a rationally defined one in which not one, but many points of view are listened to intelligently... the way to consensus and agreement is by communication in which alternate paths may be explored in a spirit of inquiry* (pp.26-27).

This is an important perspective for local newspapers to ponder, since the issue of who and what is the 'Caribbean Man' is an important yet controversial socio-political issue (Demas, 1971, Lewis, 1971).

All this is further aggravated by the fact that the 'Caribbean' is still an amorphous, culturally diverse region. Its geographical boundaries are also unclear. The *Express* editorials repeatedly talk about a 'Trinidad Man' and a 'Caribbean Man' almost in the same breath. Like many others, the *Express'* position on national identity and Trinidad pluralism appears to be ambivalent.

On March 6 1979, an *Express* editorial supports the racial exclusiveness in the calypso, the 'Caribbean Man'. Yet afterwards, May 3, 1979, another *Express* editorial appealed:

> *The primary loyalty of the people of this country must be to Trinidad and Tobago, to our constitution, to our flag, to one another.*

But this reflects the more widespread ambivalence in the Caribbean over national identity and Caribbean unity: to many the first is necessary, the second is desirable, and the two are sometimes incompatible.

Such apparent ambivalence sets up two related situations:

(1)   it could be used as a subtle convenient form of news and opinion control.

and (2)   It shows the necessity for a fuller debate on the issue of national identity as raised in the controversy.

Speaking about suppression of views in Communist countries, an

Express editorial (May 14, 1979) stated:

> *Placing the lid over the steam of national debate in the name of national development does not really work.*

The controversy was a national debate on matters of national identity. And as such, views, free of acrimony and libel, should have been fully aired.

On the television interview of March 1, Black Stalin explained that his calypso was really confined to only those of African descent.

Yet on March 7, 6 days afterwards, the editor of the *Sun* allowed a full page to *another* calypsonian (a former 'Calypso King') who said that Stalin included all races, and was *NOT* 'speaking of the African man' alone. On this basis, this other calypsonian stridently condemned an Indo-Trinidadian critic of the calypso for being 'racial'. A short protest from this critic was published the next day in the front page of the *Sun*. All this indicates the need for at least greater editorial care in guiding without suppressing controversies of this kind, 'newsroom pressures' or 'production problems' notwithstanding.

The troublesome feature in the mismanagement of news is that the suppression, or distortion even when published, is sometimes done unconsciously or as least unwittingly (Berelson, 1949). Hence this is one reason for having the editorial department as representative of the community it serves as far as is possible (Gans, 1979). This matter of representatives in radio, television, and newspaper is another issue for further study, and is in fact a current issue in multiracial communities (Kotz, 1979).

Another solution to help ensure fairness and freedom from editorial bias is to establish a newspaper ombudsman (Knepler and Peterson, 1978). A more practical alternative however, is to have a representative editorial advisory body from which guidance on such controversial issues could be obtained for the newspaper concerned.

In pluralistic Trinidad, there are no institutions like a Race Relations Board or a Human Rights Commission to referee or monitor race and cultural relations. The media then has a critical role in recognising the validity of cultural pluralism and opening up its pages to such a presence. Considering the psychology of communication and the social function in news production, such a practice cannot effectively rest on newspaper policy alone. The newsrooms must begin to represent within tolerable limits the pluralism that exists in the community as well.

One newspaper researcher, Robert Cirino (1967) explained:

> *Representatives of minority viewpoints may have the right to free*
> *speech, but at the same time they may be deprived of a real*
> *chance to get public support for their ideas in interpretations... It*
> *is certainly unfair when any representative viewpoint is excluded*
> *from the mass media... or can't compete on an equal basis with*
> *other viewpoints. But for the individual consumer of media*
> *products, it is far worse than unfair treatment. It can amount to*
> *the deprival of his freedom to think, for if he is exposed to an*
> *unfair competition of viewpoints, it means he is not being given a*
> *real choice. In essence, he is being deprived of the opportunity to*
> *make up his own mind* (p.167).

Cirino (1967) produced evidence to show that while editors claim
integrity by restricting their (or management's) views to the editorials, the news somehow generally reflect the editor's views (p.188).

It was for this reason that an editor, Norman Isaac (1966),
condemned editors 'who have permitted editorial judgements to slop
over into the news columns, who use their newspapers to play
favourites, who have too often permitted their minds to become
something like concrete: all mixed up and permanently set' (p.136).

All this suggests that as far as the role of the media on this or any
similar controversy is concerned, some hard introspection will have
to be taken with respect to what is 'the public interest', who is 'the
community', who decides what is 'sensitive', and more particularly
what are the sociological characteristics of the 'Caribbean Man', or
for that matter, the 'Trinidad Man'. The media cannot continue to
base policies on the myths which they themselves help create
wittingly or unwittingly.

Conclusion and Some Implications

As indicated early in this paper, it is not merely a matter of whether
the calypso or calypsonian is being treated with undue importance.
What concerns this paper much more is the influence of the
participants in the controversy, the pervasiveness of the controversy,
the psychological and sociological issues indirectly raised, and the
role of the media. The calypso itself merely provided the opportunity
to look at these things. A theoretical model for psychological study of
the calypso and group conflict was also laid out.

This work suggested that the two ethnic groups perceived the calypso differently mainly because they held different frames of reference. The implication is that without those frames of reference becoming reconciled or at least clearly stated, ethnic responses to issues of national identity and patriotism would always provoke controversy between the two major ethnic groups. And in this, the media has a responsible role to play in fairly accommodating and intelligently guiding the discussion. While the study suggests a need for more balanced treatment of views in such a controversy, it does not say that there was a deliberate attempt to bias the presentation of views. The study merely identified some factors which could easily lead to apparent bias and calls for greater care in editorial judgements.

It became clear during the controversy that Afro-Trinidadians were experiencing great concern over the dispossession of blacks beyond the boundaries of Trinidad and Tobago. The question of black identity with its attendant implications for self-confidence and stability was also raised in ways that seemed to justify some priority for black unity within the Caribbean.

But Indo-Trinidadians, at the same time, expressed deep concern for their rights and status within the boundaries of Trinidad and Tobago. Hence, there is someting to be said for the concerns of both Africans and Indians here.

What seems little known to non-Indians, however, is that Indians themselves are now experiencing acute cultural stress in Trinidad and the issue of their cultural identity within Trinidad is also of great concern to them. It is in this context that the *Express* editorial's views (May 3, 1979) on 'primary loyalty' to this country and those in it becomes relevant.

It appears from this study that Indians and Africans do not have enough information on the ways of thinking and concerns of each group; and consequently much of the 'racial' hostility expressed between Indians and Africans here largely develop because of the different frames of reference through which each group viewed its status in Trinidad and in the Caribbean. There seems to be a serious 'communication gap' existing between the two groups, and one which the educational system and the media could well help to close. This gap is unfortunately institutionalised by the political process. It is in this particular respect that the differences within each ethnic group must be revealed if only to avoid rampant stereotyping. For instance, within the Indian group, there is a Muslim and Christian élite closely aligned to the ruling PNM and in receipt of state favours. At the same time, some of the more political challenges come not only from the Hindu-based opposition party, but also from black groups. What all this suggests is that the socio-economic and political perceptions which each group has of one another must be brought as close as possible to the reality, rather than being embroiled in distortions and overgeneralisations. The task of the educational system and the media is thus critical in such a complex multiracial society as Trinidad. However, this study provides a viable basis for improving race relations in the society – define and discuss freely the legitimacy of each frame of reference, then build socio-economic institutions to reinforce whatever emerges as a substantial consensus.

It is unfortunate in such controversies that spokesmen from one ethnic group judge entirely the other group merely by hearing a few spokesmen from the other's domain. One must also note that within Indian and African groups there are important variations with respect to socio-economic, political, and cultural interests. In fact, it is quite possible that while as a matter of principle, an objection such as the one made in the calypso controversy could be offered, spokesmen from either ethnic group could well exploit the controversy to satisfy their narrow interests. But this alone is not enough to stifle debate, or to stop Indians and Africans from talking to each other on issues which have been historically sensitive. If as a nation, we cannot discuss our social problems openly, then we are a far way from recognising the essence of nationhood. As explained earlier, the excuse of 'sensitivity' is too often used by the status quo to suppress legitimate challenges.

Indo-Trinidians, while pressing for racial equality and recognition in Trinidad, should also be prepared to participate more in the national life of the country, and Afro-Trinidadians who now control the national institutions ought to facilitate such participation. Frames of reference on national identity between the two groups could then converge to the extent that there is equality in socio-economic and political status between them. The answer to effective nationhood and patriotism thus depends on having a shared frame of reference. This is based on the 'contact hypothesis' (Simpson and Yinger, 1974).

The other related question is: could Afro-Trinidadians derive their own cultural integrity without wittingly or unwittingly contributing to the destruction of Indo-Trinidadian culture? Maybe the entire issue of seeking cultural identity from the past needs rethinking. Cultural change, given the dynamics of a society, must come. But the problem is, in what direction must it predominantly change? And does such change always have to manifest cultural imperialism?

All in all, the cultural problems of Indians and Africans here must be shared with each group. The calypso, as a popular and effective social stimulus, could play a significant role without unduly offending the feelings of certain cultural groups in our midst.

As William James said: 'There could be no more fiendish punishment than to be turned loose in a society and remain unnoticed by all'.[36] This matter of ignoring or relegating the presence or importance of one or another ethnic group in Trinidad only instigates apprehensions by the neglected group which, like self-fulfilling prophesy, would then be viewed as 'insularity' by those who engineered the relegation. The theme of black nationalism in Trinidad calypsoes cannot continue to ignore other ethnic groups here without appearing to be quixotic at some point.

Maybe this particular calypso, 'Caribbean Man', could have escaped controversy were it not for its prize-winning status, and Stalin's television interview. There are indeed many other calypsoes which not only exclude other ethnic groups in favour of Africans, but go on to implicate other groups with negative stereotypes.[37] For example, in 'Mr. African', Mighty Explainer sings in part:

As a cosmopolitan nation, with the racial majority,
The people facing the most frustration is the black man like you
and me.
We see the Indians prospering, the Chinese
capitalising,
But the African man has his confused mind.
The Indian will like Kamal to run this country.
But black people want to kill Afro-Willie.
Mr. African, you creating your own condemnation.

The Explainer insists in the same calypso: 'I'm not preaching racialism, but let's face reality...'

Indeed, there are some controversial aspects to this calypso. Explainer's thrust is apparently different from that of Trinidad's most versatile calypsonian, the Mighty Sparrow, who proposed racial harmony and the cosmopolitan spirit in his calypso 'A Model Nation' of a decade ago. Even if the fervour of black nationalism in the calypso has intensified over the years, the calypso, as a serious, social, or political commentary faces the danger of gross over-generalisation.

The style of calypso singing, like that of newspaper commentary, must rest on some degree of generalisation. But when such generalisations turn into negative and persistent stereotyping of certain ethnic groups, it is hard to see how the ethnic group favoured in the calypso could gain its self-confidence or establish a healthy basis for ethnic unity in a cosmopolitan society. This is particularly important if the calypso is to stake its claim as the national song. This concern is also reflected in Paul Walker's advice to Stalin, but one which could be extended to other calypsonians. Walker[38] wrote:

> *Sing on Black Stalin, but please give a pluralistic yet unifying interpretation of your beautiful verses.*

NOTES

1. Henceforth called Trinidad.

2. See Appendix A for Calypso.

3. This competition is run by a government-appointed body, the Carnival Development Committee (CDC).

4. The terms, Afro-Trinidadians, Black, and 'of African descent' will be used interchangeably; so too will Indo-Trinidadians, Indians and 'of Indian descent'.

5. During the months immediately preceding Carnival (a two-day national festival of music, song, dance and masquerade), calypsonians sing at organised night shows in different tents mainly in the City of Port of Spain. These tents are sometimes shifted to different parts of the country for a night or two.

6. This is exemplified in Valentino's 'Stay up, Zimbabwe', and Explainer's 'Caribbean Integration'.

7. The Sanatan Dharma Maha Sabha, claiming representation of some 275,000 Hindus in Trinidad.

8. *Trinidad Guardian,* August 11, 1979, (p.3).

9. *Trinidad Express,* November 20, 1976, (p.3).

10. Taken from *Annual Statistical Digest,* No. 24 (1976/77) Central Statistical Office, Port of Spain, 1979.

11. For summaries of socio-economic and political status distributions, see Deosaran, R., 'Multiculturalism in Trinidad & Tobago: A Political and Psychological Analysis', Department of Sociology U.W.I., (1978). Also Ryan, S., *Race and Nationalism in Trinidad and Tobago.* (University of Toronto Press, 1972).

12. This point must be moderated by the presence of a number of black groups in opposition to the PNM, most notably the Black Power movement in 1970.

13. The historical circumstances which laid the early base for such animosity (e.g. entry of indentured labour at the end of slavery) are discussed in Eric Williams' *Capitalism and Slavery,* and *The British West Indies.*

14. A number of researchers have attempted to define the calypso. See Adams, A. 'Where Came the Calypso' *Caribbean,* 1955, 8(10); Crowley, D. 'Toward a Definition of "Calypso"' *Ethnomusicology,* 1959, 3(2), Hill, E. 'The Origin of the term calypso', *Ethnomusicology* 1967, 11(3).

15. e.g. the Rorscharch Test and Thematic Apperception Test. See *Projective Techniques* by B. Semeonoff, (London, John Wiley & Sons, 1976.)

16. See Appendix B for full text of letter. Apart from collecting the published stories, I made attempts to secure copies, either from reporters or authors concerned of the full text of the press release or letters, published and unpublished.

17. See Appendix C for copy of the original.

18. The writer of the editorial subsequently admitted that he saw the interview but felt that Stalin 'did not understand the question' posed by the interviewer.

19. Claiming representation of almost 275,000 Hindus and managing 43 schools.

20. The *Express* did not publish this attack on its editorial.

21. For example, the 20,000 member All Trinidad Sugar Estates and General Workers Union (ATSE & GWTU) held an all day seminar on the 'Caribbean Man' on March 10, 1979. The Trinidad Public Library sponsored a forum on March 22 to discuss 'Caribbean Man' and 'Om Shanti' and about 300 attended the forum.

22. These categories were developed jointly by the author and the university's deputy librarian. Actual categorisation was done by the librarian and two teachers of African and Indian descent respectively. Except in one instance, there was complete agreement among all raters. The exception was resolved by using three of the four opinions as the 'correct' one (the author and the two others). Measurement of responses (in column inches) done by a research assistant.

23. This respondent used a pen-name, *Trinidad Guardian*, April 10, 1979.

24. See Appendix D for fuller details of classification.

25. Sanatan Dharma Mahasabha (SDMS), United Labour Front leader, (Major Opposition Party), Indian Renewal and Reform Movement, All Trinidad Sugar Estate and General Workers Union; People's Representative Organisation, and the Pandits Parishad. These organisations, with the possible exception of the People's Representitive Organisation are predominantly of East Indian membership.

26. Voice of America Forum Lectures: Communication Research in the U.S., Mass Communication Series, No.1.

27. Selwyn Ryan, *Sunday Express* columnist, and Head of Department of Government, UWI, St. Augustine, Trinidad.

28. For an overview of such positions see, 'Multiculturalism in Trinidad and Tobago: A Political and Psychological Analysis', by Ramesh Deosaran (Dept. of Sociology, UWI, 1978). Also *Race and Nationalism,* by Selwyn Ryan, *op. cit.*

29. As indicated earlier, the proportion of Indians and Africans is similar; since the advent of the PNM in 1956, the government has been dominated by Afro-Trinidadians.

30. Psychological inconsistency is not necessarily the same as logical inconsistency between two or more events, attitudes, beliefs, or between a belief and an event.

31. A cognitive element is a single unit of knowledge, a single belief, or an attitude held by someone towards himself or towards some object or person.

32. This could be done subconsciously.

33. 'Facts' here mean what could be agreed upon by resorting to physical measure, or at least the denotative meaning as earlier explained by Schramm.

34. Jeremy Taylor, *Trinidad Express,* March 12, 1979.

35. Rev. Hamid's release was passed through the telex machine in San Fernando office and lodged in the *Express* Port of Spain Head Office. The Union's release was passed on to a reporter, Theron Boodan, in the San Fernando office.

36. The psychological consequences of a dominant ethnic group ignoring the pressure or contributions of other ethnic or social groups in a society and weld presented in Moscovici, S. *Social Influence and Social Change,* (London, Academic Press, 1976, ch.9.)

37. For a discussion of stereotyping, see 'Prejudice and Race Relations, and Carnival', by R. Deosaran. *Working Papers in Caribbean Society,* Department of Sociology, U.W.I., St. Augustine, Trinidad, 1978.

38. Letter published in *Trinidad Express,* March 7, 1979.

REFERENCES

ADAMS, A.	'Whence come the calypso'. *Caribbean 8*(10), 1955.
AUSTIN, R.	'Understanding calypso content: a critique and alternative explanation.' *Caribbean Quarterly 22*(2/3), June-Sept. 1976.
BAHADOORSINGH, K.	*Trinidad Electoral Politics: The Persistence of the race factor.* (London, Institute of Race Relations, 1968.)
BRERETON, B.	'The Foundations of Prejudice: Indians and Africans in the 19th century.' *Caribbean Issues,* (ed. J. LaGuerre) 1(1), April, 1974.
BERELSON,B.	'Events as an influence on public opinion.' *Journalism Quarterly.* 1949, *26,* pp. 145-148.
BLUMER, H.	'Society as Symbolic Interaction.' In *Symbolic Interaction.* Ed. J. Manis and B. Meltzer.(Boston, Allyn and Bacon, 1972.)
BRATHWAITE, L.	'Problems of race and colour in the Caribbean.' *Caribbean Issues* (ed. J. La Guerre) *1*(1), April 1974.
CIRINO, R.	*Power to Persuade.* (London: Bantam Pathfinder Books, 1967.)
COOLEY, C.	*Human Nature and the Social Order.*(New York; Free Press of Glencoe, 1956) (Reprint).
COHEN, A.	*Attitude change and Social influence.*(New York, Basic Books, 1964.)
CROWLEY, D.	'Toward a definition of "Calypso"'. *Ethnomusiciology 3*(2), May 1959.
DEOSARAN, R.	'Multiculturalism in Trinidad and Tobago: A Political and Psychological Analysis'. Dept. of Sociology, University of the West Indies, 1978.
DEOSARAN, R.	'Race Relations and Prejudice, and Carnival.' *Working Papers in Caribbean Sociology Series C, No. 3.* Department of Sociology, University of the West Indies. 1978.
DEOSARAN, R.	'Multiculturalism for democratic living.' *Caribbean Issues,* 2(1), October 1979.
DEMAS, W.	'The New Caribbean Man.' *Caribbean Quarterly,* 1971, *17*(3 & 4).
ELMS, A.	'Role playing, incentive, and dissonance.' *Psychological Bulletin,* 1967, *68* pp. 132-148.
ELDER, J.	'The male-female conflict in calypso.' *Caribbean Quarterly, 14* (3) Sept. 1968.
ENGLISH, H & ENGLISH C.	*A Comprehensive Dictionary of Psychological and Psychoanalytic Terms.* (London, Longman's Ltd, 1958.)
FESTINGER L.	*A theory of cognitive dissonance.*(Stanford, Stanford University Press, 1957.)
FESTINGER L.	*Conflict, decision and dissonance.*(Stanford, Stanford University Press, 1967.)
FESTINGER L & CARLSMITH, J.	'Cognitive consequences of forced compliance.' *Journal of Abnormal and Social Psychology,* 1959 58 pp. 203-210.
GARFINKEL, H.	*Studies in ethnomethodology.* (New Jersey, Prentice-Hill, 1967.)
GRAHAM, S & BECKLES, D	'The Prestige Ranking of Occupations.' *Social and Economic Studies,* 17 (4) Dec, 1968.
GANS, H.	'The message behind the news.' *Columbia Journalism Review,* Jan/ Feb., 1979 pp. 40-45.
GREENE, E.	'An analysis of the General Elections in Trinidad and Tobago,

	(1971).' In *Readings in Government and Politics of the West Indies,* Eds. T. Munroe and R. Lewis. (Jamaica, Dept. of Goverment, University of the West Indies, 1971.)
GREENE, E.	'Race vs politics in Guyana.' Institute of Social and Economic Research, University of the West Indies, 1974.
HARDING, J., PRASHANSKY, H., KUTNER, B., & CHEIN, I	'Prejudice and Ethnic Relations.' In *The Handbook of Social Psychology,* Eds. G. Lindzey and Aronson E. (London, Addison-Wesley Publishing Company, 1969.)
HILL, E.	'On the origin of the term calypso.' *Ethnomusicology* 11 (3), Sept. 1967.
ISSACS, N.	'Conscience and the editor.' In the *Responsibility of the Press,* Ed. G. Gross. (New York, Fleet Publishing Corp., 1966.)
JANIS, I & KING, B.	'The influence of role playing in opinion change.' *Journal of Abnormal and Social Psychology.* 1954, 48, pp. 211-218.
KOTZ, N.	'The minority struggle for a place in the newsroom.' *Columbia Journalism Review,* March/April, 1979, pp. 23-31.
KNEPLER, M. & PETERSON, J.	'The ombudsman's uneasy chair.' *Columbia Journalism Review,* July/August 1978 pp. 54-57.
LANDAU, G.	'Race relations in the French Caribbean.' In *Caribbean Issues,* (Ed. J. La Guerre), *1* (1), April, 1974.
LEWIS, A.	'On Being Different.' In *Aftermath of Sovereignity* Ed. D. Lowenthal and L. Comitas. (New York, Anchor Books, 1973.)
LOWENTHAL, D.	*West Indian Societies.* (London, Oxford University Press, 1972.
MEAD, G.	*Mind, Self, and Society,* Ed. C.W. Moms (Chicago, University of Chicago Press, 1974) (Reprint).
MILLER, E.	'Self-Evaluation Among Jamaican High School Girls.' *Social and Economic Studies,* 22 (4), Dec. 1973, pp. 407-427.
NANCOO, S.	'Mass Media roles in electoral campaign: the Trinidad and Tobago 1976 General Election.' *The Indian Journal of Political Studies.* July 1978, 2 (2) pp. 118-129.
NETTLEFORD, R.	'Caribbean Cultural Identity. Jamaica.' Institute of Jamaica, 1978.
ROHLEHR, G.	'Forty Years of Calypso.' *Tapia, 2*(1), Sept, 1972.
ROHLEHR, G.	'Calypso and morality.' *Moko,* 6 (4) January 1969.
ROHLEHR, G.	'Calypso as comment.' *Listener 101* (2596) 1979.
RUBIN, V. & ZAVALLONI, M.	*We Wished to be looked upon.* (New York, University of Columbia Press, 1969.)
RYAN, S.	*Race and Nationalism in Trinidad.* (Toronto, University of Toronto Press, 1972.)
SARASON, I.	*Personality: An objective approach.* (New York, John Wiley & Sons, 1967.)
SECORD, P. & BACHMAN,C.	*Social Psychology.* (2nd ed.). (New York, Mc Graw Hill, 1974.)
SCHRAMM, W.	Voice of America Forum Lectures: *Mass Communication Series* No. 1.
SEMEONOFF, B.	*Projective techniques.* (New York, John Wiley & Sons, 1976.)
SHOTT, S.	'Emotion and Social life: a symbolic interactionist analysis.' *American Journal of Sociology,* May 1979, 84 (6) pp. 1317-1334.
STEINBERG, C.	*The Communication Arts.*(New York, Hastings House, 1970.)
STONE, C.	'Class, race, and political behaviour in urban Jamaica.' Institute of Social and Economic Research, University of the West Indies, 1973.
THOMAS, W.	'The Definition of the Situation.' In *The Unadjusted Girl.* (Boston, Little, Brown & Co., 1931.)
WEISS, W.	'Effects of the Mass Media of Communication.' In the *Handbook of Social Psychology,* Eds. G. Lindzey and Aronson, E. (London, Addison-Wesby Publishing Company, 1969.)

Appendix A
The 'Caribbean Man'

YOU try with a federation, the whole thing end in confusion,
Caricom and then Carifta but somehow I smelling disaster
Mister West Indian Politician you went to big institution
How come you can't unite seven million
When a West Indian unity I know is very easy
If you only rap to you people and tell them like me

Chorus:
Dem is one race – De Caribbean Man
From de same place – De Caribbean Man
That make the same trip – De Caribbean Man
On the same ship – De Caribbean Man
So we must push one common intention
If for a better life in the region
For we woman and we children
Dat must be the ambition of the Caribbean Man
De Caribbean Man De Caribbean Man

You say that the federation was imported quite from England
And you going and form a Carifta with a straight West Indian flavour
But since Carifta started running morning noon and night all I hearing
Is big money talk dem Prime Ministers making
But I say no ah money could form a unity
First of all your people need their identity

Caricom is wasting time de whole Caribbean gone blind
If we don't know from where we coming then we can't plan where we going
That is why some want to be communist, some want to be socialist
A man who don't know his history can't form no unity
How could a man who don't know his history form his own ideology

De federation done dead, and Carifta going to bed
But the cult of the rastafarian spreading through the Caribbean
It have rastas now in Grenada, rastas now in Antigua
But to run Carifta you getting pressure
If the rastafarian movement upping and Carifta dying slow
Den is something dem rastas on dat dem politicians don't know.

Appendix B
Rev. Hamid's Letter

Caribbean Ecumenical Programme
St. Andrews Theological College
Paradise Pasture
San Fernando
28th February, 1979.

Dear Mr. Editor,

Kindly permit me a comment on Stalin's 'Caribbean Man'. Stalin either does not respect facts or has no place for a significant number of Caribbean people.

The fact of the matter is that right here in Trinidad not all come from the same place, nor belong to the same race, nor come in the same ship, nor made the same trip.

To add insult to injury the judges confirmed this statistical obliteration of half the population of Trinidad, where every race is said to have an equal place.

(Sgd.) Rev. Dr. Idris Hamid
Caribbean Man
SAN FERNANDO

Appendix C
Press Release

Black Stalin's prize-winning calypso 'De Caribbean Man' is both racist and sexist. It is racist because it openly pushes the view that only people of African descent here are entitled to take part in Caribbean unity.
These lines:

> *'Dem is one race*
> *From the same place*
> *That make the same trip*
> *In the same ship – De Caribbean Man'*

are nothing less than an insult to the vast number of people from other races here who have come in different ships and from different places and who are also struggling to make this unity thing work. I am sure even right thinking people of African descent will recognise the unbalanced view in Stalin's calypso. Ordinarily, the calypso could have been ignored, but the fact that it rated as top calypso this year deserves a serious comment.

Whatever ambiguities there might have been about Stalin's lyrics have been cleared up in a TV interview last Thursday when he affirmed the racial and sexist orientation of his song.

The calypso is also sexist when it says:
'So we must push one common intention..
For we woman and we children'. The calypsonian's attitude towards our women is thus exposed; that is, the Caribbean woman must wait and follow. This is brainwash, equal to colonial exploitation, and worse when done in local song. The Caribbean woman is today struggling to take her place alongside the Caribbean man, not behind him as the song implies. The Caribbean woman must be encouraged to take an active part in Caribbean leadership.

If the calypso is to be the national song, if it has to be taken as serious 'social commentary', then calpsonians must stop behaving like musical demagogues and put some deeper, more intelligent thoughts into their lyrics. Calypso judges must also stop injecting their own prejudices into their verdicts. Stalin's calypso exploits popular prejudice and the fact that it won exposes the fragility and ignorance now surrounding race relations in this region. It is a slap against the motto 'Where Every Creed and Race Find an Equal Place'.

It should be said in no uncertain terms that we – Africans, Indians, Chinese, Syrians, Whites – are all now in the same ship together. And recognition of that fact is the Caribbean spirit.

At least one good that could emerge from Stalin's song is for us to start debating exactly what is this Caribbean man that everybody is so feverishly shouting about.

Dr. Ramesh Deosaran

Appendix D

Categories	Examples of Occupations
1. Higher Professional and Managerial	Farmers and land proprietors of more than 500 acres, university professors and senior lecturers, doctors, lawyers, high court judges, engineers, owners of large commercial and industrial enterprises, directors and managers of large enterprises, chiefs of police and army, head and assistant heads of government departments.
2. Lower Professional and Managerial	Senior civil servants, headteachers of large secondary schools, magistrates, farmers with 100-499 acres, superintendents of police, senior officers of the army, assistant managers of large establishments, managers and directors of medium size establishments, university lecturers, heads of large denominations.
3. Highly Skilled	Teachers, nurses, drugists, salesmen, ministers of religion, junior officers in army, inspectors of police, other civil servants, stenographers, accountants, typists, owners of small enterprises, farmers with 50-99 acres, secretaries, clerks, highly skilled technicians.
4. Skilled	Carpenters, plumbers, cabinet makers, drivers, bus conductors, policemen, corporals, soldiers (private), farmers with 1-49 acres, dressmakers, tailors, masons, tilers, curio workers etc.
5. Semi-skilled	Factory workers, waitresses or waiters, bar-tenders, porters, office maids, postmen, machine operators, etc.
6. Unskilled	Domestic workers, watchmen, peddlars, casual workers, portworkers, fish vendors, higglers etc.

The classification of occupation was based on the following six criteria:
(i) Prestige and status derived from the job
(ii) Income derived from the job.
(iii) Responsibility required by the job.
(iv) Educational standard needed for the job.
(v) Competence required on the job.
(vi) The size of establishment where this was relevant.

Appendix E

Details of Date, Respondents, and Publications

Date of Publication 1979	Name of Publication	Organisation and/or Chief Author	Respondent's Background
February 28	Trinidad Express*	Rev. Dr. Idris Hamid	Author & Director of Caribbean Ecumenical Prog.
March 5	Trinidad Express	Dr. Ramesh Deosaran	Lecturer in Social Psychology. Supervisor-tutor in Communication Arts Programme (UWI).
6	Trinidad Express	Express (Editorial)	Editor/Management, Express Newspaper.
7	Trinidad Express	Sanatan Dharma Maha Sabha (Sat Maharaj Sec. Gen.)	Major Hindu Organisation, (SDMS) claims representation of 275,000 Hindus.
7	Trinidad Express	People's Representative Org. (Rudy Lakhan)	University Student
7	Trinidad Express	Paul Walker	Teacher, community worker
7	Sun	Hollis Liverpool	Calypsonian, Chalkdust, teacher
8	Sun	Dr. Ramesh Deosaran	(see above)
8	Trinidad Express	Holden Caulfield	George John, Editor of Express
8	Trinidad Express	Cartoon by Leitos	Cartoonist
9	Trinidad Express	Pandits Parishad (Mahadeo Sharma-Pres)	Hindu body of 120 pandits
9	Trinidad Express	Camille Ramarace	Express Sub-Editor
9	Bomb	Patrick Chookolingo	Editor, Bomb
11	Sunday Guardian	Wilton Rogers	Sociologist and Chairman of Public Library Committee, former General Secretary of ruling PNM
11	Sunday Express	Dr. Selwyn Ryan	Reader in Govt. Head Dept. of Government, (UWI)
12	Trinidad Express	Jeremy Taylor	Art and Culture critic, columnist
14	Newsletter	Kwame Mtewe	University Student
14	Trinidad Express	Hon. Basdeo Panday	Opposition Leader, United Labour Front, Lawyer and President-General of All

Date of Publication 1979	Name of Publication	Organisation and/or Chief Author	Respondent's Background
			Trinidad Sugar Estate & General Workers Union. (ATSE & GWTU)
March 18	Sunday Guardian	Beau Tewarie	Lecturer in English (UWI)
22	Trinidad Guardian	Dennis Mahabir	Columnist, former Mayor of Port of Spain
26	Evening News	Don Draper	Pen-name for ass.-editor of magazine
April 3	Trinidad Guardian	"Deosa Walked"	Pen-name for letter-writer
10	Trinidad Guardian	"Ebony"	Pen-name for letter-writer
21	The Hindu**	Sat Maharaj	Editor of Hindu, Secretary of SDMS.
May 1	Battlefront**	All Trinidad Sugar Estate & General Workers Trade Union	Battlefront Editor
9	Evening News	Valentine Brown	Senior Reporter
10	Trinidad Express*	ATSE & GWTU	Winston Dookeran, Lecturer in Economics (UWI)
11	Trinidad Guardian	Valerie John	Freelance writer
11	Trinidad Guardian (interview)	Black Stalin	Calypsonian
12	National Target	Suren Capildeo	Lawyer, columnist
15	Newsletter	Ramdath Jagessar	Journalist, Public Relations officer.

*   Submitted but not published

**   Monthly publication

Over a Hundred Years of East Indian Disturbances on the Sugar Estates of Guyana, 1869 – 1978: An Historical Overview

Tyran Ramnarine

Indians[1] first arrived in Guyana[2] in 1838 to supplement the newly freed African slaves as labourers on the sugar plantations. Except for two minor interruptions, 1838-1845 and 1848-1851, Indians continued to come every year as indentured immigrants until 1917. They were only one of several immigrant groups. West Indians (mostly Barbadians), Europeans, liberated Africans, Madieran and Azorean Portugese and Chinese also came to the Colony. But Indians became the largest group as their period of immigration was the longest and best organized. They brought about enduring economic, demographic, and cultural changes in the Colony. The 1911 census revealed for the first time that East Indians formed the largest single ethnic group[3]. Moreover, they had almost completely supplanted African and other field labourers on the sugar estates.

The plantations of Guyana had always been afflicted with insurrections and general unrest. Minor slave revolts are recorded for 1731, 1741, 1762, and 1814. More serious insurrections occurred in Berbice in 1763 and in Demerara in 1883. Emancipation in 1838 granted the ex-slaves the legal right to withdraw their labour when they thought fit. This they did in 1842 and 1847-48. The ex-slaves were victorious in 1842 when they struck against the planters who, faced with serious economic difficulties, had attempted to reduce wages uniformly. In the 1847-48 strike, however, the freedom was lost mainly because of the importation of immigrants who were providing a viable alternative. Associated with the failure of this strike is an accelerated movement of Africans away from the estates to villages. Thereafter, as Indians began replacing the Africans on the sugar estates, subsequent strikes would involve only or mostly Indians.

Very little work has been done on strikes involving Indians on the sugar estates of Guyana. This paper sets out as prolegomena to future research in that it attempts to erect historical signposts. Besides periodizing these strikes, it seeks to establish some rationale for those periodizations. Wherever time and space allow, there is some discussion of these strikes. Five periods are delineated:

(1) 1869-1917, strikes during the indenture period;

(2) 1917-1929, the end of indenture up to the formation of the Man Power Citizens' Association (MPCA);

(3) 1930-1947, the period of comparative militancy of the MPCA;

(4) 1947-1961, the challenge to the MPCA from the Guiana Industrial Workers' Union;

(5) 1961-1978, the formation of the Guiana Agricultural Workers Union (GAWU), the demise of the MPCA, and the introduction of State Capitalism in the sugar industry.

1869-1917

During the early phase of Indian immigration, planters viewed Indians as a docile and regulatory labour force. Governor Henry Light remarked in 1846 that the pliant immigrant labour force was having a 'moral' effect on the Africans in teaching them the habits of industry.[4] Indians were restoring to the plantocracy some of the command over labour that it had lost with the coming of emancipation. But from 1869, a series of strikes and disturbances started. For most of the last week of July of that year Indian labourers at plantation La Jalousie rioted over wages; on August 1st, they beat up a Portugese watchman at Leonora; on August 2nd, they fought some Barbadian labourers at Malgre Tout over rates of pay; on August 14th, they struck over wages on plantation Farm, Mahaicony, and on December 13th, at plantation Enterprise, they beat up some African police constables who attempted to arrest one of their countrymen. Thereafter, labour disturbances involving Indians on the sugar estates became a permanent feature in Guyana.

The disturbances started in 1869 as Indians began feeling the full effect of the immigration ordinances. By this time the planters had enacted with relative ease a corpus of laws designed to keep Indians on the estates a captive labour force. Indians were indentured for five years to estates where, barring severe illness, they had to provide six full days of labour per week. So effectively did the system circumscribe Indian freedom in the colony that John Jenkins, who represented the Aborigines Protection Society and the Anti-Slavery

Society during the 1870 Commission of Enquiry into the Treatment of Indian Immigrants, was moved to offer this description of their fate:

> *Take a large factory in Birmingham or Belfast, build a wall around it, shut in it work people from all intercourse, save at rare intervals, with the outside world, keep them in absolute heathen ignorance and get all the work you can out of them, treat them not unkindly, leave their social habits and relations to themselves, as matters not concerning you who make money from their labour, and you would have constituted a little community resembling, in no small degree, a sugar estate in British Guiana.*[5]

The most objectionable feature of the ordinance was that labourers who infringed the immigration laws were often prosecuted as criminals and sent to prison. Indentured Indians could not leave their estates without the permission of the managers; otherwise when caught, they could be prosecuted as deserters.

The ordinances set out procedures for the making and resolving of labour complaints between estate managers and labourers to minimize their escalation into strikes. Throughout the period of Indian immigration employers had a much higher number of complaints against indentured Indians than Indians against employers. Table 1 illustrates this point.

Table 1
Number of Complaints Between Employers and Indentured Indians. Quinquentially between 1881 and 1911

Year	No. of Indentured Indians	No. of Employers' Complaints against Indians	No. of Indians' Complaints against Employers
1881	22,879	4,256	33
1886	17,144	2,610	16
1891-2	16,700	3,911	3
1895-6	20,480	4,255	2
1901-2	14,609	3,423	5
1906-7	10,587	4,003	Nil
1910-11	9,901	2,932	2

Source: Annual Reports of the Immigration Agent General

Several reasons account for this wide disparity. During the period of the sugar depressions, 1884-89 and 1894-99, some estate managers used the complaint provision as a vindictive leverage for depressing the wage rates of indentured Indians. During the 1884-89 crisis, for instance, these managers compelled the Indians to accept the free market rates of wages which had plummetted by 33% and fell below the minimum allowed by statute for indentured immigrants. The colonial administration could do very little although managers were breaching the ordinance. Governor Charles Bruce warned that if the Immigration Department applied pressure 'without excellent judgement on the Proprietors and Managers it has been found to have the effect of multiplying prosecutions and filling the prisons with Immigrants convicted as idlers.'[6] Secondly, the process of amalgamation of estates tended to reduce 'the direct personal influence of the manager himself' and conversely increase the authority of the lower echelon of estate management.[7] The European overseers and the Indian and Creole drivers (foremen) were disposed to use their powers indiscriminately. To demonstrate and 'to show off their authority, drivers and overseers bring them (the Indians) up for the most trivial faults.'[8] A satisfactory number of Indians' complaints against their employers were inhibited by several factors. Coming from a background in which life was simply and hierarchically organized, the majority of them would have difficulty initially in relating to what might have appeared to them a complex system. Secondly, Indians generally feared reprisals from the estate authorities. The swift and violent suppression of strikes by the police made the immigrants 'really frightened to make any complaints against their employers.'[9] Testifying before the 1897 West Indian Royal Commission, the famous Bechu knew 'for a positive fact that the fear of their drivers, who keep indentured coolies so under subjection by abuses and threats, [makes] outspoken complaints...rare.'[10] Moreover, the drivers generally had a group of henchmen who could support them on fabricated charges against those who complained. Thirdly, Indians had very few opportunities to see the Immigration Agent whose duty was to safeguard the general welfare of the indentured immigrants in his prescribed district. The Agent usually 'comes around once a month, he is only there for about half an hour, and during that time all the coolies are in the field.'[11] Labourers found him further inaccessible because managers did not grant them the necessary pass to register their complaints with the Agent. Fourthly, those Indians who had the courage and the opportunity to make complaints were more amenable than the planters to a settlement 'without reference to the courts.'[12] Planters preferred the Courts because they were better able to control the labourers. They were more acquainted with the legal system, most of them were Justices of the Peace, and they enjoyed such a fraternal relationship with the magistrates that they brought undue pressure on the Indians.

The ordinance governing complaints did not work as intended. Indians could have no faith in this strike-check mechanism as they suffered much more under it than the planters. Their only alternative was open confrontation and regular use of the strike weapon to demonstrate their grievances. Indians struck work with alarming frequency throughout this period. Besides underestimating the severity of the strikes, the Immigration Agent General tended to understate the number of strikes since they might reflect poorly on his general administration. In 1889, for instance, D.W.D. Comins, who was then visiting the Colony recorded 12 strikes; the agent General, on the other hand, gave no statistics and simply stated that there was 'comparitive freedom from strikes.'[13] Thus no universally accepted average could be arrived at for the period. There is no doubt, however, that strikes occurred every year. In most cases they were of short duration from a few hours to a few days and involving only one gang. When they involved the whole estate, the strikes sometimes led to very serious injury to the labourers. For instance in October 1986, the police shot 5 Indians dead and seriously wounded 59 others at Non Pareil. At Plantation Friends 8 Indians were killed and 7 others critically injured in 1903. Rose Hall estate suffered the worst fate with 15 dead and 14 seriously wounded in 1913. These incidents occurred on individual estates without involving others from a particular district, region, or the whole Colony. Concerted action on any scale would have had dramatic consequences but it was non-existent mostly because of lack of leadership, poor communications, and pervasive management control.

At times Indians displayed admirable qualities of perseverance and they only resorted to the strike weapon as a last measure. Governor Henry Irving found that although they were 'fully alive to their rights,' they would strike only when they perceive 'a prospect of doing so with success on a question of wages, which might fall to almost any extent without complaints from them.'[14] Labourers had little faith in the established medium to channel their grievances and occasionally they sought the intervention of independent bodies in their disputes with the estate management. In 1901, a group of East Indians from plantation Versailles, disillusioned with the way the District Immigration Agent handled their complaints, overlooked him and complained to the district magistrate about the rates offered by the estate for weeding and cleaning. In another case, at plantation Success, Leguan, 93 indentured Indians besieged the district police station in 1903 to issue complaints against an overseer and a driver. These attempts, however, proved fruitless and they were referred to the District Immigration Agent whose initial indifference to their complaints was the reason for the labourers' seeking of outside mediation.

The militancy of the labourers was often provoked by the frequent illicit sexual relations between the managers, overseers, and Indian women. As early as 1869, the Government had issued a circular requesting managers to stamp out this practice. The 1870 Commission of Enquiry reported:

> *The record of complaints which we have had occasion to peruse, and even our own observations in visiting estates, have shown us that it is not all uncommon for overseers, and even managers, to form temporary connections with coolie women.*[15]

The authorities showed concern not with the moral life of the Indians but with the effect such relations might have on the smooth running of the estates. 'In every case' of such immoral relations 'the worst possible consequences to the good order and harmony of the estate' ensued.[16] The Immigration Agent General found it 'to be the secret source of dissatisfaction and disturbances.'[17] The low proportion of women to men, which remained a feature throughout the indenture period, accounts for Indian hostility against this type of relationship. Between 1880 and 1917, the ratio was on the average 40 women to 100 men on the estates. Consequently,

> *the withdrawal of even a single woman from the Coolie dwellings to the overseer's lodge is regarded with jealous eyes by her fellow countrymen, and when it is remembered that any female over childhood is already the actual wife of one of them, it is evident that no surer way could be found of sowing the seeds of discontent and riot.*[18]

This disproportion accounted for 'nearly all the serious crimes committed by coolies,'[19] especially wife assaults and murders. The most serious riot on account of illicit relationships between Indian women and managers occurred in 1896 at Non Pareil where 5 Indians were shot dead and 59 seriously wounded by the police. Evidence later disclosed that the acting manager, Van Nooten, had been living with an Indian woman and the attorney of the estate not only declined to take any action but endeavoured to protect him.

Various measures adopted by the planters did not succeed in substantially reducing the number of strikes. Managers practiced a system of divide and rule, as in slavery, in the allocation of indentured Indians. They 'purposely choose men speaking three or four separate and distinct languages not understood by each other, in order to prevent combination in case of disturbances among them.'[20] They suspected that most of the leaders of the strikes were Brahmins and took steps to stop the recruitment of immigrants from this caste. In 1890, the Planters' Association passed a resolution instructing the Emigration Agent in Calcutta 'to exclude all high caste people and Brahmins.'[21] In 1889 the pro-planter newspaper *The Argosy,* 'applauded' the prompt action of the Immigration Agent General in deporting a Brahmin priest to India for giving Indians 'bad advice.'[22] To eliminate potential leaders further, the Executive Council in 1904 decided to disallow free passages to Indians who had returned to India and to prohibit their reindenture if they did manage to return. They felt that the returning Indians 'put mischievous ideas into the heads of the new coolies on their way to the colony.'[23] To minimize and even to smother leadership, the authorities inflicted severe penalties on strike leaders. Latto (a shopkeeper), Dabysingh (a driver), and Baldeo (a labourer) were sentenced for as long as seven, six and three years' imprisonment respectively for their involvement in the 1895 strike at plantation success. At the sign of any strike, the general practice was for managers to summon the police to arrest the suspected leaders.

During the indentureship period, Indian labourers were divided into indentured and time-expired or free Indians. This division had prevented any joint action in executing strikes effectively. The free Indians received from the planters several inducements which they dearly cherished because of their dire economic position. The completion of their indenture found them, as Chief Justice John Beaumont put it, as 'paupers of a subject race, in a country which has no place for them, and exiled from their own country...'[24] These privileges included the use of pastureland for livestock, unused land for land cultivation, and the erection of houses on estate land. They

came in the form of direct personal dispensations issued by the
manager himself who then reserved 'to himself the right to cancel'
them at any time.[25]

The planters used these inducements as a lever to stifle any
incipient militancy among free Indians who consequently became a
conservative element in the estate labour force *vis-à-vis* the indentured section. Disagreements occurred frequently between the two
groups with the indentured Indians invariably being the militants. In
a dispute over wages at Enmore in 1888, indentured Indians went to
the cane fields to prevent the free Indians, who had accepted a lower
rate of pay, from working.[26] They took similar action against the free
Indians at Non Pareil in 1896.[27] In another strike at plantation
Melville in 1900, they assaulted a free Indian and chased a driver,
both of them having to take refuge in the manager's house.[28] In
another serious strike at Friends in 1903, in which the police fatally
shot 6 and seriously wounded 7, indentured Indians abandoned the
fields while the free Indians continued to work.[29]

The indentured Indians were also more militant than the African
workers who accepted fewer privileges than the free Indians. As one
witness told the 1898 Royal Commission, a strike could be organized

> *more easily amongst the indentured labourers. They can orga-
> nize a strike better (than the negroes), but then they are facing a
> much more serious situation than the negro is, because they can
> be taken before a magistrate, and if it can be shown that their
> strike was an unjust one, the magistrate can deal with it, and he
> can punish the ringleaders of it, whereas in an ordinary strike of
> negroes, of course, they can say 'we like to strike', and it is no
> offence against the law.*[30]

Over a period of time there seemed to have developed a tradition of
insurgency which was reinforced by the fresh waves of immigrants.

The militancy of the indentured Indians can be explained partly by
the dynamics associated with a servile and captive labour force and
the fact that, unlike the free Indians, the indentured Indians
depended almost exclusively on the consistently low estate wages for
their sustenance.

1917 – 39

The termination of indenture in 1917 did not bring to an end the kind
of penalties that were associated with breaches of the immigration
ordinances. All East Indian labourers then came under the 1853
Employers and Servants Ordinance. In the absence of any written

agreement, the Ordinance presumed that the labourer had a contract for one month. He could terminate his services only by the consent of his employer, for a 'just' cause, or after fourteen days notice. The planters made use of this Ordinance when it suited them.

The Immigration Department which did little during indenture to prevent strikes, did almost nothing after 1917 to defend Indian labour interests. With the termination of all indentured contracts in 1922, the staff of the Department was reduced to a bare minimum. In 1932, the post of Immigration Agent General was abolished, but some Indians still retained their former rights under the indenture system with respect to repatriation, passages, etcetera. Such functions were adopted by the Registrar-General who 'did not, however, supervise conditions on estates of concern himself with the provision made by the employer for his work people. In consequence, some retrogression was inevitable and conditions on different estates now vary considerably.'[31]

The need for representation of Indian labour interests was partly satisfied by the British Guiana Labour Union (BGLU) and the British Guiana East Indians' Association during this period. In 1922, the BGLU was registered as the first trade union in the colony. The union's principal concern was the dock workers of Georgetown who were in the main Africans. It also took some interest in conditions on the sugar estates and criticized the task work system as too exploitative. It further campaigned that Indians be paid on the same basis as other races in the Colony.[32] It had no long term impact, however, as its influence did not extend beyond those estates on the East Bank of Demerara which were within a short distance from Georgetown. It probably did serve, however, as an inspiration or catalyst for later unions in the sugar industry.

The British Guiana East Indians' Association (BGEIA) which was formally convened in 1919 to preserve and advance the social, economic, cultural, and political interests of the colony's Indians also functioned as a quasi labour union. During the economic depression affecting the colony's sugar production in the 1920s, the Association petitioned the government about the sugar workers' plight.[33] Like the BGLU, the BGEIA was Georgetown-based. It was mostly active on the East Bank of Demerara where it held meetings to discuss, in particular, demands for higher wages and the Colonization Scheme which sought to bring Indian colonists to Guyana. In spite of these activities, the Association was never powerful enough to bring any substantial improvement in the Indian lot on the estates. Besides its limited appeal to those estates close to Georgetown, its middle class leadership sought to behave in a 'responsible' manner at the expense of the workers' interests. For instance, during the 1924 disturbances at Ruimveldt estate over wages, Francis Kawall of the BGEIA attempted to dissuade the protesting workers from coming to Georgetown to lodge their complaints before the Agent General. Further, the Association did not advance issues to explain the strike but placed blame on an unnamed black Barbadian.[34]

Strikes continued unabated with the sugar industry caught in the worldwide capitalist economic crisis. Some of the most serious strikes occurred in the second half of 1935. That year had boasted a bumper sugar crop, but labourers found that they had to work harder for the same rates of pay.[35] The strikes started in August on plantation Leonora and soon engulfed a number of estates. Workers defied the police, hoisted red flags, beat drums, and drew their cutlasses in active protest. Governor Northcote hastily appointed a Commission of Inquiry which caustically criticized the prevailing state of affairs. It noted that with the abolition of the post of Immigration Agent General in 1932, the Indian labourer was 'without the assistance, safeguards, and means of ventilating grievances.' It also contrasted the employers in their highly organized Sugar Producers' Association (SPA), and labour which was entirely unorganized. Another important finding was the pervasive fear of the labourer residing on the estates. The Commission felt that no labourer gave evidence voluntarily because of fear of management victimization.[36]

Four years later, Major Orde Browne who visited the Caribbean to examine labour conditions found the general insecurity of tenure on the estates to be one of the main causes of Indian unrest. In the past indenture period, Indian labourers enjoyed the free housing that was formerly provided for the indentured immigrants. But there were no defined rights and obligations between employers with respect to residence and employment. The labourer lived and worked on the estates on the sufferance of the manager. Therefore, he could be ejected at any time, losing his home as well as his job, with little prospect of acceptance by another estate.[37] Right up to the nationalization of sugar in 1977, managers used this power to get rid of militant labourers and those whom they considered undesirable for some reason.

The absence of any established machinery for Indian workers to channel their grievances allowed strikes to continue unabated. In 1938, labour affairs came under the Department of Labour, a branch of the Local Government Department, headed by a Commissioner of Labour. It had no immediate impact in checking the strikes. A perennial grievance of the workers was the nature of the task or piece work. Labourers were assigned a specific task which was supposed to be completed within a day. This type of labour, which was almost pervasive, was also very unsatisfactory. There was no standardized task and the condition of the land varied widely. The report of the 1945 Royal Commission on this issue, although generalized for the Westindies, was very applicable to Guyana.

> *The rates of pay for particular tasks are not fixed by any general agreement or collective bargaining but usually decided on the spot. Frequently we heard complaints that labourers did not know the rates at which they were to be paid until after they had begun their task. On other occasions, when rates were being fixed on the spot because innumerable variations in soil and other conditions were likely to affect the time taken to complete a set piece of work, the discussion developed into a haggle between the labourers and the overseers. Or, more frequently, the task rates were arbitrarily decided by the overseers.*[38]

The mid 1930s which was characterized by an unusual number of strikes was followed by the formation of a number of unions. One union in the sugar industry that pre-dated the strikes was the British Guiana Workers' League which was registered in January 1931. It represented certain categories of factory and clerical workers. The most important union was the Man Power Citizens' Association (MPCA). Whether it was organized to represent East Indian sugar workers or sugar workers who, *de facto,* were mostly East Indians has not yet been established. Ayube M Edun, who Leo Despres describes as an 'East Indian idealist with a political vision of a new world order',[39] founded the MPCA in 1937. Edun had visited England in the twenties and after returning to Guyana, he propounded a philosophy he called 'Rationalist-Practical Idealism'. He published a weekly paper, the *Guiana Review,* in which he was ultra critical of the working conditions in the sugar industry. Recognition for the MPCA did not come easily or immediately. The Sugar Producers' Association recognized it after two years of further industrial unrest climaxing with the Leonora disturbance of February 1939, in which 4 Indian labourers were killed and several others seriously wounded.

1939 – 47

Official recognition of the MPCA, however, did not bring about complete industrial peace. In fact, strikes continued with almost the same frequency and intensity for the same reasons that had bedevilled the sugar industry before. In 1942, there were 31 stoppages of work at 10 different estates; 18 estates experienced stoppages in 1943; 13 estates in 1944; 11 estates in 1945; and 9 estates in 1946.[40] The MPCA for a short period provided an acceptable and effective medium of channelling the grievances of the Indian sugar workers.

The early enthusiasm and optimism that accompanied the formation of the MPCA began to evaporate as the Sugar Producers' Association (SPA) set about to neutralize it. Some members of the SPA entered into an agreement with a foremost leader of the MPCA, C.R. Jacob, under which he would cease prominent trade union activities and accept employment with Bookers at $480 per month for four years. With respect to wages, the SPA acted in almost complete disregard of the MPCA. The SPA refused the claim of the MPCA in February 1943 for a higher war bonus based on an increase of 12 cents per cwt. on Guyana sugar paid by the British Ministry of Supply and on the increased cost of living. The following year the SPA unilaterally increased the war bonus by 5% regardless of the protestations of the MPCA and the BGWL that it was too low. In 1945, the SPA again refused a claim of the MPCA for increased wages after the export price of sugar went up by $9.60 per ton. The employers illogically contended that the price increase was to meet costs already incurred.

The arrival of Cheddi Jagan in Guyana in late 1943 from the U.S. added a new dimension to labour relations on the sugar estates. Jagan first attempted to instil some degree of militancy in the MPCA. In 1945, he became treasurer of the MPCA but was forced to resign after serving only one year. Jagan claimed that the union executive moved against him because he objected to what he considered 'to be the high level of expense allowances from the funds of a poor union and, because of the tendency of the union leaders to collaborate with the sugar company.'[41] For the short while that he sat around the bargaining table with the SPA he 'saw clearly that the union (MPCA) leadership was not prepared to fight for the workers.'[42]

In spite of this set back, Jagan continued to be active among the sugar estates especially those on the East Coast of Demerara. He easily identified with the sugar workers because he himself was born the son of a driver on the Port Mourant sugar estate in Berbice where he grew up. On the other hand, the other Indian leaders whether in the MPCA or the BGEIA were generally urban based. In November 1947, Jagan contested a seat to represent the Central Demerara Electoral District No.6 in the Legislative Council. This constituency included the sugar estates on the East Coast of Demerara and so Jagan's manifesto had a special appeal to the sugar workers. Among the issues it spoke of were a 40-hour week without reduction in pay; a minimum wage law for everyone; two weeks annual holiday with pay; time and a half for overtime and double time for Sundays and holidays; and the general improvement of working conditions. In spite of a limited voting franchise, Jagan won, with the bulk of his support coming from the sugar workers. In the Legislative Council, he became the staunchest advocate for the cause of labour.

Jagan and some other leaders, who were in the executive of the BGEIA, decided to pose a direct challenge to the MPCA by establishing a rival union in 1946. The following year they had a *casus belli* in the introduction of a new system of reaping canes. Under the old 'cut and drop' system, cane cutters cut the canes and dropped them into the bank of the trench. From there they were taken by loaders who deposited them in the punts. The new 'cut and load' system combined these two operations of cutting and loading. Workers found several faults with the new system. The older workers now found it too strenuous and few of the younger ones could work more than three days per week. Logistical problems included the availability of punts and the correctness of the scales. Where the old system paid according to the area harvested, the new one paid according to weight. Management allowed a workers' representative to be at the scales, but he had to be paid by the workers themselves.

The publicising of these deficiencies and the mounting criticisms by the workers led the MPCA to take some action. It called two meetings – one for the District Secretaries and representatives of the Joint Estate Committee and the other for the representatives of cane-cutters. In the latter meeting, the cane-cutters agreed to the cut and load system with some minor adjustments and to the increse in wages by 40 cents to every ton of cane. At a joint conference, however, held with the Commissioner of Labour, the MPCA signed an agreement with management for an increase of only 7 cents per ton. Undoubtedly, the workers were dissatisified with the MPCA's handling of this matter.

1948 – 61

The rival union was called the Guiana Industrial Workers Union. It vigorously took up the cause of the cane-cutters and at the same time sought recognition from the SPA. It was most active on the East Coast of Demerara which also included the constituency of Cheddi Jagan. The GIWU was registered as a trade union on 5th of April, 1948, with Dr J.P. Lachmansingh as President, A.A. Rangela as Senior Vice-President, and J. Phillips-Gay as General Secretary. Seventeen days later, a series of strikes affected all the estates on the East Coast. Ashton Chase claims that the strikes started 'ostensibly over the system of cut and load as against cut and drop. The real object of the strike, however, was to secure recognition of the GIWU as the bargaining agent on behalf of field and factory workers in the sugar industry.'[43] Jagan, on the other hand, made no acknowledgement of this kind and simply states that 'this action of changing the system without consultation led to a four and a half month strike...'[44] The strike was most serious at plantation Enmore where the police opened fire killing 5 and injuring 12 workers.

A Commission under the chairmanship of a Judge of the Supreme Court, F.M. Boland, was appointed by Governor Charles Wooley to enquire into the disturbances. Like so many Commissions of this kind, its report defended the shooting of workers supposedly armed with sticks.

In October, 1948, the Secretary of State for the Colonies considered the Guyana situation serious enough to appoint a Commission to enquire into, report, and make recommendations on the organization of the sugar industry with special reference to the means of production, wages and working conditions. Under the chairmanship of J.A. Venn, Cambridge Lecturer in History and Agricultural Economics, the Commission submitted its final report in July 1949. It made some far reaching recommendations. It favoured the 'cut and load' system, but recommended the 'cut and drop' method when punts were not available. A novel suggestion was the setting up of a single Wages Board or Council for field and factory in the whole sugar industry. This board would comprise an equal number of representatives from both the employers and workers with neutral members appointed by the Government. Had this been instituted, wages would have been standardized throughout the industry and subsequent wage disputes would have been minimized. Understandably the SPA which had been unilaterally setting wages, in spite of the presence of the MPCA, objected to this recommendation. The MPCA, probably because of prodding from the SPA, also objected to it although the workers stood to gain much from this system.

The Commission urged the recognition of small specialized unions but ignored the claim of the GIWU. Until 1948, the SPA had only recognized the MPCA and the British Guiana Workers' League as unions representing workers in the sugar industry. Besides the GIWU, three other unions awaited recognition – the British Guiana and Westindian Sugar Boilers' Union formed in 1944, the Drivers (Headmen) Union (1945) and the Sugar Estates Clerks Association (1946). Upon the recommendation of the Commission, the SPA recognized these unions soon after. It saw the GIWU, on the other hand, as a renegade union that was duplicting the other trade unions. The Commission further argued that worker dissatisfaction with the leadership and policy of the MPCA should be met by a change of officers, not a change of the union. So the GIWU failed in its first attempt to gain recognition.

Between 1948 and 1952, the GIWU was out in the cold. During the strikes on the East Coast 50 local representatives were prevented from carrying out organizational work for the GIWU and from collecting funds for strike relief. In the end, the estate management gave them trespass notices. The leaders, including Dr Lachmansingh and Jagan, also received such notices although these estates were in Jagan's constituency. Nevertheless, the GIWU was recognized by two militant organizations – the regional Caribbean Labour Congress (CLC) and the international World Federation of Unions (WFTU).

In late 1952, the position of the GIWU had improved somewhat. Partly because of the influence exerted by the CLC, the BG Trades Union Council admitted the GIWU in its fold. At this time also a Labour Bill was introduced in the Legislative Council to solve the jurisdictional dispute between the GIWU, the MPCA, and the SPA. It empowered the Commission of Labour to conduct elections in order to decide the issue of recognition. It, however, failed to pass but, significantly, it received support from the BG Trade Unions Council. The MPCA in retaliation withdrew from the Council.

Emboldened by this limited success, the GIWU in November 1952, called another strike for recognition which proved a failure. In retrospect,. it was prematurely conceived. The factory workers did not strike. Some success was achieved only on the East Coast where the field labourers effectively crippled the estates by not supplying the factories with canes. Perhaps because of poor planning it got little support from the estates of the East Bank, the West Bank, and the West Coast of Demerara. No effort seemed to have been made to involve the Berbice estates.

The massive victory of the People's Progressive Party at the 1953 general election gave the GIWU another opportunity to press its claim for recognition. For the first time the colony voted under the universal adult suffrage and the PPP predictably won all eight seats in the sugar belt. With Jagan as leader and Forbes Burnham as chairman, the PPP assumed office on May 30, 1953. In July, Ashton Chase, the recently appointed Minister of Labour, wrote to the SPA requesting it to reconsider its attitude towards the GIWU. He informed the SPA further that the PPP intended to draft legislation which would enable workers to elect a union of their choice.

Receiving no satisfactory reply, the PPP was instrumental in the GIWU calling a general strike on the sugar estates on August 31. Ostensibly, the reasons were over rates of wages and improvement in conditions of employment, but really the aim was to win recognition for the GIWU. The strike lasted for 25 days and towards the end, the majority of unions in the BG Trades Unions Congress joined in sympathy.

Ever since the PPP came to power, the SPA had made some concessions. It withdrew the trespass notices against those who became Ministers. This had prevented them soliciting votes on the estates during the election campaign. During the sugar strike, the SPA at one stage proposed recognizing both the GIWU and the MPCA, provided they worked together towards ultimate amalgamation. It later agreed to recognize the GIWU for field labourers and the MPCA for factory workers. But the GIWU, confident of Government support, wanted to eliminate the MPCA altogether. It rejected the offer, seeking unconditional representation of all field and factory workers previously enjoyed by the MPCA. The SPA countered with a proposal that included the acceptance and execution by the GIWU of all collective agreements made with the MPCA. After scrutinizing these agreements, the GIWU rejected them and sought the right to negotiate fresh agreements with the SPA. At this stage, negotiations reached a stalemate.

Out of this dispute came the Labour Relations Bill. It was the Government's undertaking to proceed immediately with such a Bill that made the unions call off the strike. The Bill was introduced in the House of Assembly and read for the first time on September 29. Ashton Chase summarised the important provisions of the Bill. The

Bill

> *provided for compulsory recognition of trade unions based on a*
> *sliding scale according to whether the union was seeking*
> *recognition in a field in which there was no other trade union, or*
> *whether there was an existing trade union. The preference of the*
> *workers was to be ascertained through the medium of a secret*
> *ballot. But unions were free to secure recognition other than*
> *through the machinery of the Bill.*
>
> *The penalty for refusal by an employer to recognize a Trade*
> *Union that had obtained a certificate of recognition from the*
> *Commissioner of Labour was $500. There was a further penalty*
> *of $100 in respect of each day the employer was in default.*
> *Employers were also to be subject to a penalty for victimizing*
> *workers. Eviction notices, trespass notices and unreasonable*
> *transfers (e.g. in the case of the Transport Workers) came within*
> *this clause. The Courts were given authority under the Bill to*
> *order an employer to pay compensation to any worker who*
> *suffered dismissal, demotion or an unreasonable transfer (in the*
> *form of victimization).*

The GIWU and the TUC favoured the Bill but as expected, the
MPCA and the SPA opposed it. Nevertheless, on October 8, the Bill
was passed in the House of Assembly. On the following day, the
Guyana Constitution was suspended and the British troops arrived to
instal an interim government lasting three years. Another attempt by
the GIWU for recognition had been thwarted.

The MPCA gained impetus from the suspension of the Constitution. American influence in the trade union movement had been
increasing in the Caribbean since the early 1950s. Ever since its
withdrawal from the TUC in 1952, the MPCA had become affiliated
to the American-directed and controlled Inter-American Regional
Organization of Workers (ORIT). Later that year ORIT opened an
office in Georgetown and provided the MPCA with financial aid and
elaborate propaganda equipment. Following the suspension of the
Constitution, the MPCA met with some other unions and disbanded
the TUC. They formed a new organization which became affiliated to
the International Confederation of Trade Unions. They excluded any
union which was affiliated to the rival World Federation of Trade
Unions or the Caribbean Congress of Labour. This new TUC with
MPCA as its principal architect kept the GIWU out.

The MPCA was further strengthened when the nationalist movement split in 1956. Dr Lachmansingh, the most important leader of GIWU, joined the Burnham faction of the PPP. Thereafter the GIWU became discredited and its membership dwindled. In 1957, a rival union, the British Guiana Sugar Workers' Union was formed, but lasted for only a short while. It suffered from poor leadership and in July 1959 its registration was cancelled.

1961 – 1978

The PPP easily won the first elections after the suspension of the Constitution and as its term, 1957-61, drew to an end, it reopened the question of legitimate trade union representation in the sugar industry. In February 1961, it hinted at the need for legislation to guarantee workers the right to select their own unions. In May and July, the PPP sent to Georgetown batches of retrenched and other workers to picket the MPCA offices over various issues.

The PPP again won the next elections and set about immediately and vigorously to challenge the supremacy of the MPCA on the sugar estates. In September 1961, the month following the electoral victory, the Guyana Sugar Workers' Union was formed. It was renamed the Guyana Agricultural Workers' Union (GAWU) the following year and was led by a prominent PPP activist Harry Lall.

In 1963, the PPP set about again to end the jurisdictional dispute in the sugar industry. It drafted another Labour Relations Bill. This new Bill included all the features of the 1953 one but differed significantly in one area. The Minister of Labour, instead of the Commissioner of Labour, basically now had the powers to settle inter-union disputes by elections. Efforts to make the Bill law failed and left behind an 80-day general strike, burning, looting, loss of life, and racial animosity. The Bill was presented to the House of Assembly and after the first reading, the Minister of Labour held discussions with the TUC and the Employers' Associations. Consequent upon these discussions, certain amendments were made to the Bill. The government then proceeded to expedite the passing of the Bill and rejected the attempts to stall its progress. First it rejected a TUC request to postpone the second reading of the Bill so as to give it more time to consult its affiliates. Secondly, it turned down a suggestion to refer the Bill to a Select Committee of the House of Assembly. The amended Bill was passed in the House of Assembly on the 22nd of April 1963. On that very day the TUC called a general strike claiming that it objected to the wide powers that the Bill gave to the Minister of Labour. The ensuing strike lasted 80 days, and bequeathed bitter racial strife. It ended after Robert Willis of the British TUC effected a settlement. One important term for normalization was that the 1963 Labour Relations Bill would not be reintroduced in its original or in the amended form in which it was passed in the Legislative Assembly.

Upon the failure of the 1963 Labour Relations Bill, the GAWU made another attempt in February 1964 to win recognition. This time it called a general strike in the sugar industry. Serious obstacles blocked all attempts at conciliation. The MPCA refused to meet with the GAWU. It further resisted all efforts to have impartial bodies examine its books in order to establish the extent of its membership in the sugar industry. The SPA argued that it was satisfied that the MPCA had majority membership but would meet with the MPCA and the GAWU providing that they also agreed to meet. The GAWU, on the other hand, agreed to meet unconditionally. The strike ended in July 1964, without formal recognition of the GAWU.

The sequel to the 1964 sugar strike was a dramatic political change. A new electoral system, proportional representation, was introduced to replace the old one that had given the PPP power. Elections were held in December 1964 and the opposition parties, the People's National Congress and the United Force, coalesced to form the new government. For the first time there was no PPP government. Events subsequently showed that the sugar workers had lost a sympathetic friend.

Between 1964 and 1968, the sugar industry was plagued with a number of strikes as GAWU sought better living and working conditions for the workers. In an effort to arrest the situation, the government appointed Justice Cummings to investigate the grievances affecting the workers. His report was, however, rejected. In 1968, a Commission headed by Justice Guya Persaud was appointed to examine the economics of the sugar industry and make recommendations. His report, which was accepted, recommended the discarding of the one-for-all bonus scheme and its replacement with the profit sharing scheme for the workers. Under this formula, the companies received 50% of the profit and the workers the remaining 50%. In 1974, the government passed the sugar levy law which siphoned off a substantial portion of the profits leaving little or nothing for the workers. The levy is the highest in the Caribbean yielding $131 million in 1974 and about $250 million in 1975 to the government.

In 1975 GAWU called two strikes over the long term issue of its recognition and the short term one over the sugar export levy. The first strike lasting 7 weeks came during the spring crop and the second one lasting 6 weeks came during the autumn crop. In a memorandum to the Minister of Finance in 1976, GAWU pointed out that the Guyanese sugar worker was the lowest paid in the Caribbean. In spite of the increases awarded by the Crane Tribunal for 1974 and 1975, he received only about half of what his counterpart received in Barbados, Jamaica and Trinidad. For off-season, the Guyanese sugar worker received a sum equivalent to between 2 to 4 days work as compared to Barbados with a 5 day week of guaranteed employment. The strike registered heavy financial losses – G$100 million in foreign exchange and G$50 million in government revenue.

Immediately following the second strike in late 1975, the government suddenly announced that a poll would be held to select the majority union. GAWU easily won the poll and received *de facto* recognition in December 1975. The formal agreement, signed in March 1976, ended almost 30 years of jurisdictional dispute in the sugar industry. In September of that year, GAWU was admitted as an affiliate to the Guyana TUC at their biennial conference.

In May 1976, the government nationalized the sugar complex (sugar estates and business enterprises) and baptized them Guyana Sugar Company (GUYSUCO) and Guyana Stores, respectively. Little, however, changed in the corporate structure of the sugar estate in spite of the claims that they were now 'owned and operated by the people of Guyana.' The expatriate staff retained their post and maintained the old work relationship.

The sugar levy remained a thorn in the side of the sugar workers and in August 1977, it occasioned a sugar strike lasting 135 days. Soon after GAWU became a member of the TUC in September 1976, it put forward a resolution calling for the scrapping of the levy. This was later amended to 'adjusting the levy to enable workers to get their profit share on the pre-levy basis.' The resolution bore no fruit and in March 1977, the union threatened strike action but reneged so as to hold discussions with the industry and the government through the TUC. These discussions stalemated. In May 1977, the Prime Minister accused the sugar workers of wanting all the sugar profits and spoke of need for a new profit sharing formula. GAWU, on the other hand, continued pursuing the issue through the TUC, but these proved fruitless. On 24th August, it called a general strike over the question of profit sharing for the years 1974-76. On the following day, Parliament passed into law Part 2 of the National Security Act which empowered the Security Forces to institute preventative detention of persons without trial and impose the curfew.

The 1977-78 sugar strike seems to represent the ultimate in racial division in the sugar industry. Towards the end of indenture, and even afterwards, the planters had considered a certain number of Africans on the estates were necessary to prevent the Indians from combining. During the several strikes called by the GIWU and the GAWU, the sugar authorities had gone to the African villages to recruit labourers. In the 1977-78 strike, this kind of recruitment reached new dimensions. The predominantly African composed 'disciplined forces' i.e. the army, the Peoples' Militia, and the National Service provided scab labour in the government's attempt to break the strike. This served further to exacerbate relations between the two groups.

A recent development in the sugar industry has been a reversal of the ethnic composition of the middle management staff. Ever since the end of indenture, Indians had gained mobility into these middle supervisory positions through the acquisition of education and training.

In one estate on the Corentyne, Albion, GAWU points out the position has drastically changed within four years as Table 2 shows.

Table 2
Clerical and Supervisory Staff for Albion Estate

Year	% of Indians	% of Africans
1972	75	25
1974	50	50
1976	40	60

This writer has not been able to verify these figures or establish whether this is a general trend affecting the whole industry. Should there be any truth in these charges, however, the implications for the future are serious. Occupation differentiation based on race in which a minority group of the country possesses most of the supervisory positions over another group that in fact forms the majority both on the estates and in the country cannot contribute in any way to industrial peace.

The lot of the Indians on the estates is little better than what it was during indenture. Because the government provided employment in the sugar industry to the scabs, Indians are only guaranteed 3 days work per week. In the great majority of cases, only task work is given. But so rigid is the standard of work expected that labourers could spend two extra days, without payment, trying to make it acceptable.

NOTES

1. The descendants of Indians are generally called 'East Indians' in Guyana to differentiate them from the indigenous 'Amerindians'. In this paper 'Indians' and 'East Indians' are used synonymously.

2. British Guiana gained independence in June 1966 when the name Guyana was adopted. 'British Guiana', 'Guiana' and 'Guyana' are used synonymously in this paper.

3. Racial categories were removed from the last (1970) census; but considering the population trend of the previous censuses, Indians are easily more than half of the total population.

4. London, Public Record Office, Colonial Office (hereafter cited as C.O.). C.O. 111/233, Light to Gladstone, 1 May 1846.

5. J.E. Jenkins, *The Coolie: His Rights and Wrongs* (London, 1871), p.95.

6. C.O. 384/173, Bruce to Knutsford, no.4. 2 Jan. 1889.

7. J. McNeil and C. Lal, *Report to the Government of India on the Conditions of Indian Immigrants in British Guiana* (Simla, 1915), p.70.

8. Parliamentary Papers (hereafter cited as P.P.) P.P. (1898), L. (C.8657) p.75.

9. *Ibid.,* 98:1949.

10.*Ibid.,* p. 131.

11. *Ibid.,* para. 1954.

12. P.P. (1910) C.D. 5192, p.56.

13. C.O. 114/47, Report of the I.A.G., 1889.

14. C.O. 384/165, Irving to Holland, no. 102, 17 March 1887.

15. Jenkins, p.244.

16. *Ibid*

17. C.O. 114/78, Report of the I.A.G., 1897-8.

18. C.O. 114/492, Hemming to Chamberlain, conf., 6 Jan. 1897, end.

19. *Ibid.*

20. H.V.P. Bronkhurst, *Among the Hindus and Creoles of British Guiana* (London, 1888), p.18.

21. C.O. 384/177, Gormanston to Knutsford, no.68, 14 March 1890, encl.

22. *The Argosy,* 3 August, 1889.

23. C.O. 111/540, Swettenham to Lyttelton, no. 110, April 1904, encl.

24. J. Beaumont, *The New Slavery* (London 1871), p.40.

25. Jenkins, p.365.

26. *The Argosy,* 16 June 1888.

27. C.O. 111/488, Bruce to Chamberlain, no.353, 11 Nov.1896, encl

28. C.O. 111/499, report of the Inspector General of Police, 1900-01.

29. C.O. 111/537, Swettenham to Chamberlain, no.190, 20 May 1903.

30. P.P. (1910), Cd.5193, p.360.

31. Major G. St. J. Orde Browne, *Labour Conditions in the West Indies* (Cmd. 6070). 1939, p. 165.

32. Ashton Chase, *A History of Trade Unionism in Guyana, 1900-1961* (Georgetown, New Guyana Co. Ltd., 1964), p. 67.

33. *The Daily Argosy,* 3 July 1923.

34. For further discussion on this strike, see Ann Spackman, 'Official Attitude and Official Violence: The Ruimveldt Massacre, Guyana, 1924', *Social and Economic Studies,* vol.22 no.23 (Sep.1973), 315-334.

35. Hugh Tinker, *Separate and Unequal...*(London, G. Hurst & Co., 1976), p.163.

36. *Report of the Labour Disputes Commission* (Georgetown, 1936), para.9

37. Browne, p. 165.

38. Report on the West Indian Royal Commission (1945), Cmd. 6607, p.192-3.

39. Leo A. Despres, *Cultural Pluralism and Nationalist Politics in British Guiana* (Chicago, Rand McNally & Co. 1967), p.153.

40. Chase, p.140-1.

41. Cheddi Jagan, *The West on Trial...* (London, Michael Joseph, 1966), p.88.

42. *Ibid.*

43. Chase, p.141.

44. Jagan, p.109.

7 up and rum – the advertising draws attention to two of the Caribbean's enduring products based on sugar-cane

Typical canoes on the Berbice River: one has a thatched awning as protection from the sun

Participation of East Indians in the Transformation of Guyanese Society 1966 – 1979[1]

Sahadeo Debiprashad and
Dowlat Ram Budhram

*"When I described 1971 as the year of national unity...I meant
the active involvement of the overwhelming number of Guyanese
in our national goals and aims."*
Forbes Burnham[2]

Introduction

Since achieving political independence in 1966, the Government of
Guyana has embarked on a revolutionary programme to restructure
this once colonial and dependent society. Political independence
represented the basic but most important step in the drive towards
economic and social transformation of Guyanese society. The
ideological and philosophical base for this transformation is socialism
and the government has introduced and implemented some fundamental changes in its 'socialist revolution' towards the transformation.

The changes became more intense since the beginning of the 1970s.
In 1970, when the country was declared a Co-operative Republic, a
number of measures were adopted to change the existing economic
features and to accelerate economic development. The government
encouraged the development and promotion of co-operatives mainly
in the primary sector, for diversification and wider exploitation of the
country's natural resources. The co-operative was also to be the
principal mechanism through which the objectives of self-reliance
were to be realised – to achieve self-sufficiency in food supplies,
clothing and housing the nation.

With respect to the primary sector, agriculture was to be the main
source for generating wealth and economic development. A compli-
mentary policy for greater self-sufficiency in food supplies and

diversification in agriculture was implemented in 1972, when the government decided to ban several imported food commodities. State farms were established in the interior areas, investments were made in agricultural infrastructures and for the first time, agricultural science became part of the school curriculum.

As part of its overall programme towards owning and controlling the country's natural resources, the Guyana Government in 1971 nationalised the bauxite sector, one of the three important economic bases of the country. The years following witnessed a series of 'take overs' and nationalisations, culminating with the nationalisation of the giant sugar cum commercial enterprise, Bookers McConnell Ltd. Within a period of five years, the share of the state or public sector expanded from a mere 20% to almost 80% in the economy. State acquisition of many important holdings and entry into 'new' areas of economic activities has resulted in an increase from 8 corporations in 1970 to more than 30 public enterprises in 1977. In this expansion, the state has entered into almost every area of economic activity – state trading, airways, roads and transportation, telecommunications, electricity, fishing, forestry and agriculture, manufacturing and processing, insurance, banking and shipbuilding. The state thus increased its employment of people from 21.4% of the labour force in 1970 to more than 50% in 1978.[3]

The Co-operative Republic, as part of the transition to socialism, nationalised the country's school system and introduced, since 1976, 'free' education from nursery to university level. New content has been given to primary and secondary education by establishing new institutions such as the Multilateral Schools, Community High Schools and an expansion of the University of Guyana.

In the military sector, Guyana has expanded its army, the Guyana Defence Force and the Police Force. New para-military institutions such as the Guyana National Service and the Guyana Peoples Milita have been introduced as part of its socialist programme for greater mobilisation and participation of young people in national reconstruction.

The country has achieved some degree of distinction on the international arena. In the Caribbean, the country has pioneered the production of the region's cultural extravaganza, the Caribbean Festival of Creative Arts (CARIFESTA). Also, as part of its socialist philosophy, there has been an increase in trade and diplomatic relations with notable socialist countries. Within the Third World, Guyana has been playing an important role in the Non-Aligned

Movement and has supported 'the peoples of other countries in their just struggles against imperialism and colonialism...'[4]

In this process of the transformation of Guyanese society, the main declared objective of the government's socialist philosophy is to create an egalitarian society in terms of equality of opportunity irrespective of race, sex, colour or creed. 'Our aim is an egalitarian society in economic terms now that we have achieved political equality for all Guyanese', remarked the Guyanese Prime Minister.[5] Fundamentally, the socialist programme aims at making 'the small man a real man' in the society. Towards the achievement of these objectives, a Constituent Assembly has been nominated for rewriting Guyana's 'outdated' constitution to reflect these socialist aspirations.

Given this general background, we are attempting in this paper to examine the participation of East Indians at various levels in the transformation of Guyanese society. The important issues which this paper will examine are:-

(1)   East Indians in the population.

(2)   Participation in Agriculture.

(3)   Participation in the Management and Decision-Making Process in the public sector, namely
   (a)   Ministries
   (b)   Educational Institutions
   (c)   Public Corporations and Companies
   (d)   Financial Institutions
   (e)   Boards/Committees/Commissions
   (f)   Distribution of National Awards.

1.   East Indians in the Population

Previous to 1917 when East Indian immigration ended, migration was the principal factor influencing population growth in Guyana. With the introduction of East Indians (sometimes referred to as Indians) into the population of Guyana through indentureship, the country for the first time experienced natural increases in its population growth. At the 1921 census, the population of Guyana was 297,691 persons of which the East Indian population was 124,938 or 42% of the total population.

From 1921, the rate of increase of East Indians was greater than the other races in the country. Between 1921 and 1940, the death rate among East Indians declined from 31.7 to 23 per thousand mainly because of a decline in the infant mortality rate. In the same period, the East Indian birth rate increased from 27.1 to 38.0 per thousand. This rate of natural increase in the population also pushed up the rate of increase of the total population.[6] Between 1936 and 1940, the average crude rate of natural increase of East Indians was 3% per annum, and for the next five years, it had increased on the average of 1.7% per annum. The increase pushed up the natural increase of the total population by 0.8% per annum in this period.

A significant factor in the East Indian population growth has been the birth rate. Of the total births registered between 1936 and 1940, 79% of these were East Indians. In the next five-year period to 1945, the total registered births increased by 6,000 or by 148%, and East Indians accounted for 80% of this amount. In 1911, the East Indian proportion of total births had been 37.3 per thousand and by 1946 after some 40 years, this was increased to 51.3 per thousand.

Between the two main ethnic groups, East Indians and Africans, differential fertility and early marriage by East Indian women are the main factors accounting for their rate of population increase. In 1900, Afro-Guyanese were 41.8% and Indo-Guyanese 30.7% of the population; in 1960, Afro-Guyanese were only 32.8% while Indo-Guyanese were 47.8% of the total population. In 1942 when the country's birth rate was 38.2 per thousand, Afro-Guyanese were 29.8, Portuguese 22.4, and Indo-Guyanese 47.2 per thousand. At the end of 1946, there were 4.4% more Afro-Guyanese women in the child-bearing age, yet Indo-Guyanese women gave birth to 30,429 children more than Afro-Guyanese women.

Table 1 shows the population of Guyana and the percentage of East Indians in the total population. It was from the 1940s that the East Indian population started to grow at a fast rate. From 44% of the population in 1946, East Indians were 47.7% in 1960 and an estimated 51% in 1970.

TABLE 1
Population of Guyana[9]

Years	Total	East Indians	% of East Indians
1946	369,678	163,434	44.21
1960	560,330	267,797	47.79
1970	714,000	369,635	51.00
1977	812,000	406,000	50.00

Between the two census years 1946 and 1960, while the total population increased by 190,652 persons or by 51.5%, the East Indian population increased by 104,363 persons or by 63.8%. This increase in the East Indian population alone accounted for 54.7% of the total population increase. Also, we see that the average rate of increase in the East Indian population (4.6%) is greater than the rate of increase of the total population (3.7%). This pattern of differential increase was maintained in the next ten-year period 1960-70. However, by 1970, given a rate of natural increase of 3.8% per annum, East Indians were more than half of the total population. Thus in 24 years, (1946-70), while the total population increased by 93.1%, the East Indian population increased by 126.2%.

The causes of the increase in the East Indian population remain basically the same. The average age of motherhood remains about 20 years while the fertility rate is about 3.8% compared to 2.7% for Guyanese. However, other factors within the present decade have signicantly affected the pattern of increase, which is reflected in the approximate figure for 1977. There has been an outflow of many East Indians mainly to North America and neighbouring Surinam. Since 1970, large numbers of young East Indian boys and girls have been going to North America to 'try their luck.' The numbers have increased within recent times and families are now migrating, while the new trend is for many eligible Indo-Guyanese to return home for marriage so as to give their fellow East Indians a chance to migrate.

The main factor influencing this outflow of East Indians as alleged by many of those migrating is discrimination (both racial and political) in employment opportunities. Many have been 'pressured' to leave their jobs and others who are unable to obtain employment try to seek their fortunes abroad.

Finally, for the first time, the ethnic composition of the country's population was not recorded in the census of 1970. Probably the main reason for this is related to the General Election of 1968 and its implications on the pattern of voting in 1973. It is a fact that voting for political parties in the previous general elections of 1964 and 1968 was based mainly on race, and the fact that East Indians comprised nearly half the total population is perhaps not consistent with the results of those general elections.

2. Agriculture

Historically, the development and expansion of the agricultural sector has always been associated with East Indians in Guyana. The East Indian way of life has to date been predominantly rural and agricultural. Prior to East Indian indentureship, the development of plantation agriculture was based upon slavery; after its abolition and the unsuccessful attempts to employ other immigrants and labour on the sugar plantation, it was left to East Indian immigrants to fill the vacuum of labour shortage and avoid collapse of the sugar industry. As Bronkhurst noted, 'Indian immigration was looked upon as the salvation of sugar-growing British Guiana.'[10] This represented a significant and important primary role of the Indians in the early development of the agricultural sector.

A second important area of participation by East Indians in agriculture is related to the development of land settlement schemes and the rice industry. The development of land settlement schemes marked an important thrust towards diversification and expansion of a sugar-dominated agricultural sector, and it was East Indians who were mainly responsible for this. Ever since their early settlement on sugar estates, East Indians had time and again attempted to settle and cultivate lands independently of the sugar estates. Many abandoned estates and other lands were purchased (with some help from the government); this represented the early attempts by East Indians to establish and expand farming communities.

In the later period, especially during the two decades of the 1950s and 60s, when the country was governed by the PPP, East Indian participation in the agricultural sector became firmly established. The rice industry in particular was developed and was to become the third leading sector after sugar and bauxite. Dwarka Nath noted that East Indians 'not only saved the sugar estates from extinction but also established the rice industry, making it the most important industry in the colony.'[11]

With respect to land settlement schemes, it was argued that it was mainly East Indians who were given lands when the schemes were established. In fact, the entire agricultural programme of the PPP was said to be partisan and discriminated against Afro-Guyanese in particular. Indeed, when the land settlement schemes were established after 1955, the statistics reveal that the racial composition of the settlers showed 3,864 Indo-Guyanese as against 550 Afro-Guyanese.[12] However, as the ICJ Report showed, closer inspection of the methods of selection of applicants for lands in these schemes did not in any way give preference to East Indians.

> *...Land Settlement Schemes are made for the purpose of making land available to persons prepared to cultivate them, mainly for growing rice or sugar. The Indians usually happened to be the*

only persons with the necessary experience in such cultivation,
and consequently the land passed almost exclusively to them. For
this reason, there is no cause to recommend any change in the
procedures for selection of settlers. These procedures do not
appear to lead to or encourage racial discrimination.[13]

As we said above, during the PPP's term of office, the rice industry in
particular made remarkable advances. The industry in this develop-
mental stage experienced both an increase in the acreage cultivated
and productivity per acre. The main reason for the achievements of
the industry is probably related to government's agricultural policy at
the time. The hands of the government were virtually tied with
respect to the implementation of positive policies in the two foreign-
owned large sectors, bauxite and sugar. And since agriculture was to
be the base for the country's future development, the government's
alternative was to direct attention towards the domestic agricultural
sector.

The institutional framework for the agricultural sector became
enlarged to facilitate efficient functioning of the sector. Government
implemented an increase in the guaranteed price for both paddy and
rice along with increases in the prices of other agricultural commodities. Secondly, the Rice Marketing Board enlarged its physical
facilities for storage of rice. Thirdly, the Rice Producers Association,
a producers' organisation, was represented on the Board. Fourthly,
along with the increased prices for rice and paddy given, other
important incentives such as duty free gasoline, or free and subsidised
insecticides were given to farmers. Fifthly, two large and important
drainage and irrigation schemes were established and expanded at
Black Bush Polder and Tapacuma. At the same time, the Guyana
Marketing Corporation was established and offered guaranteed
prices and marketing facilities for a number of agricultural products.
Since East Indians tended to predominate in the agricultural sector,
these were the important factors which contributed to their prosperity, and to advances made by the sector.

With the change of government in 1964, there is the general feeling
that the previous agricultural programme (of the PPP) was abandoned, and that this stagnated and in some instances retarded
agricultural and economic prosperity. It is argued that the agricultural programme from 1964 discriminated against East Indians in
particular and is mainly responsible for low rate of development in
the agricultural sector.

One of the main setbacks for East Indians after 1964 was the reduction of guaranteed prices for rice bought by the Rice Marketing Board. The Board reduced the price of rice in 1966 from $24.00 per bag for super brand rice to $20.00; from $21.00 to $17.00 for first quality rice and from $18.75 to $13.80 for second quality rice. The Rice Producers' Association which happened to be a pro-PPP organisation was no longer recognised as a producers' organisation; their representatives on the Board were reduced from 11 to 3 members and were later all removed. All the incentives given (easy credit, subsidised inputs, etc.) were removed.

This 'new' programme dealt a tragic blow to the rice industry. Incidentally, it was during this same period that the Board experienced heavy financial losses. In 1964-65, the Board suffered a loss of $4.3 million and a loss of $2.8 million in 1965-66. Formerly, the Board had made such profits as $839,734 in 1961-62, $613,055 in 1962--63 and $98,906 in 1963-64. Profits were made as from 1966 only when a reduction was made in the guaranteed prices to the farmers, and it was only in 1972 that the price had increased to $22.00 after costs of production had increased considerably. In addition, the acreage cultivated was also adversely affected. Rice acreage had increased from 136,990 acres in 1957 to 316,000 in 1964 producing 163,927 tons of rice, while in 1970, 242,277 acres were under rice, producing 115,000 tons of rice.

The establishment of the two large rice development schemes at Black Bush and Tapacuma along with other schemes has always been looked upon as devices to increase the prosperity of East Indians. However rice production suffered in these areas, due not only to those factors outlined above, but also to neglect in serving the drainage and irrigation systems which are extremely vital for production. At the moment, huge sums are being spent to rehabilitate and expand the larger schemes, but many farmers have opined that it would have been less costly had these areas been serviced over the years.

Many other agricultural producing areas have been suffering the same fate and the victims are mainly East Indians. There are poor drainage, irrigation and transportation facilities for farmers' produce. Farmers claim that there is discrimination in the granting of loans and credit facilities. There are cases where machinery used for rice cultivation and harvesting are only loaned to those farmers considered to be 'sympathisers' of the ruling party. Farmers feel that low production in agriculture is mainly due to neglect. Whenever there is heavy rainfall, farmers' produce are at the mercy of floods. East Indians feel that deliberate policies are implemented to discriminate against them and that though they are the ones producing, they are the ones perishing in this transformation process to feed the nation.

There are other important instances of discrimination against East Indians. At the moment there is a differential retail price for livestock feed for poultry and pigs. Production costs for the two feeds are also different, the cost for pig-feed being lower than that of poultry. However, at the retail level, the price of pig-feed is subsidised by the revenue from poultry feed. This results in the cost of producing pork being cheaper; and since most Afro-Guyanese consume pork and Indo-Guyanese tend to consume chicken, this policy tends to discriminate against East Indians. In addition, pig farmers who are predominantly Afro-Guyanese are financed by the Agricultural Bank and the Guyana Marketing Corporation. A similar policy is implemented in the distribution of fish, except that here there is direct discrimination in the sale of fish to vendors and consumers. Lands that were once being farmed by East Indians at Ruby Backdam on the East Bank of Essequibo, were 'taken away' and given to Afro-Guyanese who formed the Rosanants Cane Farming Co-operative. Similarly at Non-Pareil, rice lands were taken away and given to Afro-Guyanese under armed protection.

Sugar Industry

One of the more important and familiar areas for racial and political discrimination is the sugar industry. Since the inception of East Indian indentureship and to date, East Indians have dominated occupations in the sugar industry. To a large extent, sugar has remained 'king' in this dependent economy and continues to direct and influence the economic life of Guyana. Favourable performances by the industry and world sugar prices are still closely linked with the government's economic programme.

The first area of concern especially to Afro-Guyanese is the 'prosperity' of sugar workers as reflected by the housing schemes established in the extra-nuclear housing areas. It is claimed that the savings of the industry are used only for financing rural facilities for sugar workers. Since the industry has now been nationalised, it is argued that the industry's savings should be used for the benefit of the entire nation rather than one sector. As such, when the sugar levy was implemented a few years ago, due to soaring world sugar prices, this reduced sugar workers' share in the industry's profits, and the argument used was that the levy must benefit the entire nation rather than sugar workers alone. Sugar workers on the other hand, looked upon this as an indirect device to reduce the size of their entitlements in the industry's profits.

Industrial relations in the sugar belt provide the more usual area of both political and racial discrimination. Historically, one would have expected that the sugar sector would have given birth to the first organised trade union activities. The first trade union, the Guyana Labour Union which organised mainly dock workers (who were predominantly Afro-Guyanese) made no attempts to organise sugar workers. The British Guiana Workers League which went into the sugar belt only attempted to organise the factory workers who were mainly Afro-Guyanese.

In the contemporary period, the industry has been the primary battleground for industrial conflicts between the government and GAWU, another pro-PPP organisation. It took almost 26 years to recognise this union which has now become the most militant one in the country. In its conflicts with the government, many of these appear on the surface to be racial rather than political as far as the government has been able to resolve them.

One instance of this was seen in the 1977 sugar strike which lasted for 135 days. During this strike, scabs were employed in the industry, members of the union were harassed and sometimes detained, the homes of many sugar workers were searched and foodstuffs were sometimes taken away under the pretext of hoarding. It was the government's claim that this strike had cost the economy almost $1 million per day and was mainly responsible for the poor performance of the industry and national economy.[14] Despite this heavy financial loss to the economy and recommendations made by the Trades Union Council to end the strike, no effort was made by the government to compromise in this matter. At the same time, the TUC (which had supported the PNC party at previous general elections) was not prepared to back implementation of a resolution at its Annual Delegates Congress in 1977, by calling a one-day token strike because of scabbing in the sugar strike.

When this strike is compared with the bauxite strike in 1979, many sugar workers feel that race is the primary factor rather than politics in resolving industrial disputes in these two sectors. Just after this strike had started, the two dismissed employees concerned were re-employed, a commission of inquiry was immediately set up and within three weeks the issues were resolved and the strike ended. Sugar workers have asked why this same 'treatment' was not meted out to them? They argue that scabs could not have been employed during the bauxite strike. A revealing instance of this occurred when a demonstration took place during the bauxite strike in Georgetown. One worker remarked: 'We nah sugar worker. Either we live or the scabs live.'

There are two other important instances worth mentioning of differential treatment to bauxite and sugar workers. Firstly, sugar workers can only obtain an interest-free loan of $3,000 for housing construction from the SILWF, a fund to which they contribute. In 1977, the Guyana Bauxite Company implemented a 'Home Improvement Scheme' for its workers, whereby workers obtain $18,000 – the first $6,000 is given as a grant; the second $6,000 is interest-free while the third $6,000 carries an interest of 3% per annum. Sugar estate 'squatting' communities which were created from the racial conflicts of the 1960s have yet to be approved by the relevant authorities for reconstruction of houses after some 15 years. In some instances, such as Bath and Meter-meer-Zorg, 'squatting' houses put up by sugar workers on vacant state lands have been demolished and workers threatened.

Secondly, while both sectors have been recognised for their important economic roles in the nation, there is some discrimination in the food distribution to the respective communities. Indians in the rural areas especially are bearing the brunt of the present food crisis. In the Linden community, there are 11 food distribution outlets that have developed over the past few years. In the sugar belt, there are only 5 such outlets for sugar estate communities that virtually stretch along 50% of the country's coastal belt. Some East Indian traders go to Linden to purchase scarce food items to resell in their own communities. There are other instances where East Indian consumers are forced to go to Afro-Guyanese villages to purchase such items; some of these are often faced with open discrimination when purchasing food.

Certain sugar estate communities which have actively participated in the demonstrations and racial conflicts of the 1960s, have now been 'cornered' and subdued by the presence of the Afro-dominated military. Strategic lands near these communities have been awarded to the military for construction of housing units and these act as buffer zones to East Indian activities. For example, there is Melanie Damishana for Enterprise, Clonbrook Front for Clonbrook Back, Vryheids Lust for Success/Better Hope and DeKendren for Meter-Meer-Zorg/Zeelugt.

A market scene in present day Guyana

The labour of fieldwork eased by mechanization

A contemporary line drawing of an old indentured East Indian Labourer from an historical photograph, Guyana, c 1889

Outside of the sugar sector, the rural people have to rely heavily on the central and local governments for providing rural facilities. The financial constraints of the central government and the ruling party's dominated district councils have not been able to provide substantial facilities to rural villages. In those cases where facilities have been provided, they were long overdue. As far as housing is concerned, some financial assistance can be obtained from the Mortgage Finance Bank. In 1977, a number of housing schemes with government's assistance were established. Of a total of 873 housing units constructed, only 31 or 6% of them were obtained by East Indians. In addition, time off from work has been given to the owners and government has in some cases provided physical facilities for the owners to construct their houses. The roads of many Indo-Guyanese villages are impassable, yet Afro-Guyanese villages such as Uitvlugt and Den Amstel have been able to obtain all-weather roads.

Despite the many pressures on East Indians in the agricultural sector, they continue to dominate and play the most positive role in the agricultural transformation of the economy. Table 2 shows the operation of Land Holdings by East Indians for six crops in a number of regions and sub-regions in Guyana. While the total acreage cultivated by East Indians is not shown here, the table gives a clear indication of East Indian domination in agriculture and their rigorous pursuit of the goal of feeding the Guyanese nation. In all the areas shown in the table, more than 70% of the operators are East Indians. East Indians have remained not only in the traditional area of rice cultivation, but they have also entered in the production of important food crops such as green vegetables and coconuts.

The active involvement of East Indians in increasing good production is reflected in the transformation of vacant land space in the rural villages into productive kitchen gardens. The rural markets of Guyana are dominated by East Indian food-crop vendors and traders. This situation also exists within the towns. It is a well known fact that the city of Georgetown and its immediate environs are heavily serviced by the vegetable farmers of Black Bush Polder and West Demerara. Black Bush Polder is the most important region for vegetable production in Guyana and it has replaced such areas as the Essequibo Islands. It also remains the leading area in the production of rice, and it is for these reasons that Black Bush Polder is referred to as the 'food basket of Guyana.'

TABLE 2
Operation of Land Holdings by East Indians, 1978[15]

04/01/01 – Upper Corentyne

Crop	Nos of Farms	Acreage	Nos of Farms operated by East Indians	Percent
TOTAL	3,803	24,042.5	–	–
Rice	3,357	21,280.3	2,985	88.9
Coconuts	1,227	2,705.0	1,189	96.9
Sugar Cane	1	51.0	1	100.0

04/01/02 – Black Bush Polder

Crop	Nos of Farms	Acreage	Nos of Farms operated by East Indians	Percent
TOTAL	2,792	20,598.2	–	–
Rice	1,298	18,896.6	1,089	83.8
Coconuts	1,213	836.3	1,058	87.2
Green Vegetables	752	509.2	673	89.4
Citrus	322	13.1	213	66.1

04/02/01 – Lower Corentyne

Crop	Nos of Farms	Acreage	Nos of Farms operated by East Indians	Percent
TOTAL	5,065	36,944.9	–	–
Rice	4,234	31,633.1	2,762	65.2
Coconuts	1,447	3,871.2	1,221	83.3
Green Vegetables	48	186.2	27	56.2
Sugar Cane	3	427.2	2	66.6
Citrus	6	29.3	4	66.6

03/02 – Mahaica-Mahaicony-Abary

Crop	Nos of Farms	Acreage	Nos of Farms operated by East Indians	Percent
TOTAL	4,461	86,405.1	–	–
Rice	3,286	75,369.5	2,731	83.5
Coconuts	605	9,060.9	447	73.8
Green Vegetables	102	183.3	73	71.5
Citrus	4	2.5	1	25.0
Pineapples	45	46.6	29	64.4

03/03/01 – East Coast

Crop	Nos of Farms	Acreage	Nos of Farms operated by East Indians	Percent
TOTAL	5,208	11,617.0	–	–
Rice	297	2,788.5	183	61.6
Coconuts	2,334	5,629.9	873	80.2
Green Vegetables	407	362.8	315	77.3
Citrus	12	10.5	7	58.3
Pineapples	1	.2	1	100.0

02/01 – West Demerara

Crop	Nos of Farms	Acreage	Nos of Farms operated by East Indians	Percent
TOTAL	3,516	23,607.6	–	–
Rice	1,477	9,030.6	1,389	94.0
Coconuts	7	11.5	5	71.4
Green Vegetables	32	99.0	28	87.5
Sugar Cane	821	8,386.3	801	97.5
Citrus	237	460.0	168	70.8
Pineapples	192	511.6	132	68.75

3.   Participation in the Public Sector [16]

In this section, we will attempt to look at participation of East Indians
in the administrative/decision making process at a number of levels.
We feel that with the thrust towards socialism, various groups of
people whether they are ethnic, political or religious groups etc.,
should at all levels actively participate in the decision-making process
and management of the nation state. At the same time, the groups
should represent the broad ideals of the masses and the programmes
should transcend the barriers of race, creed or sex. After all, the
socialist philosophy is very consistent with the principle of mass
participation.

(a)   Public Service – Ministries

Table 3 shows the senior management and administrative structure of
all ministries and other departments of the public service.

TABLE 3
Public Service – Senior Administrative and Executive Ranks, 1979

	Total Nos	I	A	0	Percentage		
					I	A	O
Ministers[17]	29	7	20	2	24	69	7
Other Senior Positions	66	31	25	10	47	38	15
Permanent Secretaries[18]	29	2	25	2	7	86	7
Principal Assistant Secretaries[19]	38	14	21	3	37	55	8
Personnel[20]	22	5	17	–	23	77	–
Accounts[21]	19	9	8	2	47	42	11
Other Departmental Heads[22]	139	19	102	18	14	73	13

Of the seven East Indian ministers three are regional ministers and
one of them a Minister of State. The second category of 'Other
Senior Positions' shows a larger number of East Indians. Over the
years, East Indians have climbed slowly out of their rural isolation to
participate actively in the professions. The positions of this category
are mainly important professions within the public service. In the

magistracy, 10 out of 19 magistrates are East Indians; of the 8 principal Auditors and 8 Assistant Auditor-Generals, only 2 of the latter are Afro-Guyanese.

The other categories of the table show that few East Indians can be found in the administrative positions of the Public Service, except the heads of the Accounts divisions. Most of the positions are occupied by Afro-Guyanese. In 1973, there was only 1 Indian Permanent Secretary as against 2 in 1979. Thirty-seven per cent of Principal Assistant Secretaries and only 23% of the heads of the Personnel Divisions are East Indians. In the Accounts Divisions, 47% of heads are East Indians. This position and, in general, the accounting profession tends to be dominated by East Indians. In the Ministry of Finance and Auditor General's Department, more than 60% of all the senior positions are occupied by East Indians.

(b) Educational Institutions

Table 4 shows the ethnic composition of the heads of the main educational institutions including education officers. None of the higher institutions of learning is headed by an East Indian. In the recent additions of multi-lateral schools and Community High Schools as part of a revolutionised education system, none of the heads of the former and only 20% of the latter are East Indians. Only in the secondary schools do we find a high percentage of East Indian headmasters.

TABLE 4
Ethnic Composition of Heads of Main Educational Institutions, 1979

	Total Nos	I	A	O	Percentage I	A	O
1. Higher Institutions of Learning	9	–	9		–	–	100
2. Multilateral Schools	5	–	4	1	–	80	20
3. Community High Schools	25	5	19	1	20	76	4
4. Other Secondary Schools	40	23	15	2	57.5	37.5	5
5. Education Officers[23]	20	6	14	–	30	70	–

Of more importance however is the racial imbalance of education officers in the country. This is an important administrative position in the education system since education officers have much influence on the appointment and promotion of staff. Theoretically, all appointments should be made by the Teachers Service Commission. Even when this is so, there is racial imbalance in the composition of the Commission. Of a total of 10 members, only 2 of them are East Indians. We can therefore conclude that while a number of institutions might be headed by Indo-Guyanese, direct supervision and overall control are done by predominantly Afro-Guyanese.

TABLE 5
Corporations – Senior Administrative and Management Ranks, 1979

	Total Nos	I	A	O	Percentage		
					I	A	O
Boards of Directors[24]	270	53	170	47	20	63	17
General Managers	37	7	24	6	19	65	16
Deputy General Managers[25]	27	3	18	6	11	67	22
Personnel	36	7	25	4	19.4	69.4	11.2
Accounts	36	17	18	1	47	50	3
Other Divisional/Dept Heads	277	71	153	53	26	55	19
Branch Managers[26]	70	15	47	8	21	67	12

(c)   Corporations/Companies

The establishment of a large number of corporations and companies by the state is seen as a positive step towards state control of the economic activities of the nation. Prior to the nationalisation of Demba in 1971, there were only 8 corporations in the public sector. Today, there are some 38 corporations and companies (including financial institutions) under the umbrella of the Guyana State Corporation. The list reveals that nearly every economic activity is under some form of direct government control through a corporation/company.

Unlike the public service, the structure of the public corporations are more akin to those of private enterprises. All the corporations are under the control of the Guyana State Corporation which has a number of executive chairmen, each being responsible for a number of corporations. Each corporation is governed by a Board of Directors and the administrative responsibilities and direct supervision being done by a General Manager. Appointment of staff and the salary structure are to a large extent more lucrative than the traditional public service.

Table 5 shows the ethnic composition of the upper management/ administrative structure of all corporations/companies in the public sector. Here again, we see that with the expansion of the public sector, East Indians have not been able to occupy the important management occupations of these enterprises. Out of a total of 8 Executive Chairmen, only 1 is an East Indian. Of the directors on the corporations' boards, only 53 or 20% of all the members are East Indians. Of the enterprises, 4 corporations including the 3 sub-companies of the Guyana Liquor Corporation alone account for 27 board members or 51% of all the East Indian directors. This means that there are only 26 Indian directors on the boards of 29 corporations. There are 8 corporations with no East Indian board members, 17 having 1 member and 4 corporations with 2 members each. At the same time, the 17 corporations have a total of 88 Afro-Guyanese members or 73% of the total board members of those enterprises.

For the position of General Managers, there are only 7 Indo-Guyanese compared to 24 Afro-Guyanese occupying this position. Of this number, 4 of them or 57% of the East Indians are General Mangers of 4 sub-companies of 2 corporations. Of the other categories in the table, the same situation as in the Public Service occurs. East Indians are fairly represented in the accounts positions. In the expansion process of many corporations, there are more Afro-Guyanese branch managers than Indo-Guyanese.

(d)   Financial Institutions

Table 6 shows the racial composition of the management/ administrative structure of the financial institutions in the public sector. There is perhaps greater ethnic imbalance in the financial sector as the table reflects. No East Indian has yet been able to occupy the positions of General Manager or Deputy General Manager since the establishment of any of these financial institutions.

TABLE 6
Ethnic Composition of Management/
Administrative Structure, 1979

	Total Nos	I	A	O	Percentage		
					I	A	O
Board of Directors	40	6	30	4	15	75	10
General Managers[27]	5	–	5	–	–	100	–
Deputy General Managers	4	–	4	–	–	100	–
Personnel	5	–	5	–	–	100	–
Accounts	5	2	2	1	40	40	20
Other Departmental Heads[28]	37	7	23	7	19	62	19

(e)   Boards/Committees/Commissions

TABLE 7
Boards/Committees/Commissions – Ethnic
Composition of Members, 1979

	Total Nos	I	A	O	Percentage		
					I	A	O
Chairmen[29]	44	5	35	4	11	80	9
Members	487	97	365	25	20	75	5

To assist in the day-to-day functioning of the various institutions and agencies in the public sector, a number of committees, commisions etc., have been permanently created to undertake this task. Table 7 shows the racial composition of chairmen and members of 42 such boards, committees and commissions. In both categories of the table, there is an overwhelming majority of Afro-Guyanese membership. On 7 of these bodies, there are no East Indian members while on 14 of them there is 1 East Indian member each. Of more importance however, is that the 5 East Indian chairmen are found on the less important bodies such as the Government Lotteries Control Committee and Visiting Committees of the Prison.

Of the 4 Commissions directly responsible for the appointment and promotion of staff for a large part of the public sector, all the chairmen are Afro-Guyanese; 16 of the other members are Afro-Guyanese compared to 4 Indo-Guyanese out of a total of 25 members. Of the 38 officers appointed in the National registration exercise (which normally compiles the list of voters), only 9 of them are Indo-Guyanese compared to 28 being Afro-Guyanese.

(f)   National Awards

Table 8 shows the racial composition of the recipients of national awards from 1975 to 1979. Of the total number of awards given, only 28% were East Indian recipients compared to 60% being Afro-Guyanese. On a year by year basis, 29% of the recipients were East Indians in 1975, 30% in 1976 and 1977, 24% in 1978 and 26% in 1979. Of those receiving the highest award, the Cacique's Crown, only 2 East Indians out of a total of 15 people in this period have received it so far.

TABLE 8
Recipients of National Awards – Orders of Guyana (1975-79)

	Total Nos	I	A	O^{30}	Percentage		
					I	A	O
Cacique's Crown	15	2	10	3	13	67	20
Golden Arrow of Achievement	42	8	32	2	19	76	5
Medal of Service	95	32	50	13	34	53	14
TOTAL	152	42	92	18	28	60	12

Given the data and the issues discussed so far in this paper, two important areas of participation by East Indians have been identified. These are participation in the agricultural and public sectors. In the agricultural sector, the historical pattern has remained the same. The Indians have demonstrated their superior capabilities as tillers of the soil. They have converted swamps and savannah lands into productive agricultural holdings, and have laid the important base for any agricultural transformation in the economy. However, before concluding, it would be important to address our minds to some important issues with respect to public sector participation by East Indians.

The opposition and other pressure groups in the society have always spoken of racial discrimination being practised by the Burnham-led government and that this accounts for out-migration of many East Indians and non-cooperation by those in the society. Coercion and fear are responsible for those who 'actively' participate. On the other hand, given the low level of participation from our data, can we say that Indians are not perhaps qualified enough to occupy such administrative/management positions? As the ICJ report indicated, is it for historical and social reasons and not because of discrimination against them that fewer East Indian managers are in the public sector?[31] Does the situation still hold that East Indians are more interested in private enterprise than in Government service?

Over the past decade or so, the spread of modern education and improved communications have positively influenced the desire of East Indians for social and economic mobility in the society. While they have been in the forefront battling for justice on sugar estates and pioneering increased agricultural production, they have not been content to remain isolated in rural villages and farming communities. East Indians have slowly progressed from being 'coolies' to entering into important trades and professions in Guyana. In 1965, out of a total of 165 medical practitioneers, 85 were East Indians; of the 220 legal practitioners, 110 were Indians. Today, there are 63 medical practitioners of which 37 are East Indians while there are 82 East Indian legal practitioners of a total of 126. Of a total of 91 land surveyors employed in the public service, 58 of them are East Indians. Between January and June 1979, of a total of 87 specialist appointments in the public service, 44 of them were East Indians.[32] These figures merely illustrate the successful attempts by East Indians to enter the various professions in the society.

The opportunities for East Indians to be employed and promoted within the public sector are not abundant. Two important departments which recruit personnel, the Labour Exchange and the Redeployment Secretariat are both dominated by Afro-Guyanese. A Central Recruitment Agency which was recently established to discharge the functions of these two departments is also heavily manned by Afro-Guyanese. In October 1978, 42 Indo-Guyanese who were casual workers at the Guyana Pharmaceutical Corporation were dismissed and replaced by 38 Afro-Guyanese.

A similar situation prevails with respect to middle and upper management personnel. Fewer opportunities for specialist training are given to East Indians, thus reducing their chances for promotion. Out of a total of 45 students enrolled in the Diploma in Accountancy programme for public sector employees at the University of Guyana, 23 students are Indians. Total applicants for this programme were 138 of which 75 of them were Indians. Only 23 were eventually released for the course. Of 6 important specialised training seminars held for public sector managers in June 1979, only 37 or 24% of the trainees were East Indians. Since the emphasis of these institutions within recent times is on upper and middle management training, then East Indians would tend to have few opportunities for upward mobility within this structure.

Conclusion

In this paper, we have attempted to examine the role of East Indians and their participation at various levels in the transformation of the Guyanese society. It is not the purpose of this paper to 'air' the grievances of East Indians, but to look objectively at the role of East Indians *vis-a-vis* other groups in the society. While it is not the specific objective of the paper to look at racial discrimination, we feel that it is an important factor affecting any wider participation by East Indians.

In the programme for socialist transformation, East Indians continue to play the most important role in the agricultural sector. They are perhaps the true pioneers in the thrust for self-reliance and self-sufficiency. Unfortunately, public sector participation does not reflect this characteristic feature. Various management/ administrative levels of the public sector reflect a serious racial imbalance with Afro-Guyanese dominating occupation of the various positions. And, when rewards are given in the form of national awards, East Indians are very much under-represented.

Given such a situation prevailing in Guyanese society, some important observations should be noted. The attempt to transform the society along socialist lines is seriously questioned by East Indians and this would tend to perpetuate racial antagonism already existing in the society. The battle for social and economic mobility will increase the possibilities of conflicts along racial lines.

Various pressures on East Indians and racial imbalances in the decision-making processes of the state are important ingredients to generate such conflicts. The general feeling among East Indians is that a deliberate policy is implemented to reflect this racial imbalance. They also express the opinion that the task of feeding and repaying the debts of the nation are their responsibilities, while at the same time they derive few benefits and rewards in the process.

The above situation would definitely reflect a retrograde step in the process of nation building. The transition to socialism is therefore generating its own seeds of disintegration and societal destruction. What is recommended and expressed in other circles is that a truly socialist programme be implemented which would eventually transcend the problems of race and class barriers in the society. As long as this is delayed, socialism for Guyana would also be delayed.

NOTES

1. This is part of a wider study on 'Social Mobility of East Indians in Guyana'. The data in this paper was collected from a survey conducted from April to June 1979 by the authors. The data on Agriculture (Table 2) was obtained from a survey on land use in Guyana conducted by the Ministry of Agriculture in 1978. All other data are as at July 1st, 1979.

2. Forbes Burnham, *Address to the 14th PNC Delegates Congress,* 1971.

3. See 1970 population census, Vol 4, Part 3.

4. Independence Anniversary Speech by the Chinese Foreign Minister, *Guyana Chronicle,* Page 1, Saturday July 14, 1979.

5. Forbes Burnham, *op cit.*

6. Sukdeo, Fred, 'Malaria Eradication and Population Growth in Guyana' University of Guyana, March 1973.

7. *ibid.*

8. *ibid,* p. 31.

9. The figures for 1946 and 1960 were obtained from the population census reports of British Guiana, 1946 and 1960. The total population figures for 1970 and 1977 were obtained from the Bank of Guyana Annual Reports, 1972 and 1977. Figures for the East Indian population are approximate and are based on the natural rate of increase.

10. Bronkhurst, HVP, *The Colony of British Guiana and its Labouring population.* (London, 1883, p. 128.)

11. Nath, Dwarka, *History of Indians in Guyana,* 1975, Vol I, p. 203.

12. International Commission of Jurists (ICJ), *Report of the British Guiana Commission of Inquiry – Racial Problems in the Public Service,* October, 1965, p. 104.

13. *ibid,* p. 105.

14. See the Budget Speech for 1978 presented by Frank Hope, Minister of Finance on February 27, 1978, and an article by M Hamaludin in the *Sunday Chronicle,* February 26, 1978, p.19.

15. Holdings do not include those operated by such institutions as Guysuco, Guyana Rice Board, etc. All data in the table as at August 1978.

16. Three ethnic categories only are used in this paper. The abbreviations are I – Indo-Guyanese. A – Afro-Guyanese, and 0 – Others. 'Others' include Chinese, Portuguese, Mixed, etc.

17. Includes Ministers of State and Regional Ministers.

18. Includes Secretary to the Treasury, Executive Secretaries of the Ministry of National Development, Deputy Auditor General, Deputy Director of Public Prosecutions, Secretary to the Office of the President and Deputy Solicitor General.

19. Includes Secretary to the Cabinet, Confidential Secretary to the Prime Minister and Principal Administrative Assistants in the National Development Ministry.

20. This position refers to the Head of the Personnel division such as Chief Personnel Officer or Principal Personnel Officer as the case may be.

21. This refers to the Head of the Accounts division.

22. These are heads of the various departments/divisions within the ministries. Also includes Regional Development Officers.

23. Includes Senior Education Officers and Supervisors.

24. Does not include members of Guystac's Board.

25. Includes Vice-Presidents of Guystac. Some departmental heads of some corporations act in this position.

26. Includes such positions as Ranch Managers of the Livestock Development Corporation, Estate Managers of Guysuco, etc.

27. Includes the Governor, Bank of Guyana.

28. Includes branch managers of the various banks.

29. There is no chairman for National Registration (Officers). There are 2 chairmen for the Boards of Review for the Inland Revenue Department and 3 chairmen for the 3 visiting Committees of the Prisons.

30. Includes such institutions as the National Service.

31. I.C.J. report, *op cit,* p. 61.

32. Such positions as Chief Draughtsman, Physiotherapist, Meterologist, etc.

Depression in the 'Tin Roof Towns'

Economic Problems of Urban Indians in Jamaica 1930 – 1950

Verene Shepherd

Between 1845 and 1916, approximately 37,000[1] East Indians were imported into Jamaica in an attempt to satisfy the planters' desire for 'bound' and 'controllable' labour which emancipation and the subsequent revolt of the peasantry had denied them. These Indians worked under five-year contracts on the several sugarcane and banana estates throughout rural Jamaica, earning subsistence wages and subjected to numerous labour laws, contravention of which fetched punishments ranging from fines to imprisonment.[2]

At the end of the Indian's indenture, he legally became a 'free' man. This freedom was limited, however, for while he could move from estate to estate, he could not emigrate or return to India until he had completed a further five years of continuous residence in the island. At the end of this ten-year period of compulsory residence, time-expired Indians then became entitled first to completely free, and later to assisted return passages to India.[3] However, the majority of time-expired Indians settled permanently in Jamaica as a result of the inefficiencies in the repatriation arrangements and the inducements offered to get them to remain in the island. Indeed, it was the opinion of the majority of planters in the West Indies that it made very little economic sense to repatriate Indians once they had become acclimatized and seasoned labourers. Consequently, of the total number of Indian labourers imported into Jamaica, only 38.10% were eventually repatriated.[4]

As in Trinidad and Guyana, the bulk of this settled East Indian population in Jamaica continued, well into the twentieth century, to be concentrated in the rural areas. Kelvin Singh records that in Trinidad in the late 1920s, and largely because of economic factors, '...the majority of Indians...whether they liked it or not remained within the latifundial environment of the sugar belt....'[5] Lesley Key notes that up to 1921, East Indians formed only 10% of the population of Georgetown and 15% of New Amsterdam.[6] The 1911 Census for Jamaica recorded that in that year, 94.4% of the total East Indian population were rural dwellers.[7]

Nevertheless, an urban East Indian population did develop in Jamaica. This comprised time-expired Indians who from the latter part of the nineteenth century began to move to Kingston and St. Andrew in search of more remunerative employment. The earliest record of an urban East Indian community in Jamaica was the census of 1881. This census revealed that 200 East Indians, comprising a mere 0.5% of the total population of the city, resided in Kingston. By 1891, the urban East Indian population totalled 900 and by 1911 it had increased to 967 or 5.6% of the total East Indian population.[8]

The migration of rural Indians to Kingston and St. Andrew was much lamented by the planters and was opposed by the Protector of Immigrants who in his report for the fiscal year 1914-15 remarked:

I consider that the tendency of Immigrants who have completed their indenture to leave the country parts and engage in casual work in Kingston, is prejudicial and should be discouraged.[9]

There were three fundamental grounds on which the objection to internal migration was based. In the first place, planters complained that rural-urban migration removed a valuable source of labour from the agricultural districts, particularly as the labour supply had already been diminished by the development of the peasantry and the emigration of native and ex-indentured immigrant labourers to Cuba and Central America. After 1916, moreover, the customary addition to the labour force through new importations of Indian contract labourers ceased. Secondly, it was feared that this movement would lead to competition with local labour '...which has always regarded coal and banana carrying, (two occupations of the urban poor), and such occupations as its own prerequisite,'[10] – a fear which turned out to be groundless since urban Indians mainly engaged in market gardening. Thirdly, according to the Protector, '...it reduces the inclination of the Immigrant to seek regular employment and weakens his capacity as a wage earner.'[11] This latter comment reflected the age-old attitude of the planter class that regular labour consisted only of labour on the estate.

Despite opposition to the urban migration of Indians, this movement not only continued unabated, but accelerated between

1930 and 1938 – a period fraught with socio-economic problems for all sections of the labouring population, regardless of ethnic origin. Indeed, the 1930s were difficult years throughout the world. The decade began with a financial crisis in New York and London, with confidence in banks and governments undermined. It was characterised by employer-employee conflicts which the absence of active Trade Unions made more difficult to solve. Colonial agricultural countries such as Jamaica, moreover, shared in the worldwide economic depression reflected in massive unemployment and underemployment, low wages, poor working conditions, poor health and educational facilities and poor and inadequate housing. The situation was compounded by the ineffective Crown Colony System, the removal of which was increasingly being called for by the rising coloured and professional classes. For the rural agricultural labourers, Panama disease in the banana industry and the imposition of the sugar quota created undue hardships. Despite the repeated warnings to keep out of an already overcrowded Kingston, many of these displaced rural agricultural workers trekked to the urban area in search of casual jobs. According to the report of the Indian Official, J.D. Tyson, published in 1939, though East Indians suffered along with the rest of the island population from the general wave of unemployment which existed in the 1930s, '...to this had been added, in the case of the East Indians, a growing competition, even in fields hitherto regarded as his own, from West Indian labour returning from Cuba and elsewhere, with some training and experience in estate work.'[12] Consequently, Afro-Jamaicans, traditionally preferred by the planters, allegedly obtained work over the heads of East Indians. East Indian women were particularly hard hit, the majority being lucky to obtain even two days' work per week. Such displaced Indian labourers, unable to find alternative employment in the rural parishes, joined the exodus to Kingston; so that by 1943, as the census of that year indicated, 1,279 East Indians resided in Kingston, a percentage change of between 100 and 199.9 from 1911. The growth in St. Andrew was even more phenomenal; in 1943, approximately 2,769 Indians were enumerated there. These figures, combined, represented 2.6% of the total population in the City and 18.9% of the total East Indian population in Jamaica.[13]

East Indians in Kingston settled first in Smith Village (now Denham Town), and Bachan Pen or Back-O-Wall, (the present Tivoli Gardens). They later inhabited several other areas on the fringes of the city including Hindu Town (Penwood Road), Trench

Town (formerly Trench Pen), Cockburn Gardens, and Franklyn
Town. They also settled in areas along the Spanish Town Road
extending as far as Six Miles.[14] Those who settled in St.
Andrew were located in Constant Spring, Whitehall Avenue, Molynes Road Area,
August Town, and Hagley Park Road.[15] These settlements were
never exclusively East Indian enclaves, though in a few cases East
Indians formed the bulk of their inhabitants. Close to 75% of the
population of Smith Village in 1938, for example, was East Indian.[16]
In fact, Smith Village in 1938 contained the majority of the East
Indian population in Kingston.[17]

While East Indians in St. Andrew were able to erect fairly
habitable dwellings, those in Western Kingston lived in veritable
slums. These slum conditions were created through overcrowding
and were characterised by illiteracy and crime. Homes consisted of
thatched huts and shacks made of every conceivable type of material.
A part of Smith Village was described in the 1890s as:

> ....a poor and tumble-down quarter...with narrow and uneven
> streets on either side of which are ruinous looking houses with the
> stamp of poverty upon them written clearly in the crumbling
> walls and windows where rusty tin takes the place of glass.[18]

In the 1940s, Smith Village was said to have been inhabited and
frequented by so many 'denizens of the underworld' that a police
constable on hearing that he had been transferred there immediately
doubled his life insurance policy![19] Trench Pen was described as the
'Tin Roof Town' – a description befitting most of the dwellings of the
urban poor – on account of the fact that since zinc was rare, many of
the shacks were roofed by flattened petrol tins.[20]

In the period under review, the economic condition of all who
inhabited these 'Tin Roof Towns' was predictably harsh. In the case
of the Indians, as will be later shown, the cultivation and sale of
vegetables and flowers, the major economic activity favoured by
most of them, was beset by many problems. Those who set up shops,
cultivated tobacco, reared cattle or engaged in a variety of non-
agricultural occupations such as the jewellery trade, fared better in
these troubled years; but such people were very few. Tyson reported
that in 1939:

> compared with the East Indian community in British Guiana and
> Trinidad, I found the East Indians of Jamaica backward, as a
> community, and very helpless, numbering among them barely a

> *dozen professional men and merchants, practically no civil*
> *servants, or even teachers ... except for a few scattered*
> *storekeepers, the community is still an agricultural and labouring*
> *one...*[21]

This paper will, however, focus largely on the urban market gardeners, dwellers of the 'Tin Roof Towns' who suffered greatly on account of extortionate landlords, high land rents and water rates, a discriminatory Kingston and St. Andrew Corporation Law, slum clearance activities and unemployment. Some attention will also be paid to the unemployable who in the period 1930-50 became increasingly destitute and had to seek poor relief.

The main income-generating activity of Indians in Kingston was market gardening. The Protector of Immigrants had lamented the fact that despite the availability of Crown Lands in the rural areas, time-expired Indians exhibited a preference to purchase ready-made vegetable gardens in Kingston '...where they can earn a modest living at the expenditure of a minimum amount of energy by cultivating market garden produce.'[22] This description is reminiscent of that applied to Afro-Jamaican peasants, who were characterised as lazy, because they preferred to work on their provision grounds than on the estates. Nevertheless, as long as they could, East Indians in Kingston rented quarter to half acre lots on which they not only erected a humble dwelling, (in some cases the land was rented with a dwelling already built), but planted a variety of vegetables including cabbage, lettuce, beet, garden eggs and callaloo. Flowers were also cultivated on these plots; in fact, the cultivation and sale of flowers seem to have been East Indian specialties. An Afro-Jamaican inhabitant of Smith Village told a vistor to that area in the 1890s that whenever there was a wedding or similar function, '...the Coolie agriculturalists supply all the flowers and decorations, for this is their speciality and they certainly make excellent gardeners.'[23]

These vegetable plots seem to have been not only well laid out, but if an eyewitness account is to be believed, even better planted and tended than those cultivated by the few Afro-Jamaicans who engaged in market-gardening. The aforementioned visitor to Smith Village, remarking on the East Indian vegetable plots said that:

> *...nothing is wasted; there is strict economy everywhere and the*
> *most ordinary cultivation round the house is done with a certain*
> *rustic science that makes the most out of the soil and*
> *surroundings.*[24]

Each type of vegetable was planted in a different bed, each bed, the visitor continued, '...being better watered and tended than those of the negroes, whose idea is rather to have a wilderness of mingled products from which they are glad to take whatever happens to be right at the time.'[25]

East Indian market gardeners disposed of their goods either by selling them to the Chinese shops in downtown Kingston or piling them in baskets which they carried on their heads from house to house.[26] Most of these sellers were women. In the 1890s, one such seller was described as follows: '...heavy silver bangles...glistened pleasantly against the soft brown of her skin... On her head was poised a basket laden with vegetables of every description; bunches of fresh lettuce, garden eggs and other similar products.'[27]

East Indian market gardeners had several economic problems with which to contend in the period 1930-1950. The first was the high rent rates which increased by the system of slum clearance and rehousing undertaken by the Central Housing Authority. In his evidence before the Moyne Commission, Mr. Jhangai of the East Indian National Union had stated that, '...landlords today take advantage of the tenants.'[28] Not only were the rents charged for usually rundown buildings extortionately high – being 10/– to 30/– a month – but non-payment of rents led to eviction at short notice '...or otherwise their property is levied upon to pay the rent and they are given notice to quit instantly. In some cases the pipe is locked off so that no water could be obtained for the vegetable garden.'[29] Such an evicted person lost his entire investment including his garden, which the landlord promptly sold/let to another tenant. Inability to communicate fluently in English usually prevented the evicted tenant from seeking legal advice in the matter. Some of these very landlords were East Indians who allegedly had no sympathy for their less fortunate countrymen. There were at least three large East Indian landowners in Smith Village, for example; they owned 62 acres of land on which close to 3,000 people lived, each acre being subdivided into five lots.[30] As very few of these lands were actually purchased by the Indians, the majority of whom were too poor to afford them, they consequently had to put up with the insecurity of land tenure which could lead to eviction.

In an attempt to alleviate the problems of the urban poor a general clearance of slums was undertaken by the Government after the 1938 riots which had erupted across the island as a protest against poor living and working conditions. The Government also attempted to rehouse those affected by such slum clearance. In fact an extensive building scheme was undertaken by the Central Housing Authority in the latter part of the 1940s. Western Kingston slums, the 'tin roof towns', were the first to receive attention. Those affected by slum clearance, however, suffered grave economic problems. This was because the acute housing shortage created resulted in a steep increase in rent rates. This led East Indians and others in these areas to complain to the Government that they were under 'the hells of oppression'; Spanish Town Road lots, for example, for which they used to pay 4/– per month, suddenly rose to 29/– per month.[31] They also complained that no two square chains of vegetables planted on the same lots could hope to yield revenue to pay the required rental and leave enough profit on which to live.[32]

The system of slum clearance caused other problems besides that of increased rent rates. For one thing, though compensation at a rate of between £50 and £100 per 'house' was paid by the Government for the loss of houses, such compensation was often inadequate to enable the people in these areas to afford new accommodation. This was on account of the exorbitant prices charged for dwellings in the new housing schemes built to relocate them. For example, Denham Town, created out of the slum area of Smith Village, initially became a settlement for the lower middle class as the urban poor could no longer afford to live there. The latter, therefore, simply moved to other areas such as Trench Pen where they proceeded to erect shacks once more.[33] When Trench Pen slums were cleared, less than 10% of the displaced from the area were able to afford the new houses built to absorb them.[34]

East Indian vegetable gardens and plantain fields were occasionally destroyed in the interest of slum clearance. East Indians in Cockburn Pen suffered in this way when slum clearance was undertaken in that area and the construction of houses by Bellrock to house the homeless began. As in the case of Smith Village and Trench Pen, the Indians in Cockburn Pen complained that though compensation was offered, this was grossly inadequate. For example, only 3d. per root was paid for each gungo tree destroyed, 1/– per root for plantains and 60/– per square chain or 1d. per root for okras.[35] Furthermore, where plots were destroyed for the purpose of laying roads, no compensation was paid.[36]

Urban East Indian market gardeners were affected by two other developments in the 1930s. The first was the ban placed on the house to house sale of vegetables, a measure which came into effect in 1931.

The second was the general metering of water in the Corporate Area. By the Kingston and St. Andrew Corporation (K.S.A.C.) Law, Section 136, of 1931:

> *any person who shall expose or exhibit for sale in the urban or suburban district of the Corporate Area any fresh meat, poultry, game, fresh fish, turtle, vegetables, ground provisions or fruit elsewhere than in a public market or in a shop licensed...for the sale of such articles shall forfeit a sum of ten pounds for every day in which he shall so offend.*[37]

Although a proviso to the Law later exempted the sellers of poultry, game, fresh fish, fruit and ground provisions, the ban on the door to door sale of vegetables remained until 1945.[38] This held good despite repeated requests by the leaders of the East Indian Community for the removal of this clause from the Law;[39] especially in the light of reported police harassment of Indian sellers, many of whom pleaded ignorance of the Law. The East Indian Progressive Society further claimed that racial discrimination was practised by the police in making their arrests for this offence, since non-Indians who sold a variety of goods on the street were not equally harassed by the police.[40] This was denied by the Colonial Secretary who claimed that no East Indians had been arrested for the house to house sale of vegetables, though a few had been prosecuted for causing obstruction on the sidewalk. Fines for these offences ranged form 2/6 to 5/–.[41]

Despite the denial by the Colonial Secretary, the Protector of Immigrants Papers contain the verbatim evidence of an East Indian woman, Beatrice Setal, who claimed that she and three others had been charged under the K.S.A.C. Law, Chapter 11, Section 137, for 'exposing for sale vegetables at a place other than a public market or shop licensed for that purpose',[42] although they claimed to have been selling their produce to a Chinese shopkeeper. The following is Setal's statement:

> *This morning about 6.30 o'clock myself and three other East Indian girls were supplying greens and vegetables to Chinees (sic) in a Chinees shop at 115 Barry Street ... Constable Hewitt who is an employee of the K.S.A.C. came to the door and said, "Hai, unno don't run", and took our names. He then told us to go to the Sutton Street Police Station-*
> *.......There was a Black woman also selling fowls in the*

Chinees cookshop, but they let her go and prosecuted us.[43]

Despite the fact that the selling of game and poultry was not in contravention of the Law, such racial discrimination persisted. Indeed, the 1930s were characterised by deteriorating race relations between East Indians and Afro-Jamaicans. Formerly, racial hostility was directed mainly at the Chinese who dominated the commercial life of the island and who were obviously prospering in the midst of the poverty of the majority of the labouring population. East Indians, however, had largely escaped racial attacks. Despite the fact that Indians and Blacks harboured feelings of superiority towards each other, such racial feelings remained at the covert level and consequently, all official reports indicated that both ethnic groups co-existed harmoniously. This apparent racial harmony existed largely because up to the 1930s, Afro-Jamaicans, unlike Afro-Guyanese, did not feel threatened by the presence of East Indians. The return of migrants from Cuba and Central America, the wave of unemployment, and the resultant competition for scarce jobs in the 1930s exploded this myth of non-racialism between Indians and Blacks. The former were increasingly called aliens and complained of racial discrimination.

Great economic problems were also created for East Indian market gardeners by the programme of general metering of water by the Water Commission in the Corporate Area. This began in the late 1930s and extended over a five to seven year period.[44] The E.I.P.S. claimed that East Indians who used to live by growing vegetables and selling them had gone out of employment by the hundreds as '... they cannot afford to pay for metered water.'[45] A similar observation had been made by Thompson of the E.I.N.U. in his evidence before the Moyne Commission in 1938. According to Thompson, '...the water meter system of the vegetable crops has come in and that has choked out their means of earning a livelihood.'[46] Indians in Kingston reported that the only market gardeners not affected by the high water rates were those who had wells on the land rented, such as those in Bachan Pen. Bachan Pen was owned by an Indian, Mr Tewari, who had migrated to Jamaica from Guyana. He first settled in Clarendon where he became a big landowner. The family later moved to Kingston where they invested in land in West Kingston. Many East Indians rented land for housing and vegetable gardens from the Tewaris. On the death of the elder Tewari, however, his children decided to use the land for non-agricultural purposes, particularly as hundreds of East Indian market gardeners were unable to meet their rent obligations. The Tewaris felt the land could be utilized in more economically viable ways. Hundreds of East Indians were therefore forced to search for other lands in areas where the water rates were cheaper. In this they were assisted by the E.I.P.S which formed the East Indian Syndicate Ltd. for the purpose of purchasing ten acres of land at a place which eventually came to be called Hindu Town, situated on Penwood Road. The displaced Indians from 'Tewari Lands' were encouraged to purchase quarter acre plots on easy repayment terms. It is reported, however, that Indians in Hindu Town failed to meet their financial obligations with the result that the E.I.P.S. was forced to sell the land to those who could afford to pay in order to reclaim their investment.[47]

Some East Indians who were unable to find cheaper lands on which to continue their market gardening moved out to St. Catherine to engage in cane farming or rice growing. Others who had sufficient capital but were forced to move out of 'Tewari Lands', moved up into St. Andrew where they grew tobacco or reared cattle. The large majority, however, found themselves unemployed and thrown at the mercy of the landlords. Thompson of the E.I.N.U. had observed in 1938 that '...there is very little that they can do...and they have found themselves in the hands of the iniquitous landlords, particularly among the Indians. The Maraghs have realised their true position and they have held...a big stick over their heads...They cannot remove immediately so they have to be subdued there under any condition...'[48]

Two solutions were proposed by the E.I.P.S. in the 1940s to help to alleviate the economic plight of the urban East Indian poor. The first was that the Lands Department buy up available properties, cut them up into small parcels, provide irrigation facilities, and allot them to East Indians for growing vegetables; the price of such allotments was to be collected in instalments.[49] Some of the properties suggested were Baxters Land (Waltham Park Road), Drews Land (Four Miles, Spanish Town Road), and Motto's Land (Molynes Road). Despite repeated representations to the Lands Department, however, no such lands were purchased by the government to facilitate Indian market gardeners. There were two explanations for this. In the first place, the properties suggested were expensive. Baxters Land, for example, which comprised 85 acres, was going for £3,000, Drews

Land, (75 acres) for £2,000, and Motto's Land (176 acres), for £4,400.[50] The Lands Department therefore informed the E.I.P.S. that the government could not make funds available for the purchase of these lands.[51] The Commissioner of Lands, Captain Burnett, did however inform the E.I.P.S. of the Government Land Settlement Schemes in the rural parishes where for a deposit of 10% of the total cost of lots, those people wanting lands could purchase same. These lands were cheaper than lands in the Corporate Area, being available from £7 an acre.[52] Burnett was informed by the E.I.P.S. that the majority of Indians could not afford the required 10% deposit and that thus should be waived. In response the E.I.P.S. was told that this could not be entertained, and that East Indians wanting land were expected to go through the same channels as the native population. Moreover Government opposed any attempt to give special treatment to East Indians in Government Land Settlement Schemes or other areas on the grounds that '....they are but a small minority in the community and ...must attempt to fit in in everyway that they find possible.'[53]

Urban Indians did not, however, evince very much interest in rural land settlement schemes. Of the 158 East Indian applicants for consideration in such schemes forwarded by the E.I.N.U. to the Administrator General's Department in 1942, only 24 or 15.2% were from the Corporate Area.[54] However, most of these were ineligible for benefits, since the general policy in the Land Settlement Scheme was to allot a holding of not less than three acres. The majority of East Indian applicants, however, could afford only quarter to half acre lots. In fact, of the 158 applicants, 52.5% applied for half-acre lots. Only 1.93% requested three to five-acre lots.[55] Up to 1942, therefore, urban Indians had failed to benefit from the Government Land Settlement Scheme.

The second solution to the economic plight of urban East Indians proposed by the E.I.P.S. was that Indians be given jobs under the Government Relief Work Scheme administered by the Labour Bureau. After a labour survey in 1939, the government had decided to institute special works for the relief of the unemployed in parts of the island where the need was greatest. Funds for this project were provided partly by the Government of Jamaica and partly by an imperial grant. In 1940, the Kingston Employment Bureau was set up to register the unemployed and issue employment tickets.[56] Unemployed East Indians in Kingston and St. Andrew increasingly sought the assistance of this Bureau, and a few were in fact able to procure jobs. When the Government in connection with its War Food Programme established its own vegetable gardens at Majesty Pen, East Indian relief workers were used to cultivate them, despite the complaint that this created unfair competition with those Indians who were cultivating vegetables on their own account.

Relief work in other areas such as on the roads was more difficult to procure. East Indians claimed that this was on account of the great discrimination practised by ticket distributors who favoured the Afro-Jamaicans. They charged that '...even ex-criminals and people of desperate character are given relief work over the heads of honest, hardworking East Indians.'[57] This was refuted by the Labour Advisor who instructed all East Indians to register in person at the Department where they would be issued with tickets and given jobs when they were available.[58] He did admit, however, that East Indians often had difficulty in actually getting their names registered in the Bureau since they were frequently 'elbowed' out of the queues by Afro-Jamaicans.[59] To avoid this, East Indians needing jobs were asked to apply to the Protector who in turn would submit their names to the Employment Bureau. They would subsequently be called in specifically to be registered and ultimately to receive their employment ticket.[60]

Registration did not guarantee jobs, however. Mr Payne, Managing Director of the Bureau stated that only about 20% of East Indians obtained jobs through the Bureau, because the majority were only fit to do agricultural work, unavailable in the Corporate Area.[61] In 1940, for example, 247 Indians registered for jobs.[62] Of this number, 198 qualified for agricultural jobs only.[63] By the end of the year moreover, 234 were still unemployed.[64]

Finally, a word must be said about those urban Indians who through old age, illness or permanent physical disability fell into the category of the unemployable and were rendered destitute. These increasingly applied for Poor Relief. Otherwise known as public assistance, this was administered by the local authorities, that is, the K.S.A.C. and the Parochial Boards under the control and guidance of the Board of Supervision – a statutory body with an Administrative Secretary appointed under the Poor Relief Law. The local authorities operated through Poor Relief Committees which made weekly allowances of between 2/– and 10/–, depending on need and size of family and dependents.[65] The chronically sick and disabled, considered to be better served by indoor relief, could get Alms House accommodation, which was available in each parish. Each year, hundreds of letters requesting poor relief poured into the Immigration Office from urban Indians, mainly from the old, infirm and destitute.[66] Such applicants were often given letters, endorsing their requests for poor relief, to be taken to the Inspector of Poor at Half-Way-Tree. The majority requested outdoor relief even if they qualified for indoor relief. The major reason for this is clearly stated in the following letter from the Protector to the Inspector of Poor:

> *The bearer of this letter, Budha of Hindu Town...states that she is sick, destitute and unable to work to earn her living and applies for Poor Relief.*
>
> *Owing to her Hindu religion, Eastern customs and habits of religion, she does not wish to be sent to the Poor House, but will be grateful to receive outdoor relief.*[67]

The Protector was no doubt referring to the aversion to beef (Hindus) and pork (Moslems) which Indians had. East Indians claimed that no attempt was made in these Alms Houses to provide alternative food. In fact, they claimed that a 'diet test' was often applied to determine whether Indians should in fact be admitted to Alms Houses. The Alms Houses, however, generally refused to cater specially for East Indian inmates even though the East Indian organisations continued to press for these. Separate cooking facilities and utensils for Indian inmates, for example, were advocated.[68] In addition, older Indians could not speak English fluently, and since there were no interpreters in the Alms Houses, their problems were compounded. The number in receipt of outdoor relief consequently exceeded those receiving indoor relief. In the year 1946-47, there were 51 East Indians in the Alms Houses in contrast to 139 who were getting outdoor relief.[69] In any case, outdoor relief was said to have been cheaper for the K.S.A.C. since the recommended rate of maintenance for East Indians was 5/- per head per week – less than the rate of maintenance in the Poor Houses.[70]

Thus, although up to 1950 the East Indian community in Jamaica was largely a rural one, an urban East Indian community did exist. This community consisted of time-expired and free Indians who wanted to escape plantation life and seek more remunerative employment in the city. Though this rural-urban migration was frowned on by the planters and by the Protector of Immigrants, it continued unabated. Indeed, it accelerated in the period 1930-1938 as rural agricultural labourers – Indians and Afro-Jamaicans alike – sought to alleviate their depressed socio-economic condition, engendered by the decline in sugarcane and banana production in this period, by seeking jobs in the Corporate Area of Kingston and St. Andrew. The majority of urban Indians resided in Western Kingston where they engaged primarily in market gardening. Several factors combined to render this urban East Indian community an economically depressed one. Chief among these were the high rents charged by landlords, some of whom were Indians; the slum-like conditions of their dwellings; the ban on the house to house sale of vegetables imposed in 1931; the metering of water and the shortage of houses resulting from the system of slum clearance. Consequently, unemployment and destitution plagued urban Indians – as indeed it did many of the Afro-Jamaicans. Some measure of assistance was found in the Government Relief Work Scheme and the Poor Relief System The only Indians who escaped this overall picture of mass misery were the few professionals, merchants, shopkeepers, jewellers, landlords and a few odd Indians who managed to move out of West Kingston into St. Andrew where they engaged in tobacco farming and cattle rearing.

NOTES

1. As a result of the wide variation in the figures given in the main sources consulted for the study of East Indian immigration into Jamaica, this total may differ from that used in other studies. Roberts and Byrne's figure of 36,412, (which only represents the period 1845-1914), comes closest to the present writer's findings. To this total has been added the 615 Indians who came on the *S.S. Dewa* in 1916. (see G. W. Roberts and J. Byrne, 'Summary Statistics on Indenture and Associated Migration Affecting the West Indies, 1834-1918', reprinted from *Population Studies*, Vol. 20, No.1, July 1966, p. 129)

2. For more detailed information on the system of Indian indentureship in Jamaica, see Harinder Singh Sohal, 'The East Indian Indentureship System in Jamaica, 1845-1917', unpublished Ph.D. Thesis, University of Waterloo, Canada, 1979.

3. Jamaica's legal obligation to provide back passages ended in 1928, though the last shipment of return immigrants was actually made on the *Sutlej* in 1929.

4. A similar trend was observed in other West Indian Colonies. For example, between 1843 and 1917, only 66,140 or 27.7% of the 238,909 Indians introduced into British Guiana, returned to India. See Roberts and Byrne, *op. cit.*, pp. 129-132.

5. K. Singh, 'East Indians and the Larger Society', in *Calcutta to Caroni: The East Indians of Trinidad,* ed. John La Guerre, (Longman Caribbean, Trinidad and Jamaica, 1974), p. 53.

6. L. Key, 'East Indians and the Afro-Guyanese: Village Settlement Patterns, and Inter-Group Relationship, 1871-1921', Paper presented at the Fourth Conference of Caribbean Historians, U.W.I., Mona, April 9-14, 1972, p. 27.

7. Jamaica: 1911-1912, Governor's Report on the Blue Book and Departmental Reports, (Blue Book Report), Protector of Immigrants Report, 1911-12, Abstract O, p. 78.

8. *Ibid.*

9. Blue Book Report, 1914-15, Protector of Immigrants Report, Sec. 19, p. 287.

10. *Ibid.*

11. *Ibid*

12. J. D. Tyson, *Report on the Conditions of Indians in Jamaica, British Guiana and Trinidad, 1938-39,* (Government of India Press, Simla, 1939), p. 33. Tyson was deputed to give evidence before the Moyne Commission on behalf of Indians in the above mentioned colonies who were not considered sufficiently articulate in the English Language to give their own evidence.

13. Central Government File, (C.G.F.), 1B/9/136, Protector of Immigrants Report, 1944, Protector of Immigrants Papers, Jamaica Archives.

14. *Ibid*. Also personal interview with Ivan Blake, former member of the East Indian Progressive Society, (E.I.P.S.), December 4, 1983. The E.I.P.S. was one of three East Indian Associations formed between 1930 and 1940 to represent the needs of the free Indian Community. The other two were the East Indian National Union and the East Indian Association of Jamaica.

15. *Daily Gleaner,* (Jamaica), December 2, 1938 p. 19, evidence of Mr H. Cox the East Indian National Union, (E.I.N.U.), before the Moyne Commission.

16. *Ibid.*

17. Ms. 59, Livingstone Collection Scrap Book 1, National Library, Jamaica.

18. *Jamaica Times,* March 24, 1945, p. 1.

19. *Jamaica Times,* February 3, 1940, p. 3

20. Tyson, *op. cit.,* p. 33.

21. Protector of Immigrants Report, 1914-15, *op.cit.,* Sec. 36.

22. Livingstone Collection, *op. cit.*

23. *Ibid.*

24. *Ibid.*

25. C.G.F., 1B/111/31, 'Laws Affecting East Indians'.

26. Livingstone Collection, *op. cit.*

27. *Daily Gleaner,* December 2, 1938, p. 19, evidence of Mr. S. J. Jhangai before the Royal Commission. It should be noted that while Afro-Jamaicans engaged in a series of strikes and riots in 1938 to protest similar poor social and economic conditions, East Indians largely stayed aloof from such action, preferring to utilize the existing East Indian Associations to articulate their grievances and seek redress. Indeed, in contrast to the militancy shown by Indians under indenture who often struck and rioted for better working conditions, free Indians were remarkably docile.

28. *Daily Gleaner,* December 2, 1938, p.19, evidence of Mr Emanuel Raout of the E.I.N.U. before the Moyne Commission.

29. Evidence of Jhangai, *op. cit.* There were no regulations regarding rents in this period.

30. *Jamaica Times,* October 14, 1950, p. 1.

31. *Ibid.*

32. *Jamaica Times,* March 31, 1945, p. 5.

33. *Jamaica Times* March 3, 1945, p. 3.

34. *Jamaica Times,* July 8, 1950, p. 1.

35. *Ibid.*

36. C.G.F. 1B/9/111/31, 'Laws Affecting East Indians', *op. cit.*

37. *Ibid.*

38. C.G.F. 1B/9/111/31, Secretary of the E.I.P.S. to the Mayor and Council, K.S.A.C., October 7, 1940.

39. E.I.P.S. to Ritchie, Protector of Immigrants, December 19, 1941.

40. C.G.F. 1B/9/111/31, Colonial Secretary to the E.I.P.S., October 28, 1940.

41. C.G.F. 1B/9/111/31, evidence of Beatrice Setal, written by P. Arms, Interpreter, May 6, 1941.

42. *Ibid.*

43. *Jamaica Times,* June 1, 1940, p. 1.

44. C.G.F. IB/9/111/31, Dukaran to Ritchie, July 1, 1940.

45. *Daily Gleaner,* December 2, 1938, p. 19, evidence of W. H. Thompson before the Moyne Commission, 1938. Also Personal Interview with Mr Thompson, March, 1983.

46. Personal interview with Ivan Blake, *op. cit.*

47. Evidence of Thompson, *op. cit.*

48. Dukaran to Ritchie, *op. cit.*

49. *Ibid.*

50. C.G.F. 1B/9/111/31, 'Report of a meeting between F. A. Stockdale, Government Comptroller and A. O. Ritchie', October 5, 1941.

51. C.G.F. 1B/9/111/31, Report of 'Report of P.J. Arms of a meeting between the E.I.P.S. and the Commissioner of Lands', April 26, 1941.

52. C.G.F. 1B/9/11/31, Report of Stockdale, October 11, 1941.

53. C.G.F. 1B/9/111/31, Administrator General to the Commissioner of Lands, November 20, 1942.

54. *Ibid*

55. Jamaica Annual Report, 1946, p. 12.

56. C.G.F. 1B/9/156, Fred Payne, Managing Director, Kingston Employment Bureau, to the Protector of Immigrants, January 24, 1941.

57. C.G.F. 1B/9/156, Labour Advisor to the Protector, February 15, 1941.

58. C.G.F. 1B/9/111/29, 'Report by P. J. Arms of a meeting between F. A. Stockdale and the Protector', February 20, 1941.

59. *Ibid.*

60. *Ibid*

61. C.G.F. 1B/9/89, Requests for Employment through the Immigration Department.

62. *Ibid*

63. *Ibid.* 67.1% of those unemployed lived along the Spanish Town Road. (See C.G.F. 1B/9/156, Labour Advisor to Administrator General, January 4, 1941).

64. Jamaica Annual Report, 1948, p. 57

65. C.G.F. 1B/9/154, Letters of Application for Poor Relief.

66. C.G.F. 1B/9/108, Arms to the Inspector of Poor, February 4, 1947.

67. Requests of the East Indian Association of Jamaica (E.I.A.J.), to Tyson, 1939, Tyson Report, p. 38.

68. Arms to the Inspector of Poor, *op. cit.*

69. C.G.F. 1B/9/111/31, Arms to the Mayor, K.S.A.C., June 6, 1941.

The Evolution Of The Social, Economic and Political Position Of The East Indians In Surinam, 1873 – 1980

Sandew Hira

An analysis of the social, economic and political position of any ethnic group in Surinam is implicitly also an analysis of the interethnic relations in that society. Therefore, our treatment of the position of the East Indians in Surinam is basically concerned with the question: which factors determine the position of any ethnic group in this former Dutch colony? . Thus, the paper is more than a factual sketch of the position of the East Indians in Surinam. It penetrates to a deeper theoretical problem, namely: what are the primary driving forces behind the evolution of interethnic relations?

We can single out two basic answers to this question. One answer seeks the primary driving forces in a specific psychological constitution of an ethnic group (it's 'nature', 'mentality' or whatever label one attaches to this constitution). The other points to a material base (socio-economic and technological factors) for the position of an ethnic group. This paper does not offer a 'solution' for the problem, but only adds fuel to this age-old controversy by offering an analysis from a materialist point of view. We will try to show that the position of the East Indians in Surinam has, by and large, been determined by material rather than psychological factors, that a materialist analysis is able to provide a coherent framework for the analysis of the ethnic relations in Surinam. In this framework psychological and other non-materialist factors do play a certain role in the determination of ethnic relations, but within the boundaries created by the material base.

A. The Homogeneous Mass, 1873-1916

Since the abolition of slavery in the British colonies it became increasingly clear to the Dutch that if they did not follow suit they might be crushed by the free competition in sugar production. For the free colonies were able to produce cheaper sugar thanks to the abolition of dear slave labour.[1] Although slave labour was not profitable for the planters and those who lived off them, neither was free labour. The abundance of land for free labourers and the rise of the non-agricultural sector (gold-digging and, later on, rubber production) made it impossible for planters to rely on the ex-slaves. However, some ten years before the abolition of slavery in Dutch Guiana the planters began to experiment with another form of labour-organization. In 1853 the import of indentured labourers from China and Madeira began. But it was only from 1873, after a ten-year period of apprenticeship, that a mass import of indentured labourers – now from British India – occurred.

Between 1853 and 1939 the Dutch colony imported more than 74,000 contract-labourers: 1% from Portugese Madeira, 3% from China, 4% from other Carribean colonies, 46% from British India and 44% from Indonesia (Java). One-third of the British Indians and more than 20% of the Javanese returned to their country.[2] The influx of labourers from British India stopped in 1916, but import from Java, which started in 1890, continued up until 1939.

Coolie-labour performed a specific function in the colonial economy.[3] It enabled the planters to put a temporary brake on the decline of the plantations. Planters' capital used contract-labour for three purposes. First, contract-labour solved the problem of irregular labour of the ex-slaves. The Africans could only be attracted to a week, a month or at the most a one-year engagement with the planters. So when harvest time came, it could well be the case that ex-slaves were withdrawing from the plantations to cultivate their own small plots of land or refusing to renew their contract if their wages were not raised. The five-year contract with the coolies took care of this problem. Second, coolie-labour exerted a downward pressure on the free wages. A comparison of the free wages on plantations with free labourers only, and plantations where free and contract labourers were employed, shows that the free wages on the latter was lower than on the first.[4] Third, contract-labour was substantially cheaper than free labour. This was the result of the combination of piece-work with a long-term contract.

The five-year contract ensured the coolie a daily wage of 40 cents for women and 60 cents for men (Surinamese money). In 1920 these rates were raised to 60 and 80 cents respectively. The wage rate was based on a certain amount of piece-work. In practice however, this amount was hardly reached, either as a result of deliberate maladministration by the planters or because of the fact that the amount was just too high. Radjen Bhagwan Bali, a Surinamese historian, revealed that in fact the actual wage received by the coolies was even well below the standard of living, at least for women and children. Bhagwan Bali calculated that an extreme minimum of only food and clothing on a daily basis would cost 30 cents for grown-ups and 15 cents for children in 1874. In the period between 1875 and 1891 the wage-rate of women never rose above the minimum. In fact, it was 30-50% below this minimum! The children's wage rose above the minimum only in 1879 and 1891; in general it fluctuated between 20% and 60% of the minimum. The male's wage was at the maximum 30% above the minimum, which by the way was still one-third less than the prescribed wage of 60 cents. The reason for this system was given by the agent-general Cateau van Roosevelt in a letter to the governor of Surinam: 'it was generally hoped that they [the coolies] driven by hunger would by themselves do more labour'.[5]

The social position of the indentured labourers was conditioned by the development of the plantation sector. The plantations gradually lost ground to the peasantry and the non-agricultural sectors (gold-digging, rubber production and bauxite). Although the immigration of the coolies did slow down the decline of the plantations, it could not prevent the direction of its development. This was reflected in the social position of the plantation worker. The proportion of field and factory workers in the total population diminished from 55% in 1873 to 27% in 1904 and eventually to 18% in 1931. On the other hand the ratio of indentured to free labourers rose from 0.41 to 1.5 in the period between 1873 and 1904.[6] Coolie-labour rapidly replaced (African and other) free labour. In so far as free labour was used there existed a division of labour between the indentured and free labourers. The free labourers got the highest paid jobs (the digging of irrigation works and drainage canals) while the coolies had to stick to lower paid work. The British consul in Paramaribo, Annesley, wrote: 'If a coolie is beginning to make 60 cents a day regularly, he is put to some other work, where he cannot earn more than 40 cents a day.'[7] And as he was under contract, the immigrant was obliged to accept the task.

The division of labour was not only a matter of concern for an individual plantation. It was a general rule in the colony that coolie-labour was not to be used outside the plantation sector. In fact, it was forbidden for the contract labourers to work in rubber and gold production.

Life on the plantation was very hard. The workers on the cocoa plantations were better off than the workers on the sugar plantations. During harvest time especially – when the cane must be cut and manufactured into sugar – the workers had to endure long working days.

The social position of the coolie was not only expressed in the lower wages that they received, but also in the bad housing condition and medical care. Most coolies lived in the old slave barracks. These were often not even rebuilt to accommodate the new immigrants. Because many barracks were situated near swamp areas and marshy islands, diseases sometimes took epidemic proportions, especially in the first two decades of the immigration period.

As usual in class societies women had to suffer most of that 'new system of slavery'. Females formed about one-third of the coolie population. Indian women went together with the men into the fields, did the same work, but earned less. The babies and small children remained behind in the care of old women or an older brother or sister. They received inadequate care during pregnancy, and some-times they were forced to work even in the last months of their pregnancy. Women were often sexually abused by the planters and their officers, and sometimes also by Indian men. The women who came unmarried to the colony had a strong independent spirit. The quarrels between men and women often took a violent form ending in the burning or cutting of the women. [8]

The ethnic group that stood at the other end of the social system was not formed by the Africans, or 'Creoles' as they are called in Surinam, but by the whites. Elout van Soeterwoude, who visited the colony in 1884, gave the following description of the white planter-manager: 'He gets up at around six, half past seven, drinks a cup of coffee, wanders through the buildings or goes to sit on the veranda to watch the coolies and blacks preparing to go to work. At eight he sets down at the table and consumes a meal consiting of bread, eggs, salted fish and ham and bacon. Next he goes into the field to see how the work has been done and what has been done yesterday, sets up new tasks etc...Around noon he returns home, and while his errand boy strips his footwear off, he uses a swivel – we would say a cold cognac-grog. Then breakfast is brought. After that he retires into his bedroom to contemplate his labour of the morning. At four he uses a cup of tea, and if he is not too tired, there follows a walk along the coolie – and nigger – lines; but usually he makes this inspection from the veranda. Next he rests from the heat of the day and the exertions of the afternoon stretched in his rocking-chair...and calmly and uncomplaining waits for the moment – around eight, half past eight – when "a piece of food" will give him the necessary strength to go to bed to spend the night.' [9]

The relationship between Indians and Creoles was not specifically marked by tensions in contradistinction to the relationship between the Indians and the Whites. The latter were in the eyes of Indians and Creoles the oppressors. Although within the colonial economy the Creole free labourers were better off than the Indian indentured labourers, there was hardly a question of competition between the two groups or anything like oppression of one by the other. This became clear in the periods of political upheaval, as will be seen in all the pre-war political conflicts.

The coolie-worker did not have any political rights. He was forbidden to leave the plantation without a pass signed by the manager, so he was curtailed in his movement outside the plantation. Even though there were no formal regulations forbidding the organising of workers on the plantations, the practise of bloody repression of any attempt to unite the coolies made it clear that even this right did not exist for the indentured labourers. The coolies had the right to bring their complaints about the planters or managers to court. But in practice there were a lot of obstacles. They could not obtain a pass or often if they got one, it was only for Sundays when the offices were closed. When finally they managed to reach the authorities, it appeared that their charges were not accepted. A white man was rarely confined, while the coolie was quite easily thrown in jail. Corporal punishment was introduced in 1875, when it became clear that the coolies were protesting their fate on the plantations. Physical and psychological torture was quite common in the colonial jails.

Still, this did not stop the Indians from staging protests against their treatment. Small strikes involving a few workers occurred from 1873. Uprisings involving a whole plantation – most of them were bloodily repressed – occurred in 1873, 1875, 1876, 1877, 1878, 1883, 1884, 1885, 1891 and 1902. *None of these involved conflicts between Indians and Africans or another oppressed ethnic group.* In fact, one coolie-uprising (1876: plantation De Resolutie) began with the demand for the replacement of an oppressive coolie-overseer by a creole. In the plantation-uprisings it was always the white planter-manager assisted by the army which confronted the fighting coolies, who were sometimes led by women. One of them, named Tettary, died while leading a group of women fighting an army detachment which came to repress a revolt in 1884. [10]

B. The Rise Of The Indian Petty Bourgeoisie, 1916-1940

The period between the abolition of slavery and World War II is characterized by the decline of the plantations and the rise of petty commodity production, on the one hand, and a shift towards non-agricultural export production, mainly bauxite, on the other. In 1900, 90% of the total agricultural output was produced by the plantations and 10% by the small peasantry. By 1940 the reverse was the case. Sugar was still the number one export product at the beginning of the twentieth century. In 1940 bauxite was the most important export product. [11] In Paramaribo (the main city) the economic activity consisted of small-trade handicraft production.

The economic activity of the Indians after the period of indentureship was largely confined to peasant production. In an effort to keep the Indians in the colony the government issued small pieces of land in return for giving up the right to return to British India. These lands could become the property of the Indians after a few years of cultivation. The forest had to be cleared by the coolies themselves. And in the west of Surinam, polders, such as Boonackerpolder, Hamptoncourtpolders, Henarpolder and Sawmillkreekpolder, were built out of swamp-land by the coolies. In 1903 there were 1,972 Indians holding a total of 14,182 acres of public land in free use or leasing or in property. In 1911 there were already 4,250 Indians controlling 30,448 acres of land. [12]

Some Indian peasants were self-subsistence producers. Others were selling part of their produce on the market. In some districts – especially around Paramaribo – these peasants produced vegetables and other horticultural goods. They also sold milk and meat to the city people. In the outer districts many peasants produced rice partly for themselves and to a larger extent for the export market. Only a few Indians were involved in handicraft. In Paramaribo most Indians were cart-drivers, tailors, shopkeepers or small traders. The general trend before World War II in the development of the economic position of the Indians coincided with the general trend in the development of the colonial economy as a whole: a rise of petty commodity production.

There was still a social division of labour between the different ethnic groups. The Whites and light-coloured Creoles were in the commanding heights of society. They were to be found in high governmental posts and the managerial offices of the private agricultural and non-agricultural companies. The Creoles in Paramaribo were in the lower echelons of the governmental apparatus and the handicraft sector. Outside the city many Creoles were working as wage-earners at the bauxite and rubber companies – later on rubber production was wiped out by the Great Depression – and the few small industrial enterprises for the production of commodities such as cigarettes, soft drinks, ice-cream and the like. In agriculture most Creoles were involved either in small subsistence production or in the production of cocoa (this product was for a few decades one of the most important export products of the small peasantry until a disease destroyed the whole cultivation). The production of coconut and coconut-oil was also a matter for the Creoles. The Indians were strong in the rice-sector.

The social weight of the Indians clearly increased in the second phase of their development, although the relative proportion of Indians in the total population remained more or less the same. In 1921, out of a population of 112,300, 50% was Creole, 28% was Indian and 17% was Javanese. In 1939 the corresponding figures were 45%, 29% and 21% of a total population of 156,000.[13] But after indentureship the different ethnic groups concentrated in specific districts, so that each district was ethnically defined. In 1939, district Marowijne (2% of the total population) and the coconut producing district Coronie (3%), had a 90% Creole population. The population of the main city Paramaribo (35%) was made up of 79% Creoles, 10% Indians and 2% Javanese. Commewijne (16%) was overwhelmingly Javanese (67% against 18% Indian and 13% Creole). Saramacca (6%) was more Indian (49% against 23% Creole and 20% Javanese), as was Nickerie (10% of the total population; 49% Indian, 27% Creole and 20% Javanese).[14]

Although already in the period between 1873-1916 there were some social differences among the contract labourers and among the free immigrants, in the period after indentureship the stratification process in the Indian community was accelerated. The peasantry was not one big homogenous mass. There were, for example, different categories of Indian peasants. Among the rice cultivators in Nickerie and Saramacca there was a small layer of rich peasants owning rice hulling works (there were 133 in 1939) and tractors. They also acted as middlemen buying up the produce of the small peasants.[15] In

Commewijne, Indian middlemen owned cars in the late twenties. In Paramaribo free Indian immigrants coming from the neighbouring British Guiana (they formed 8% of the total Indian immigrants in 1921) made their way up through trade to the higher social strata of Paramaribo. In 1925, more than 30% of the houses belonging to Indians were owned by this category. [16] Indian shopkeepers and traders in Paramaribo formed a small but rich category. Their sons were able to acquire western education (the daughters stayed at home) which enabled them to get better positions in society. However, the mass of self-employed Indians in or outside the agricultural sector consisted of rather poor people struggling to earn a living, like most of the other oppressed ethnic groups.

Apart from the social differences the Indian community was also divided along other lines. Religion was one. In 1940 70% of the Indians were Hindus, 20% were Muslims and 10% were Christians. The Christian churches exploited children's homes and arranged for young Indians to study in Paramaribo. Thus they were able to gain some influence among the Indians. The difference between city and country was also reflected in the Indian community. Although the mass of Indians were as poor as, for example, the black Creoles, there were more rich Indians in the city than in the countryside. City Indians were also more in touch with public life. Often they had a more progressive attitude concerning traditions.

The difference between the sexes was decreased in one sense. While almost one-third of the Indians brought to Surinam were female, in 1939 their share in the Indian population increased to 47%. [17] But after indentureship more hardship fell on the Indian women. They were not only taking part in the production, but the household work was augumented by the absence of the system on the plantation whereby others could look after the younger ones.

Even in this phase the relation between Indians and Creoles was not specifically marked by ethnic problems. However, there were some tensions. Creole small peasants in Commewijne for example, complained about the Indian middlemen who paid too little and took too much. In the city poor black Creoles renting houses from rich Indians also complained about the high rents. On the other hand Indian small peasants selling their produce on the market to Creole wage-earners – especially in the depression-period of the twenties and thirties – were dissatisfied with the Creoles who did not want to pay enough for the Indian goods. Many poor Indians in and outside the city came across the light-coloured Creole administrator, teacher or civil servant, who acted as bureaucrat. Complaints about them could also be heard. Still, these instances took a subordinate place in the ethnic relations before World War II, as is again showed in periods of political upheaval. The main adversary of the Indian was the white man and his armed gangs.

After 1916 the Indians acquired some civil and political rights. Although they were foreigners in a legal sense – they had British nationality – they were formally eligible to all civil posts and had active and passive franchise. From 1927 on, all Indians born in Surinam got Dutch nationality. Thus at that time most Indians became Dutch. Between 1901 and 1936 there existed a parliament, whose members were chosen by 2% of the population, because only those who paid a certain amount of taxes and with a certain level of formal education were allowed to vote.[18] In 1930 the first Indian, a Catholic, C.R. Biswamitre, was elected to parliament. In 1936 the election system was changed. From then on five out of ten members were appointed by the governor. Two of those appointed were Indians.

While the (Creole) working class was beginning to organize itself into trade unions, the (Indian) petty bourgeoisie was organizing itself into different competing religious and cultural unions. Among the Hindus a majority formed the Sanathan Dharm, while a minority of about 20% formed the Arya Samaj. The Muslims also had different competing religious groups of which the Sunnis were the largest. In 1910 the first (conservative) cultural union was formed: the Surinaamsche Immigranten Vereeniging (Surinamese Immigrant Union). A year later the more progressive Surinaamse Brits-Indiers Bond (Union of Surinamese British Indians) was founded with a white woman, Mrs. Grace Schneiders-Howard, as a leading advisor.

But mass politics in those days was not a matter of unions, but of the unorganized mass. In 1910 the so-called Killinger-affair caused a stir in the colony. A group of coloured Surinamese around the (white) police-inspector Frans Killinger had planned a *coup d'état* that should have resulted in the ousting of the Dutch and the proclamation of a republic. An Indian, Jatan, was a member of this group. He was to mobilise the Indian workers at the plantation Marienburg for the night of the great attack. The group was betrayed, and the plan was aborted. At the public trial, mass gathering of thousands of Surinamese, including Indians, showed that Killinger's group enjoyed the esteem of many Surinamese, including Indians and Creoles.

In 1931 a mass uprising of unemployed Creole workers and tax-weary Indian peasants involved hundreds of Indians fighting a landowner and the police. When the uprising in Paramaribo was already bloodily surpressed, a hundred and fifty Indian peasants gathered to march to the city. But a strong police force dissuaded them from doing so.

The following year a Social-Democratic Workers Party under the leadership of the Creole Liesdek attracted a lot of Creole women and Indian peasants to its meetings. The party was dissolved due to repression by the police.

In 1933 another mass uprising occurred when a socialist of Creole origin, Anton de Kom, managed to bring Creoles, Javanese and Indians together in mass mobilizations. De Kom was arrested. The mass movement demanding his release was bloodily repressed. One of the two dead and six out of the twenty-two wounded were Indians.[19]

These examples show that in periods of political upheaval the main contradiction was between the colonial government and the oppressed workers and peasants, that is to say, in the period before the war. Profound changes were to take place in and after the war.

C. The Rise And Fall Of Ethnic Politics 1940-1980

Post-war Surinam is characterized by profound social, economic and political transformations. The old plantation economy collapsed. Although there are two distinctive periods in the economic development of the country, the post-war phase is clearly one of rapid capitalist economic development. The main features of this phase are:

a) a massive influx of foreign investment, to a large extent of Dutch and American capital. Dutch capital was mainly introduced in the form of development-aid which accumulated to Sf 380 million (Surinam guilders) for the period between 1947 – 1975 (by the way, the transfer of profits from Surinam was almost three times this amount in the same period). But American capital came out of the war as the hegemonic force in Surinam.

b) a rapid rise in the production of the commodities produced by the modern capitalist sector. For example, at the outbreak of the war Surinam produced 0.6 million tons of bauxite. In the seventies production-levels of above 6 million were reached. In 1940 padi-production was around 30 metric tons a year. In the seventies it fluctuated around 160 tons.

c) the rise of an infrastructure supporting this capitalist development. A network of banks was set up (central bank, commercial, saving and investment banks). The tax system was adjusted in a manner which facilitated the influx of foreign capital. The role of the state in the economic development of the country was strongly expanded.

d) the reorganization of production along lines compatible with international economic developments. Thus, the traditional plantation crop, sugar, was replaced by rice, while mining (bauxite) became paramount in the economy. This reorganization was accompanied by the introduction of modern technology (mechanization in agriculture).

The main features of the post-war social development are:

a) the rise of the working class. Modern agriculture, mining, the weak but growing industrial sector, the banking sector, the internal and external trade and the state, employ large groups of wage-earners.

b) the differentiation of the working class itself. A wage-earner is not necessarily a poor, almost starving, person. Within the class of wage-earners there is a substantial group of people forming a middle layer that is relatively well off. Most of them work in the highly modern mining and financial sectors.

c) the differentiation of the petty bourgeoisie. The rural petty bourgeoisie, the peasantry, is splitting up in three main groups. One group of peasants is forced to sell their land to their creditors (often middlemen). They form the rural proletariat. Some of them still have a piece of land while working as wage-earners. Another group is still trying to make a living on their land (in the peasantry this is still the largest group). Finally, a small group of rich peasants owning land and other (modern) means of production employ wage-earners. This group is strongly integrated into the rest of the modern capitalist sector.

d) the rise of a compradore bourgeoisie. The large influx of foreign capital created a group of entrepreneurs who live off the remuneration for the favours extended to foreign companies and people who act as their local representative. The local importers are the largest group, although there is also a group of people acting as local representatives of foreign industrial companies.

e) a class of local entrepreneurs who are not specifically representatives of foreign business, but have their own company, began to grow in the seventies.

The political development of Surinam after the war is characterized by:

a) the introduction of universal suffrage in 1948.

b) the rise of powerful social organisations of the new classes, especially the trade unions and the organization of employers.

c) the organization of political parties along ethnic lines, and the subsequent rule of these parties.

d) the growth towards formal independence (which began with internal autonomy shortly after the war ended) in the proclamation of the Republic of Surinam in 1975.

Within the post-war social, economic and political development we can distinguish a distinctive period with its own important features. From the mid-sixties the local industrial base of the economy was broadened through the expansion of the local market and the accumulation of private capital by small local entrepreneurs and some representatives of foreign capital. From the seventies, a national local bourgeoisie with its own base of accumulation independent of foreign capital emerged. Another feature of this period is the beginning of mass emigration, especially to Holland, where now one-third of the population lives. And last but not least, in this period the first political groups emerged which did not base themselves primarily on ethnic groups but on an anti-imperialist ideology, the first being the nationalist, followed by different socialist organisations.

What has been the position of the Indians in this period? The number of Indians grew from 46,000 in 1939 to 142,000 in 1971 of a total population of 385,000. Their relative share in the total population increased from 29% to 37%.[20] While in 1939 10% of the population of Paramaribo consisted of Indians, in 1964 this number was raised to 26% and further increased in the course of time.[21] Because of the fact that the statistical system no longer provides data on ethnic groups we can only give some rough indication of the position of the Indians in the economy. However, these scanty data do give an indication of the direction in which this position is evolving.

The economic position of the Indians is characterized by their dispersion over all sectors of the economy. According to an enquiry of 1964, 15% of the Indian men and 6% of the Indian women were employed as civil servants. Before the war there was scarcely an

Indian in the civil service. The same pattern can be discerned in all sectors where before the war no or only a few Indians were employed. In 1964 the mining sector employed 3% of the Indian men and 1% of the women. Manufacture employed 9% of the men and 4% of the women. Construction employed 6% of the men and no women. The trade and banking sector employed 30% of the men and 23% of the women. [22]

In 1964 there was still a large group of Indians working in agriculture, but the number of people working in agriculture was drastically reduced (by more than 50%) in 1980. And these people were going into the new economic sectors emerging after the war. Among the unemployed and those who have not been able to sell their labour-power and have to make a living out of hustling, there is a growing number of Indians. Many of them have migrated from rural areas to the towns and mingled with the hustlers. So the working class was by 1980 not exclusively Creole. However, this class is still marked by a predominance of Creoles. For example, in 1964 there were still three-times more Creoles than Indians in the mining sector and twice as many in the civil service. Although the predominance of Creoles is undeniable in certain sectors, the direction of the evolution of the position of the Indians in Surinam is a growing influx of Indians into economic sectors where traditionally no or only a few Indians were employed. The peasants in the districts of Nickerie, Saramacca and Surinam are still of Indian origin, while in other districts such as Caronie and Para these peasants belong to the Creole ethnic group. The rural proletariat is mainly Indian, although in Nickerie, bordering upon Guyana, the immigrating Guyanese workers that are employed in large-scale agriculture count among them also a few Creoles.

In the ruling classes an interesting development took place after the war. Before the war the importers and the planter class consisted of Whites, Lebanese and light-coloured Creoles. After the war the planter class disappeared and the compradore-bourgeoisie was expanded with people from other ethnic groups. The large group of importers consist now of Indians, Chinese, Lebanese and Creoles operating independently and in competition with each other. Within this class the Lebanese, Chinese, Whites and light-coloured Creoles played an important role, but in the course of time some Indians built up a strong position in this class as did some Creoles. As a consequence of this development the compradore bourgeoisie was not solely made up of one ethnic group.

As entrepreneurs from different ethnic groups accumulated capital there came a phase in which people of different ethnic groups put together their capital to invest in profitable sectors. So from the end of the sixties we see companies arising where the board of directors and owners include people from different ethnic groups. These enterprises are often located in construction, manufacturing and even in the trade sector. In agriculture a similar process is developing. Through political control of, or connections with the state, people of different ethnic groups managed to get hold of large pieces of land to be used for modern rice-production. For example, in 1976 a public scandal around the issuing of 42,000 acres of land, originally meant for small peasants revealed that this land came into the hands of fourteen big landowners. These landowners included persons of Indian, Javanese and Creole origin.[23]

The post-war evolution of the social and economic position of the Indians in Surinam can be summarized as follows. A more or less parallel structure of class and ethnic groups is being broken down. The ruling class is more and more made up of different ethnic groups. Up to the end of the sixties these different groups were also each others' competitors, but the parallel structure began to break down. Now the position of the Indian sector of the ruling class is more than ever characterized by a growing cooperation with economic partners of other ethnic groups. Among the working class and the petty bourgeoisie the parallel structure is also torn down. These processes are clearly expressed in the existence of multi-ethnic trade-unions and employers' organisations. None of these organisations are based upon one ethnic group.

In politics a paradoxical situation was created after the war. While in the social and economic field the ethnic barriers were broken down, in politics the ethnic factor played an increasingly important role. The first political parties were organized along ethnic lines. In May 1946 the first political party was formed by Indian Muslims: The Moeslim Partij Suriname (Muslim Party of Surinam). Since then scores of parties have been formed along ethnic lines. The parties based upon Creole voters seldom carried in their name a reference to the ethnic group. The largest and oldest of these parties is called the Nationale Partij Suriname (National Party of Surinam). The various 'Creole' parties differed not in programme but in electoral base. The differences might be of a religious (Catholic or Protestant) or social nature (light-coloured middle-class or dark-coloured working class). And of course, there were differences in leadership rather than in programme or electoral base. Most 'Indian' and 'Javanese' parties carried in their name references to the ethnic group to which they appealed. The largest and long-standing 'Indian' party, the VHP changed its name several times, although the abbreviation stood for Vatan Hitkari Partij, a Hindi-name meaning 'Party to Promote National Welfare'. Of course, Hindi is not understood by Creoles. Later on the name was changed into Verenigde Hindostaanse Partij (United Indian party) and in the seventies the reference to the Indian community was removed. The abbreviation now stands for Verenigde Hervormingspartij (United Reformation Party).

In political debates, and especially during elections, it seems as if the actual policies of these parties are based upon the interest of an ethnic group as a whole. They appeal to the cohesion of the respective ethnic group. But as one student of ethnic politics noticed during a field-work study in Surinam: 'I have interviewed political leaders, members of parliament and ministers, to get behind the importance of ethnicity as a mean for mobilization...It appeared otherwise that there was a discrepancy between utterances of these leaders in front of me and their public statements. While talking to me they were very tolerant and well-balanced; during political campaigns they held impassioned, somewhat racist speeches in regard to other ethnic groups'.[24]

How can we account for this seemingly contradictory situation in which in the social and economic field the ethnic barriers are broken down, while in politics they are erected, and then in such a way that in the actual policy it is secondary to the use in the propaganda of the parties? The explanation can be found in a combination of factors. The first factor is the nature of the compradore-bourgeoisie. A compradore does not have an independent base of accumulation, because he does not own an enterprise. He is more a representative – sometimes formally and sometimes materially (as is the case with importers) – of a foreign company. So for his living he depends on the favours he can arrange for his boss. Thus the competition between the compradors is not based on profitable production or selling of commodities but on the extent to which they are able to provide the favours needed by foreign companies. Second, the strong position of the state in the economic development of the country (through development-aid and through the incentives it gives to attracting foreign capital) makes it an essential element in providing favours for foreign enterprises. Third, the control over the state after the war was regulated through the mechanism of a parliament elected by universal suffrage. The party that controls the majority of parliament controls the state. So the material position of the compradore was conditioned by the extent to which it could manipulate the elections, thus the parliament, and thus the state. Fourth, in the process of breaking up the parallel structure of class and ethnicity there arises a contradiction between what is called in dialectics the general and the particular. The struggle itself between the general and the particular contributed to the rise of ethnic politics in Surinam. This needs some explanation.

The first Indians moving to the city consisted of a group of poor landless peasants and a group of well-to-do persons who exploited houses in which poor black Creoles were living. In a general sense this was one of the first steps in the breakdown of the parallel structure. In a particular sense, the black Creole was now confronted with an Indian who exploited him through high rents. The Indian workers on the other hand were confronted with light-coloured or sometimes even black Creoles as rulers in the lower echelons of the civil service and the non-agricultural companies. And these were the first barriers to overcome in the process of spreading out in all sectors and layers of the society. The general process of integrating into all sectors of the society was achieved through a struggle that conditioned the consciousness of the different social layers. So in the working class the black Creole worker saw the emerging rich Indian charging him high rents, without seeing directly the influx of Indians into the same social position as he or she occupies. On the other hand the landless Indian moving into other economic sectors has to fight the light-coloured Creole boss to obtain a decent living. And through the transmission of capitalist competition into the working class black Creoles and Indians found themselves competing for jobs, housing and other facilities. In the upper classes an almost similar process was developing. The economic base for the white planter class was falling apart, and the direct rule of the Whites fell with it. The Indians who moved up into the upper class had to compete with the light-coloured Creoles, the Chinese and Lebanese, but also with the group of well-to-do black Creoles which was also moving up. The difference between the black and light-coloured Creole was only one of the shade of colour. From the Indian point of view they formed a more or less homogeneous group. In the normal (capitalist) competition between the compradors, the Creole compradore would try to prevent the Indian from moving up, while the Indian compradore would have to consolidate his position at every step. This process is clearly reflected in the political propaganda of the parties basing themselves on the different ethnic electorates. The 'Indian' parties emphasize in their propaganda the aggressiveness of the Blacks who do not grant the Indians a better economic position. The 'Creole' parties on the other hand stress the danger of an exploitative domination of the Indians. Thus both parties bring their electorate together on the basis of the specific interests of the compradore and the tensions arising in the lower class as a result of the breaking up of the parallel structure of class and ethnicity. Lastly, the nature of the racist ideology after the abolition of slavery plays a specific role after the downfall of the white planter class. During slavery racist ideology postulated the premise that a black man or woman was not a human being, but a non-human totally different from the 'normal', that is white, human being. So a black person should not behave as if he or she were a human. Wearing shoes or learning to speak the master's language was forbidden for the Blacks. This ideology corresponded with a system of exploitation based mainly on physical repression of the labourer. After slavery racist ideology changed. The black man or woman was indeed a human being, but an inferior one. He should be a 'normal' human being, and the way to achieve that was to be like the white man. A colour-scale was introduced according to which black was bad and white was good, and the lighter the colour, the better the person. Blacks were to straighten their hair and to learn the Dutch language. And this ideology corresponded with a system of exploitation based on market relations and ideological attachment of the Blacks to the Whites.

Now, after the white colonialists left Surinam to operate behind the curtains, the colour-scale played a role in ethnic politics. In the colour-scale the brown Indians took an intermediate position, and thus according to the ruling ideology he was considered to be better than the black Creole. The Indian compradors promoted the colonial view according to which Indian culture was more close to the 'normal' white culture. On the other hand, black Creole compradors made use of the anti-colonialist feelings to gain political positions upon the light-coloured Creole compradors and the Indians. According to this propaganda the Whites and the Indians masses were traitors of the country. The combination of a compradore-bourgeoisie state that is operating politically through a parliament elected by universal suffrage, a state with a strong intervention in the economy, the uneven breaking-up of the parallel structure of class and ethnicity and the role of racism in a society like Surinam, account for the rise of ethnic politics.

This explanation is reinforced by the periods preceding and following the rise of the ethnic bourgeoisie. As explained above, during political upheavals before the war Indians and Creoles fought together, not with each other. In fact, shortly after the war the Indians who were to become leaders in ethnic politics were behaving in strikingly non-ethnic ways. One of these leaders (of the Sanathan Dharm, a pillar of the VHP) was an active member of the nationalist movement at the end of the forties and the beginning of the fifties. Even during the rise of ethnic politics the leaders of the different ethnic parties could go along with each other after the elections, if not in a government-coalition then certainly in business. Even on a personal level, warm and cordial relations were maintained.

In 1980 it became clear that the rule of the compradore bourgeoisie was coming to an end. On the 25th of February non-commissioned officers perpetrated a *coup d'état*. This was political turbulence of the highest order. Still it did not produce ethnic tensions in the first place. Political differences were not expressed with references to ethnic interests, but with references to national or social interests. The old, political parties mobilized against the new forces on the basis of fear for communism. And the new rulers, people from different ethnic origins, justified their actions with social instead of ethnic arguments. Of course there were still ethnic arguments being used in informal discussions, but the main political contradictions were expressed in social instead of ethnic relations, contrary to two decades ago. This itself is the result of two factors.

As we have explained elsewhere, the driving social force behind the *coup* was the rising national bourgeoisie, a group of entrepreneurs that differs from the old compradore bourgeoisie. They have their own base of accumulation. They own enterprises producing commodities. They might find themselves in competition with foreign companies producing similar or substituting commodities. Many of these enterprises are multi-ethnic. Capitalists of different ethnic origin have pooled together their capital to put up an enterprise. So this class does not have a material base for promoting ethnic tensions, contrary to the compradore bourgeoisie.[25]

Furthermore at the end of the seventies the breaking up of the parallel structure of class and ethnicity had reached a point where the general was expressed in the particular. In other words, the different ethnic groups were dispersed over most social and economic sectors to such an extent that the social-economic relations were being expressed in politics without the intermediary of the ethnic conscious-ness. Thus, the nationalist movement was becoming very strong, up to the point of getting the leadership of two important trade union federations and ministers in the government. At the same time the left-wing socialist parties began to grow, while the employers' federation was openly intervening in politics with declarations on the political situation in the country. Bourgeois political parties with different ethnic electorates went into elections (1973, 1977 and preparing for 1980) as a political combination fighting rising communism. Since 1980 this pattern of politics in Surinam has been maintained.

History once again showed that the material base – though also through non-material factors – determine the evolution of ideological and political forces.

NOTES

1. See S. Hira (1982), pp. 75-82 on the nineteenth century debate in Holland concerning the abolition of slavery.

2. Calculated from J.E. Ismael (1949), table I; E.F. Verkade-Cartier van Dissel (1937), table XXIX and XXX and E. Snellen (1933), appendix.

3. The term coolie has often been used in a derogatory sense, even among the Indians. Nowadays young Indians proudly use this term to indicate their identification with the 'wretched of the earth'. They would rather be identified with the coolie who with blood, sweat and tears built the country than with those Whites and Indians who on the back of the coolie managed to rise to the status of exploiter.

4. The Colonial Reports give ample statistics on this matter. For example, in 1884, the year of the sugar crisis in Surinam all wages went down, but still the downward pressure of the indentured system could be felt. On plantations where contract labour existed besides free labour the (free) Creole man earned 90 cents a day and the women 61 cents. On plantations with only free labour the Creole man earned 92 and the women 64 cents. The free immigrant worker on the first plantation earned 93 and 71 cents, while on the latter plantations they got 97 and 91 cents (men and women respectively). The contract labourers got 71 and 61 cents on average.

5. Radjen Bhagwan Bali has done some excellent research on the social, economic and political position of the Indians in the period 1883-1902. His results will soon be published in his dissertation entitled 'Some causes of the subordination of the British-Indian immigrants in Surinam, 1873-1902'. According to Bhagwan Bali famine among the Indians occurred from time to time.

6. Calculated from the relevant Colonial Reports.

7. Cited in R. Bhagwan Bali, manuscript.

8. For examples see R. Bhagwan Bali, ms.ch.III and S. Hira (1982), ch. IV.2

9. Elout van Soeterwoude (1884), pp. 48-49.

10. A historical overview and analysis of the struggle of the Indians against colonialism can be found in R. Bhagwan Bali (manuscript) and S. Hira (1982), Chapter IV.2

11. NOP (1965), p. 16, table 18.

12. J.D. Speckmann (1965), p. 41

13. Calculated from ABS (nd), p.4

14. Calculated from Eswin (1956), p.7

15. See S. Beck (1924), pp. 20-23 and H. Luning and P. Sital (1979), p. 209

16. G.A.de Bruijne (1976), p. 51

17. Calculated from Eswin (1956), p. 7

18. J.A.E. Buiskool (1946), 154. Between 1902 and 1940 the highest number of potential voters was 1972 (in 1939). The highest percentage of valid votes was 72% (in 1938).

19. See S. Hira (1982). ch. IV.4 for the Killinger-affair and ch. V for the revolts of the thirties. The date on the Social-Democratic Workers Party we have collected from some files of the intelligence service. It will be published in a separate publication being prepared on the early history of the socialist movement in Surinam.

20. Encyclopedie (1977), p. 279 and Eswin (1956), p. 7.

21. G.A. de Bruijne (1976), p. 91 and 197.

22. *Idem*, p. 62.

23. De Vrije Stem from 23 October 1976.

24. F. Derveld (1982), p. 24.

25. Our analysis of the background and development of the *coup d'état* in Surinam is published in S. Hira (1983a). An extract in English appeared in S. Hira (1983b).

BIBLIOGRAPHY

1. Beck, S. (1924): *Lezingen over Surinaamsche problemen. Paramaribo.*

2. Bhagwan Bali, R. (1984): *Enkele oorzaken van de subordinatie der Brits-Indische immigranten in Suriname, 1873-1902. Manuscript.*

3. Bruijne, G.A. de (1976): *Paramaribo. Stadsgeografische studies van een ontwikkelingsland. Romen/Bussum.*

4. Buiskool, J.A.E. (1946): *Suriname nu en straks, een sociaal-economische en staatkundige beschouwing. Amsterdam.*

5. Derveld, F. (1982): *Politieke mobilisatie en integratie van de Javanen in Suriname. Gronigen.*

6. Elout van Soeterwoude, W (1884): *Onze West. Den haag*

7. Encyclopedie (1977): *– van Suriname. Amsterdam/Brussel.*

8. Eswin (1956): *Suriname. Enige statisieken over de jaren 1931 to en met 1952. 's-Gravenhage.*

9. Hira, S. (1982): *Van Priary tot en met De Kom. De geschiedenis van het verzet in Suriname, 1630 - 1940. Rotterdam.*

10. Hira, S. (1983a): *Balans van een coup. Drie jaar 'Surinaamse revolutie'. Rotterdam.*

11. Hira, S. (1983b): 'Class formation and class struggle in Surinam: the background and development of the coup d'etat', in: F. Ambursley and R. Cohen: *Crisis in the Caribbean. Kingston/Port of Spain/London, pp. 166-190.*

12. Ismael, J.E. (1949): *De imigratie van Indonesiers in Suriname. Leiden.*

13. Luning, H. and P. Sital (1979): 'The economic transformation of small holder rice farming in Surinam,' in: M. Cross and A. Marks: *Peasants, plantations and rural communities in the Caribbean. Leiden, pp. 193-219.*

14. NOP (1965): *Nationaal Ontwikkelingsplan Suriname, deel 1. Paramaribo.*

15. Reports: *Colonial – Several years.*

16. Snellen, E. (1933): *De aanvoer van arbeiders voor den landbouw in Suriname. Wageningen.*

17. Speckmann, J.D. (1965): *Marriage and kinship among the Indians in Surinam. Assen.*

18. Verkade-Cartier van Dissel, E.F. (1937): *De mogelijkheid van landbouwkolonisatie voor blanken in Suriname. Amsterdam.*

The Sex-Ratio Disparity And Its Consequences Under The Indenture In British Guiana

Basdeo Mangru

Many immigrant societies seem to experience initially a shortage of women. It was clearly evident among the immigrant workforce introduced into British Guiana (Guyana) from a variety of sources to fill the vacuum created by the gradual withdrawal of the emancipated labourers from plantation agriculture. Given the restraints on family emigration imposed by caste, custom, the protective joint-family system and the socio-cultural pull of the Indian village, it was hardly surprising that Indian women emigrants were so scarce. Nor was emigration overseas a spontaneous movement since it was dictated largely by socio-economic conditions and the demands of the different seasons. But the shortage of Indian women remained a feature in most recipient colonies throughout indenture and it was prolonged for spurious reasons and with disastrous consequences in the immigrant camp. The two published works on the Indian diaspora in British Guiana, which were largely pioneering studies, (D. Nath, *A History of Indians in British Guiana* and P Ruhoman, *Centenary History of the East Indians in British Guiana 1838-1938*) refer to this disquieting aspect of indenture but an in-depth examination is yet to emerge. This essay attempts to fill a definite gap in the literature in its analysis of the various reasons for the shortage of Indian women and its impact on the indentured immigrant community in British Guiana.

Procuring the prescribed proportion of Indian women for the sugar colonies was a perennial problem to the colonial Emigration Agents at Calcutta and Madras. As emigration progressed specific quotas were fixed. In 1857 the ratio was 35 women to 100 men, rising progressively to the high level of 50 to 100 in 1860. Simultaneously a Convention between France and England relating to the export of Indian labour to the French colonies reduced the proportion to 25 to 100 because of 'this comparitively new emigration' and the likelihood that a larger quota would be difficult to obtain. Protests from the British colonies against what seemed an unfair advantage forced the Indian authorities to grant similar concessions.[1]

In 1868, following consultation between the Colonial Office and
the India Office, the proportion was once again raised to the original
1860 level apparently to redress the sex imbalance in the importing
colonies and alleviate its concomitant evils. The requirement produced sharp criticisms from a variety of sources which believed it was
prohibitive and would necessitate the enlistment of a 'low and
immoral' class of women detrimental to any scheme of settlement and
colonization. One of the critics, Sir Clinton Murdoch, Chairman of
the Colonial Land and Emigration Commission which supervised the
movement of population overseas, argued that a proportion of 40 to
100 could be obtained without drafting women of 'degraded habits'.[2]
By fixing a realistic quota, he contended, the problem of detaining
men for prolonged periods and at considerable expense because the
stipulated number of women could not be procured would be
minimized. Couples forming 'temporary attachments' during their
sojourn at the depot would not be forcibly separated nor women
arbitrarily removed from one batch to augment another. Murdoch's
suggestion was implemented and it remained unchanged until the
demise of indenture in 1917. As a concession against unforeseen
recruiting difficulties colonial agents were permitted occasionally to
despatch a reduced quota provided the deficiency was counter-
balanced at the close of the emigration season or at the beginning of
the next.[3]

Several factors accounted for the difficulty in recruiting women in
sufficient numbers. Not only were there few families disposed to
leave their *janmabhumi* (motherland) and sever traditional family
ties but there were few unattached women because of the Indian
custom of child betrothal and marriage at puberty. In Bengal in the
1880s, for example, over 93% of the general Hindu population were
listed as married before reaching the age of 14 while among the
higher castes every Hindu girl was 'practically a wife or a widow'
before attaining that age[4], for Indian parents seemed to believe that
by contracting such early marriages they would be blessed by the
Gods. Respectable women of both high and low castes seemed
reluctant to emigrate unless accompanied by their husbands or close
relatives. Indian men, too, seemed averse to expose their wives and
daughters to unknown lands.[5] They seemed to detest a system which
subjected their wives to a prolonged depot detention and to a
searching medical examination for venereal diseases. Consequently
Indians were generally recruited individually often in search of
industrial employment and without the knowledge of their wives or

parents.

Indian women who regularly boarded emigrant vessels comprised principally 'young widow and married and single women who have already gone astray, and are therefore not only most anxious to avoid their homes and conceal their antecedents, but were also at the same time the least likely to be received back into their families'.[6] Prostitutes from Calcutta and other large Indian cities were shipped largely to augment the numerical shortage and minimize demurrage. During famines which occurred with increasing frequency in the latter half of the nineteenth century women of higher social status, emaciated from hunger, often opted to emigrate with their families rather than face starvation. Low caste families emigrated freely during these periods of economic distress but usually it was among those reemigrating, or induced to leave, that families predominated.[7]

The perennial shortage of Indian women on the estates produced considerable tension and provided the key to an understanding of the problems Indian immigrants faced in establishing a stable family life. The Guianese authorities exacerbated the problem by consistently refusing throughout indenture to grant both Hindus and Muslims the same marriage rights as Christians. Under the Heathen Marriage Ordinance 10 of 1860, before a marriage was contracted the parties were required to sign a declaration that no impediment existed against the proposed union either by previous or existing marriage, consanguinity or parental dissent. If no objections were raised the district Magistrate gave each a certificate to produce to the Immigration Agent-General in Georgetown who validated the marriage and issued a marriage registration certificate at a fee of two dollars.[8] The Consolidated Ordinance XXV of 1891 made provisions for the marriage of East Indians by a Stipendiary Magistrate, Christian Minister, Hindu Priest or Muslim Moulvi thereby rendering it unnecessary for the contracting parties to travel to Georgetown. Where the marriage was to be solemnised by an Indian priest the Immigration Department would forward the 'no impediment' certificate, signed by the Immigration Agent-General, to the district Immigration Agent who would summon the parties before him. The priest was merely required to sign and witness the date of marriage. Within seven days the certificate had to be delivered to the Immigration Agent-General under heavy penalty. When all such technicalities were fulfilled the marriage was registered and a certificate issued.[9]

Such formalism and officialism the Indians considered contrary to their religious rites. The 'no objection' certificate and other needless obstacles tended in their view to deter registration and promote the contracting of invalid marriages. Largely illiterate and custom-ridden, Indians regarded a marriage celebrated with due publicity and performed according to established rights and customs legal whether registered or not. Charles Freer Andrews who visited the Caribbean in 1929 pointed out that for generations Indian villagers had accepted the customary form of marriage without registration and emphasized that 'the very publicity of Hindu marriage is equivalent to a kind of registration'.[10] Consequently the immigrants' customary marriages were considered invalid as only a few were registered. Between 1860 and 1871 an average of 12 were registered annually under the 1860 ordinance and 7 between 1904 and 1914, which meant that the majority of Indian children were registered as born out of wedlock and therefore illegitimate. As such they experienced considerable difficulties over succession to intestate properties. Several marriages went unregistered because one or both of the contracting parties were below the prescribed legal age limit, 13 years for girls and 15 for boys. Before 1891 the high registration fees and the inconvenience and expense incurred in travelling to Georgetown proved an additional deterrent.[11] Many Indians who already had wives in India seemed to regard the registration of marriage 'as of no importance whatsoever'.[12]

The refusal to recognise the validity of Indian marriages solemnised in accordance with custom and religion tended to weaken the marriage ties and facilitate the desertion of unfaithful wives to form new matrimonial connections. In a letter to the *Argosy* entitled 'An East Indian Grievance', S. Mohamed Baksh articulated the general disquiet of the Indian community over the apparent inadequacy of the law.

When a wife deserts a husband or a husband a wife we are helpless at law. If a man or woman go to the police or the magistrate or the Immigration Department the first question asked is: 'Were you married by English law?' and if the reply is in the negative the applicant is told, 'We can do nothing for you'. The faithless one is thus at liberty to do what she likes in the violation of the religious marriage vows, and the aggrieved one, if he be a poor, ignorant East Indian labourer, then sets thinking how he can achieve his own revenge with results which the criminal annals of the colony show. I know many of the atrocities for which East Indians are convicted, sent to prison and hanged would be prevented were the law but to recognise the validity of marriages according to the law and custom of East Indians.[13]

Fifty years were to pass before the Guianese authorities provided legislative remedy to this widespread Indian grievance.[14]

The tendency of European overseers, and even estate managers, to form temporary connections with Indian women not only aggravated the shortage but produced considerable tension in the immigrant camp. Such immoral relations were undoubtedly fostered by the estate organizational system which kept young, single overseers 'in a state of enforced celibacy', circumscribed their movements even during leisure and placed them in regular contact with an Indian indentured population of 37,066 in June 1869, of whom one-third were women, scattered over the sugar belt. One could hardly fail to visualize the problems inherent in a situation where Indian women by their mode of dress seemed to reveal to estate subordinates 'more physical charm' than what they had been accustomed to in Britain.[15] Such liaison, apart from constituting a serious breach of estate discipline, tended to produce conflict and undermine the employer-employee relationships. The Royal Commission which instituted a minute inquiry into all aspects of indenture observed: 'The withdrawal of even a single woman from the Coolie dwellings to the Overseers' lodge is regarded with jealous eyes by her fellow countrymen; and when it is remembered than any female above childhood is already the actual wife or partner of one of them, it is evident that no surer way could be found of sowing the seeds of discontent and riot'.[16]

Although such 'reprehensive' conduct was frowned upon by the authorities, the intimate relations between overseers and Indian women were 'not uncommon'.[17] The Royal Commission reported several cases of such cohabitation while touring the sugar estates. They found at Plantation Friendship and Sarah in Essequibo[18] an Indian woman 'of unmistakable appearance' occupying rooms in the overseers' quarters. At Plantation Bath, West Coast Berbice, the Deputy Manager was 'keeping' an Indian woman whose husband had returned to India, while at Plantation Anna Regina, Essequibo, the manager was cohabiting with the wife of an indentured worker.[19] The illicit sexual relations between Gerad Van Nooten, Deputy Manager of Plantation Non Pareil, West Coast Demerara, and an Indian woman Jamni, seemed the principal cause of the riots there in 1897 when 5 Indians were killed, including the woman's husband Jungli, and 59 seriously wounded. Although Van Nooten admitted the liaison both W.P. Ebbels and H. Garnett, Manager and Attorney respectively of the estate, not only refused to discipline him but endeavoured to condone his action.[20]

In such a predominantly male immigration the sex disparity could have been alleviated through inter-racial marriages but there seemed little evidence of such unions under indenture. Even today the percentage of mixed marriages in Guyana is comparatively small. Observing the 'Gladstone Coolies' not long after their introduction in 1838 Governor Henry Light, whose administration spanned the eventful years 1838-1848, seemed sanguine about East Indian-Creole relations: 'The magnificent features of the men, their well shaped though slender limbs, promise well for the mixture of the Negress with the Indian'.[21] A decade later Dr George Banyon mentioned a few children at Plantation Lochaber, Berbice, who were offsprings of such unions but it was the rare exception rather than the rule as the evidence clearly demonstrates.

Governor John Scott observed in 1871 that although Indian-Creole relationships seemed cordial there was 'no general social intercourse between them, such as would tend to bring about more intimate relations'.[22] The *Creole,* organ of the black population, found Indian immigrants 'intensely clannish, they keep to themselves, and mix with no other race'.[23] In James Crosby's somewhat exaggerated view 'the Indian immigrants never, and the Chinese but seldom intermarry with any other race than their own'.[24] Governor James Longden noted the 'repugnance or at least indifference' which Indian men had shown to Creole women.[25] Attorney General W.F. Haynes Smith, too, referred to this social distancing but also cited cases of Indian women cohabiting with the Chinese, Portuguese and Englishmen.[26] In 1897 J.E. Tinne, who had extensive mercantile and planting interests in British Guiana, underlined the lack of social intercourse between the Indians and the Creoles in terms of strikes or disturbances on estates: 'They are totally different people, they do not intermix'.[27]

The virtual absence of any visible form of social contact could be explained largely in terms of religion. Although caste distinction and religious prejudices were weakened somewhat, the continuous influx of batches of immigrants with their language and traditions tended to strengthen Hinduism as well as Islam. The new arrivals provided the link between village India and estate residents and acted as a stimulus to their flagging religio-cultural awareness. Indians were thus reluctant to risk social chastisement from fellow immigrants by marrying women of another race. Moreover, the majority regarded themselves as exiles and were not disinclined to claim a return passage, hoping to be readmitted into caste by performing certain expiatory rites. Marrying a woman of a different race, or for that matter a low caste Indian woman, and taking her to his village was unthinkable as it would most likely involve the severing of family ties and connections and certainly caste expulsion.

The disproportion of the sexes, non-recognition of customary marriages, erosion of traditional restraints and marriage customs, produced serious social problems in the indentured community in several of the recipient colonies. These promoted unsettled habits, lowered the standard of morality, produced unhealthy competition, made seduction more likely and fostered a feeling of jealousy which made the immigrants oblivious of the consequences of their actions. More importantly, they produced an alarming incidence of wife murders which plagued the indenture system until its demise and prompted intense criticisms in India. The official statistics showed 23 murders of Indian women by their husbands or reputed husbands in the period 1859-1864, 11 between 1865-1870, 36 between 1884-1895[28] and 17 between 1901-1907. There were also 35 cases of cutting and wounding of Indian wives with the hoe and cutlass between 1886-1890. The Reverend Robert Duff of the Church of Scotland drew attention not only to the frequency of such outrages but to the fact that they were 'accompanied with such circumstances of cruel barbarity as to make the blood run cold at the bare recital of them'.[29]

Despite periodic attempts to whitewash the problem, the evidence demonstrates forcefully that nearly all the serious crimes among the indentured population were directly traceable to the sex-imbalance. Crosby, the indomitable Immigration Agent-General, was convinced that the shortage of women was 'the great exciting cause of the lamentable quarrels and wife murders' among Indians despite various preventative measures.[30] Governor Scott considered it one of the primary causes for the criminal outrages on Indian women for it provided the 'main root of the loose domestic relations' among the Indian population and accorded the women 'a value and influence' which they would not otherwise possess.[31] Governor Longden echoed similar views.

Others sought to explain the prevalence of the crime purely in terms of the 'degraded class of women' imported and the contempt in which they were held, the revengeful spirits and 'ungovernable passions' of

Indians, the loss of jewellery and wounded self-esteem on being deserted by unfaithful wives. When a desertion occurred the wife, not the seducer, was seen as the offender and had to pay the extreme penalty 'not for the act itself, but for its manner'.[32] Clearly these factors were contributory not fundamental ones. Although a proportion of Indian women were referred to as 'not of a reputable class' both Scott and Longden doubted whether contempt *per se* was the motivating factor.[33]

Perhaps to provide some justification for the crime, which constituted a grave blot on indenture, or appease overseas criticism, Scott and others claimed that uxoricides were likewise prevalent in India, a claim which Lord Kimberley, Colonial Secretary, regarded with serious doubt.[34] Indeed, a superficial analysis of the statistics on wife murders in the three Presidencies and principal provinces of British India might seem to confirm Scott's contention. In the 1866-1870 period the Indian Government returns showed that wife murders comprised .0007% of the total population, and jealousy, neglect of children or household duties, returning to parents without consent, quarrels about food preparation and serving meals seemed to be the motivating factors.[35] This percentage did not differ very significantly from the Guianese statistics which showed that wife murders comprised .0710% of the Indian population between 1859-1864 and .0209% during 1865-1870.[36] What must be emphasized is that the Indian Government figures embraced women of all classes in the society whereas the Guianese were based largely on the lower agricultural and labouring classes which comprised the overwhelming majority of colonial recruits. In fact there was no separate classification of wife murders in India which could be traced in the criminal statistics at the India Office. Murdoch provided an apt explanation:

> *I do not think it possible to institute any comparison between the prevalence of wife-murder in Indian and in the Westindia Colonies, –first, because our information from the Westindies is incomplete; and secondly, and chiefly, because the Indian statistics cannot show proportion of wife-murders committed in the class which corresponds with the Indian emigrants to the Westindies. In the Indian population...is included not only a much larger proportion of women and children than in the emigrant population, but also the whole of the more respectable classes of every description. To initiate a comparison between the crimes especially of violence committed by such population, and the similar crimes committed by a population exclusively of the*

lowest class, is entirely delusive.[37]

A minority opinion even contested the overwhelming evidence that the crime had originated from the paucity of women. Both Immigration Agent-General A.H. Alexander and Emigration Agent R.W.S. Mitchell claimed that the scarcity of women had 'comparitively little' to do with the crime. In the former's view 'whether women are many or few, the men will always bear animosity to the particular women on whom they have spent their money'.[38] He apparently ignored the fact that it was the serious sex-imbalance which facilitated seduction and encouraged desertion with the jewels with which the husbands had bedecked their wives and which made minor orchestration 'with each gentle movement of the wearers'.[39] Additionally both tended to equate the barbarity of some of the crimes with those in India where, they alleged, 'the aggressors show a refinement of cruelty' unknown in British Guiana. They cited reports in the Indian press which showed husbands torturing their wives with hot iron tongs, pulling out their teeth and caning them mercilessly. In Bombay 'biting off a wife's nose continues to be a favourite amusement.'[40] But while there seemed little evidence of such forms of torture on the Guianese sugar estates the hacking of unfaithful wives to pieces with the hoe, shovel or cutlass was not uncommon.

The number of wife murders, albeit small percentage-wise, produced considerable alarm both locally and abroad. That the problem demanded urgent remedial action was beyond dispute especially as it could provoke questioning of the entire immigration system. The measures devised to counter the problem were initially preventative and subsequently curative.

In December 1863 the colonial authorities issued an official proclamation admonishing immigrants in unambiguous terms that the perpetrators of such acts would be liable to the maximum penalty of death by hanging and that it was a misconception that violent crimes could be justified by 'previous provocation'.[41] Apparently many immigrants were under the erroneous impression that a plea on the grounds of provocation 'will either excuse or at least palliate any crime'. As such the capital punishment would tend not only to lose its impact but appear 'capricious and cruel'.[42] As the outrages continued more positive measures were instituted. A circular despatch in March 1865 from the Colonial Office to estate proprietors, attorneys and managers emphasized the importance of proper estate management and supervision which, it claimed, constituted 'the most effective means' of combating the crime. The despatch threatened in thinly veiled terms to withhold further allotment of immigrants in cases where employers failed to exercise effective vigilance over their work force.[43] A subsequent circular instructed estate managers to notify the district Stipendiary Magistrate promptly when a wife deserted her husband for another man. The officer was correspondingly empowered to remove either the husband or the wife to a distant plantation, particularly when threats to murder or maim were reported, subject to the Governor's approval.[44]

The response from estate managers initially disappointed the colonial authorities. While some displayed 'a laudable desire' to conform to official directives many seemed reluctant 'to trouble themselves with the domestic squabbles of their Coolie labourers'. They were apparently more concerned with manipulating labour and maximizing profits. It was alleged that the murder of Baumee who deserted her husband Maudhut could have been avoided had the proprietor taken prompt action to separate the young couple.[45] Governor Francis Hincks, a planter sympathiser, denounced their 'continued remiss', warning that any defect in the system could be exploited by its opponents abroad.[46] He reiterated the necessity for stricter estate vigilance to detect the termination of marital connections and for swift action to separate the parties, and threatened to impose a substantial fine on managers in all cases of wife murders in which their actions were not exonerated. Scott, Hincks' successor, expressed optimism that managers would eventually realise that their interests demanded that the crime 'be assiduously suppressed'. Indeed, in the period 1864-1868, the crime rate fell by over 50% despite the fact that there was a significant increase in immigration and 7 of the 11 murders committed occurred in 1864 alone.[47]

The execution of three Indians for murder a few years later produced fresh criticisms from Lord Granville, Colonial Secretary, who questioned the effectiveness and adequacy of the supervision and vigilance expected of managers. He instructed Scott to appraise estate proprietors or attorneys whenever the manager 'appears chargeable' with serious neglect.[48] But immigration authorities were equally culpable as evidenced in the case of Tenegree, an indentured worker of Plantation Helena, East Coast Demerara, whose wife Anundai deserted him for a 'pleasanter life' with another man on the same estate. It would seem that Tenegree reported the desertion to the district Immigration Agent expecting either his wife or the seducer to be removed but apparently no effective action was taken. Anundai's murder was the inevitable result. The press denounced the 'unaccountable neglect' by both government and estate authorities and mounted a vigorous campaign for clemency which resulted in the commutation of the death penalty to life imprisonment.[49]

The Royal Commission which attributed the crime to the 'constitutional jealousy of Orientals exaggerated....by the great inequalities of the sexes' expressed little faith in transfers, the principal preventative device adopted at the time, as a panacea for the disputes and quarrels of Indians. They advocated measures which they believed would strike at the very root of the evil – flogging as a punishment for men and for women, the 'disgrace' of having their heads completely shaved.[50] Scott had echoed this view a year earlier when he underlined the inefficacy of capital punishment as a deterrent on Indians as against men of other nationalities. J.F. Trotter, Acting Immigration Agent-General, expressed succinctly and cogently the need for an alternative to capital punishment:

> *The Coolie looks with stoical calmness at the prospect of death on the Gallows, and apparently goes to his doom with indifference, looking upon his death in that form as a matter of fate; he has, however, the most acute fear of the cat-of-nine-tails, and it is probable that were this the punishment inflicted the fear of the ultimate consequences to himself would, in nine cases out of ten, prevent him from committing the awful crime of murder, of which he so often stands accused, and for which he so frequently suffers the extreme penalty of the law.*[51]

Trotter advocated a combination of life imprisonment and whipping – thirty three lashes on a fixed day annually for five years after commencement of imprisonment on the plantation where the crime was committed.

The use of the whip as a deterrent received additional support from Chief Justice Chalmers while passing the death sentence on Goja for the murder of his wife Saukalia. His remarks from the bench constituted a grave indictment of indenture: 'the cases of murderous revenge by Coolies upon their women are so frequent as to justify allegation that there is here a serious blot on the system of Coolie Immigration and labour'. He continued: 'the cases which result in convictions for murder do not represent the whole of the evil; for some are of such a nature as to afford room for the verdict of manslaughter, and others, although a comparatively smaller number, result in severe wounds and maiming but fall short of being fatal'.[52] Chalmers recommended flogging where the capital punishment was not effected and in all cases of manslaughter as he also believed Indians regarded the death penalty 'with perfect apathy'. For serious wounding flogging should be administered publicly at the scene of the crime and repeated at stipulated intervals. Such forms of punishment, he argued, would subject the perpetrator to 'a new disgrace' as Indians seemed to fear the whip 'on account of the indignity as well as the pain'.[53]

These various suggestions received close scrutiny in the Colonial Office. The Colonial Land and Emigration Commission raised strong objections against shaving but favoured flogging for the seducer. R. Ebden in the Colonial Office stressed that subjecting the seducer to the whip 'would be putting the ignominious punishment on the right shoulders'. Kimberley's response was terse: 'I cannot sanction either flogging or shaving'.[54] In the absence of an official explanation for the Colonial Secretary's decision one can only surmise that such forms of punishment would seem an affront to Indian dignity and national self-respect, wholly inconsistent with contemporary penal legislation and reminiscent of the infamous slave system.

Consequently the colonial authorities were forced to utilize transfers with increasing frequency. Between 1869 and June 1870 a total of 88 transfers arising out of threats or strong suspicion of intended violence were effected as against a mere 17 in the 5 years ending 1868. Scott ascribed this phenomenal increase to the active cooperation of estate managers with official directives.[55] In the 10 years 1881-1890 transfers resulting from 'wife cases' averaged 34% and 29% between 1899/1900 and 1905/1906.[56] While transfers were executed for misconduct, insubordination, or abandonment or amalgamation of estates, jealousy in some cases accounted for over 50% of them. But transfers could only prove effective if threats of violence were actually detected for, in Scott's view, it was hardly the man who loudly reiterated his threats who would most likely carry them out 'but rather the man who broods over his grievance and seeks his revenge without making any great demonstration of his purpose'.[57]

Not infrequently transfers were used indiscriminatingly and the husband rather than the seduced evicted from the plantation. Crosby was convinced that in several cases if a thorough investigation was made the seducer would be transferred and the woman reunited with her husband. 'I have been much distressed', he complained, 'to be obliged to separate people who have been living together ten or twelve years, and have had children'.[58] But even if the seducer were removed the aggrieved man still remained vulnerable to the jeers and ridicule of his co-workers and wounded self-esteem might prove a powerful factor in goading him to fatal violence.

In the majority of cases the crime was confined to indentured Indians, committed generally in the first few years after arrival and provoked by one long resident in the colony and presumably better off economically to be 'more lavish in presents of jewellery and other articles of personal adornment'.[59] The prospect of a life of comparative wealth and comfort in contrast to the rigours and drudgery of plantation labour was a temptation often too difficult for a woman to resist. That the crime was linked largely to the indentured population was because it was among them that the sex-imbalance was most acute. Chief Justice Beaumont who had practical, official knowledge of the workings of the indenture system stressed that the crime was largely absent among unindentured Indians who in the 1860s comprised one-third the resident estate population. Whereas in the 1890s the sex-ratio in the indentured camp remained constant at 41 to 100, among the non-contract resident workers it averaged 54 to 100.[60] A decade later it was 44 to 100 and 62 to 100 respectively.

Besides transfers, the colonial authorities advocated the implementation of measures designed to enable the injured husband to recover damages from his succesful rival, thereby making him less disposed to seek personal revenge on his wife. Additionally the law should compensate the husband by cancelling his registration of marriage and imposing such a heavy fine on the seducer that the crime would be 'distinctly recognised as ignominious'[61]. Legislative measures giving practical effect to some of his views were incorporated in Consolidated Ordinance 25 of 1891 which amended the Heathen Immigration Ordinance. An immigrant found guilty of enticing a woman or unlawfully harbouring the wife of another was liable to a maximum penalty of $24 or imprisonment with hard labour for three months or both. When a wife deserted her husband the Stipendiary Magistrate could issue an order protecting his earnings from the time of desertion.[62]

In the 1860s and 70s the measures adopted to combat the crime had been largely preventative and seemed to treat the symptoms rather than the fundamental cause of the crime. From the mid-1870s the authorities adopted a more judicious policy aimed a finding a permanent solution. Besides augmenting the proportion of women they simultaneously wanted to attract a better quality. Criticisms regarding the type of women imported had not been wanting.

Immigration officials and others often referred to their 'loose and depraved character' and condemned the Emigration Agents for shipping 'the sweepings of the Bazaars' of Calcutta and other large Indian cities.[63] The Colonial Land and Emigration Commissioners had to emphasize time and again the advantages of enlisting a respectable class of women even if additional expenses were incurred. Despite such criticisms the evidence suggests that prostitutes were only shipped when the requisite quota could not be obtained and thus the percentage must necessarily be small.

In June 1877 the planters passed a resolution calling for the importation, free of indenture, of Indian widows and betrothed women who, they claimed, having lost their husbands or intended husbands were less disposed to remarry, despite the legalization of widow – remarriage, and 'by religion and custom are condemned to live apart'. The proposal in fact had been mooted by Henry Firth, the colony's assiduous Emigration Agent at Calcutta, who claimed that the women were accustomed to lead 'pure and blameless lives' and were prepared to 'exchange the condition which they were forced to endure' in India for 'one of freedom elsewhere'.[64] In discussing the scheme the Combined Court, the colony's financial body, stressed that while the introduction of a better class of women would not completely obliterate the 'passion of jealousy' there would at least be 'less ground for its demonstration'.

Acting Governor William Young commended the scheme as the crime continued unabated, thirteen alone between 1873 and 1875. He believed that by their introduction the 'whole social and moral condition' of the Indian population would be improved and 'true Colonization' promoted. He continued:

> *It is a gratifying sight in this Colony to witness the numerous instances of industry and thrift to be found amongst the free Coolie women, and to observe their intelligence in the management of the little property they and their Husbands may have acquired. In many instances their Husbands seem to leave all business details to their Wives, and the Wives seem well worthy of the trust. It is the women in most cases who are to be seen paying in money to the Savings bank, or making lodgments of money for remittance to India.*[65]

He advocated positive action to improve the 'moral status of the Coolie woman'. Only by recognizing their traits of character and initiating measures to develop them, Young contended, that 'civilization and morality' could be substantially improved among the Indian population. The Indian woman was not physically capable of strenuous plantation exertion but, claimed Young, she was industrious and by devoting herself to domestic duties she could exercise 'a civilizing and humanizing influence on those around her'.[66]

The enthusiasm displayed for the scheme contrasted with the lukewarm response from the Indian Government which expressed strong reservations about the mode of implementation. The project, in fact, never materialised even though the 1891 population census of India showed a total of 22 million widows under 21 years of age. [67] Mitchell's report of 1903 showed that he was still experiencing problems in despatching the requisite porportion of women. Even if the scheme had commenced, early marriages, caste inhibitions, ignorance and fear of the unknown, and innate love of home, could still have proved insurmountable barriers.

Another scheme to obviate the shortage produced equally disappointing results. Under it single men under contract would be encouraged to contact relatives and friends in India to select prospective brides who on arrival would be indentured to the same plantation . Proprietors were instructed to publicize the plan but only six applications were reportedly made of which three were rejected on the grounds that the men already had wives and families. The *Argosy* attributed the apparent indifferent response to the failure of Indians to recognise what had been done on their behalf.[68] The equalization of the sexes thus became a post-indenture feature left to be solved by a natural increase in the Indian population. This correction process was slow indeed as women living in a state of polyandry could hardly be prolific and it was further delayed through the extraordinary low birth-rate on the plantations.[69]

The scarcity of women was exploited by some parents who exacted the 'best price obtainable' for their young daughters' hand in marriage. In September 1869 the *Royal Gazette* reported the prevalence of a system whereby parents sold their young daughters to men old enough to be their fathers or grandfathers.[70] According to Haynes Smith they then 'laboriously enlarge the private parts of the poor child by mechanical means until she is ready for the aged purchaser'.[71] The absence of love and affection in such marriages tended to result not infrequently in adultery and eventually murder. The marriage of Seecharan, a comparatively wealthy Indian of 50, to the pretty 11 year old Etwarea is a case in point. Seecharan, in return for the girl's hand in marriage, agreed to give the parents a cow and calf, $50 in cash and to make a will leaving his substantial property to his wife and expected children. Initially the marriage seemed successful but on reaching sixteen, with her sexual desires stimulated, she 'began to lend a willing ear to the blandishments of several young men'.[72] Moody, silent and brooding over his wife's suspected infidelity, Seecharan stayed away from work, sharpened his cutlass and completely severed Etwarea's right arm. She died two days later and Seecharan was convicted and subsequently hanged. Another 'atrocious and deliberate crime' involved Tellock, 'a miserable looking object' who bought a young girl from her parents and murdered her because she allegedly refused to live with him. It appeared that the action of Tellock, who was presumably a tribesman, was based on the notion which seemed to prevail among certain tribes in India, that the girl was his property and he could do whatever he liked with her.[73]

The refusal to recognise Indian marriages performed under traditional rites and customs meant that a girl thus sold hardly enjoyed the security of a legal status. She could be re-sold subsequently to another purchaser prepared to offer a more attractive 'bride price', very often with disastrous consequences. During discussion of the Indian marriage amendment bill in January 1886 the tragic case of young Goirapa came to light. She was married 'Coolie fashion' to Yadakana who later suspected that her parents intended to remove her from the matrimonial home and sell her to a prospective buyer. Realising that he had no legal claim over his wife, Yadakana murdered her to prevent such a sale.[74] On the other hand, Bindharry of Plantation Richmond, Essequibo, by 'discreet management' disposed of his three beautiful daughters at 'excellent prices' and returned to India with more than £1,000, besides a quantity of jewellery.[75]

The shortage of women affected other apects of life in the Indian community. It accelerated the weakening and modification of caste consciousness by facilitating inter-caste marriages. The breaking down of caste distinctions had actually commenced during depot residence in India and continued on the voyage where the cramped conditions made it difficult to observe untouchability or practise certain rites. People of different castes and religions not only shared common facilities but were allocated duties indiscrimately. On the sugar plantations employers disregarded the nuances of Indian culture and made no distinction in job allocation. It was not uncommon to find men of higher castes being supervised by low caste sirdars (headmen). Major D.W.D. Comins, Protector of Emigrants at Calcutta, found during his visit to British Guiana in 1891 little evidence of caste distinctions. He reported marriages or cohabitation between high caste Chattris, Rajputs and Thakurs and low caste women.[76] An extract from the Marriage Register showed the marriage of Soorujbally, 'Chuttry' to Paragiam 'Chamar', and Drikpaul, 'Chuttry' to Bhugia, 'Mossulman'. Mitchell, now Immigration Agent-General, claimed that an interpreter in the Immigration Department was the offspring of a Kahar and a Dom,[77] 'the lowest of all castes'.[78] Andrews description of the 'coolie' lines in Fiji seemed to mirror that in British Guiana: 'Castes, creeds, races, religions were joined and jumbled together in chaotic confusion. Mohammedans cohabited with Hindus, and Sweepers with Brahmins'.[79] Caste modification, on the other hand, tended to facilitate occupational mobility and create new avenues of employment for those whose occupation in India was circumscribed by caste.

Additionally the paucity of women made polyandry almost an acknowledged system. Very often an Indian woman was found to have two husbands and to be unfaithful to both.[80] At Plantation Rose Hall in Berbice the most persistent complaint against Jugmohan, a Brahmin and Head Driver, was that he regularly supplied women to single men on a temporary basis and at an agreed fee.[81] Scott commented on the loose domestic relations among the indentured population: 'It is not uncommon for a woman of this class to leave the man with whom she has cohabited for another, and then for third, perhaps for a fourth, and sometimes to return to one of those she had previously deserted; and this she does in most cases with impunity'.[82] This tendency seemed to unsettle the traditional submissive role of Indian women as they began to adopt roles which gave them greater prominence in the immigrant community.

That uxoricides among the Indian immigrant population were the direct result of the evils inherent in indenture and its administration could hardly be refuted. An artifical immigration system, as indenture undoubtedly was, which resulted in a serious sex-ratio imbalance among those introduced, uprooted them from the stability and security of a communal village life and placed them in an environment where the women were vulnerable to outside pressure and influence, was bound to create conflict and tension. Such an immigrant community was unlikely to develop a high order of morality. In clamouring persistently for indentured immigration, the plantocracy, preoccupied with profits and labour control, hardly ever considered the Indian character or studied conditions in India. While the scarcity of women invited intense competition there seemed little evidence of any concerted attempt to increase the supply beyond the requisite quota imposed by law. Even at the height of the anti-indenture campaign in India the Emigration Agents remained indifferent to the problem. This seemingly nonchalant attitude was reflected in the conduct of some estate personnel who not only studiously ignored official directives but actually contributed to the immorality on estates. The knowledge that Indian women were leading immoral lives in the recipient colonies deeply offended an Indian public that set great store by the chastity of its women folk. Their plight became the most explosive feature of the indenture system and provided the articulate Indian nationalists with a powerful weapon against its continuation.

NOTES

1. Govt. of India to Govt. of Bengal, no. 2040, 19 Oct. 1860. Bengal Emigration Proceedings (hereafter B.E.P.), 2 Nov. 1860, 2.

2. C. Murdoch to India Office, 30 June 1868. B.E.P. Sept. 1868, 3.

3. C.O. 319/55. F. Rogers to CLEC, 2 Dec. 1868 & 1 Feb. 1869.

4. C.O. 384/165. Memorandum of Guianese Govt. on the Marriage Amendment Bill, 10 Jan. 1886.

5. T. Warner to CLEC, no. 76, 22 April 1865. B.E.P. 5 Jan. 1866, 46.

6. Reporter of Protector (of Emigrants), 1879-1880.

7. D.G. Pitcher, 'Report on System of Recruiting Labourers for the Colonies', 1882, para 79.

8. Ord. 10 of 1860.

9. C.O. 113/8. Ord. XXV of 1891, articles 151-153.

10. C.O. 111/689/75141/30. C.F. Andrews, 'Impressions of British Guiana', 1930.

11. C.O. 114/29. Immigration Agent-General, report for 1880.

12. C.O. 111/345. Gov. Francis Hincks to Duke of Newcastle, no. 89, 4 May 1864.

13. The *Argosy*, 30 June 1906.

14. See Ord. 35 of 1957.

15. The *Argosy*, 30 Oct. 1880 and 26 April 1884.

16. P.P. 1871, XX, (393). Royal Commission Report, para 308.

17. The *Royal Gazette*, 23 Sept. 1869.

18. In 1831 the three separate colonies (counties) of Essequibo, Demerara and Berbice were united to form the colony of British Guiana, popularly known as Demerara.

19. Royal Commission, Report 1870, Appendices Pt.II, p. 86.

20. C.O. 111/492. Immigration Agent-general to Gov. A. Hemming, 4 Jan. 1897.

21. C.O. 111/162. Gov. H. Light to Lord Glenelg, no. 7, 11 Jan. 1839.

22. C.O. 111/386. Gov. J. Scott to Earl of Kimberley, no. 106. 18 July 1871.

23. The *Creole*, 10 Nov. 1873.

24. C.O. 114/26. Immigration Agent-General, Report for 1874.

25. C.O. 384/111. Gov. J. Longden to Earl of Carnarvon, no. 199, 16 Sept. 1876.

26. C.O. 384/165. Minute on Marriage Bill, 3 Feb. 1887.

27. P.P. 1898, L., (C.8655), p. 47.

28. Compiled from Immigration Agent-General, Annual Reports.

29. R. Duff, *British Guiana* (Glasgow, 1886), p. 320.

30. C.O. 114/27. Immigration Agent-General, Report for 1875.

31. C.O. 111/376. Scott to Kimberley, no 100, 15 Aug. 1870; C.O. 111/386.

32. H. Mitchell to Colonial Secretary, Feb. 1873.

33. Walcott to Herbert, 6 Sept. 1871. B.E.P. Nov. 1871, 12.

34. Colonial Office to India Office, 26 Aug. 1871. B.E.P. Nov. 1871, 12; C.O. 111/386. Scott to Kimberley, no. 106, 18 July 1871.

35. See India Emigration Proceedings (hereafter I.E.P.), Sept. 1872, 5 & 11.

36. *Ibid.*

37. Minute of Murdoch, 18 Oct. 1872. I.E.P. Jan. 1873, 1.

38. Immigration Agent-General, Report for 1900/1901.

39. The *Argosy,* 15 March 1884.

40. Immigration Agent-General, Report for 1900/1901.

41. C.O. 111/342. The *Official Gazette,* 12 Dec. 1863.

42. C.O. 111/342. Hincks to Newcastle, no. 199, 17 Dec. 1863. Encl.

43. The *Royal Gazette,* 14 March 1865.

44. See Ord. 4 of 1864, art. 125.

45. C.O. 111/334. Hincks to Newcastle, no. 21, 3 March 1862.

46. C.O. 111/369. Hincks to Duke of Buckingham and Chandos, no. 162, 19 Nov. 1868.

47. *Ibid.,* no. 177, 18 Dec. 1868. See also C.O. 111/371. Scott to Granville, no. 43, 1 March 1869.

48. C.O. 112/42. Granville to Scott, no. 206, 30 April 1870.

49. The *Royal Gazette,* 30 April and 7 May 1872.

50. P.P. 1871, XX, (393), pp. 187-191.

51. C.O. 114/27. Immigration Agent-General, report for 1876.

52. C.O. 384/139. D. Chalmers to Gov. H. Irving, 3 Aug. 1882. Encl. in Irving to Kimberley, no. 320, 1 Nov. 1882.

53. *Ibid.*

54. *Ibid.* See minutes of Kimberley, 10 and 15 Dec. 1882.

55. C.O. 111/376. Scott to Kimberley, no. 100. 15 Aug. 1870.

56. Compiled from Immigration Agent-General, Annual Reports.

57. C.O. 111/376. Scott to Kimberley, no. 100, 15 Aug. 1870.

58. Royal Commission Report, vol. 1, p.40. Minutes of Evidence.

59. C.O. 384/144. Gov. H. Irving to Earl of Derby, no. 339, 5 Dec. 1883.

60. Compiled from Immigration Agent-General, Annual Reports.

61. C.O. 384/139. Chalmers to Irving, 3 Aug. 1882.

62. Ord. 25 of 1891, arts. 155-160.

63. C.O. 384/106. Longden to Carnarvon, no. 218, 20 Oct. 1875.

64. C.O. 384/115. Gov. W.A. Young to Carnarvon, no. 138, 25 June 1877.

65. C.O. 384/123. Young to M. Hicks Beach, no. 133, 24 May 1879.

66. *Ibid.*

67. Report of Mitchell for 1905/06. By the end of indenture in 1920 the estimated number was 25 million widows.

68. The *Argosy*, 11 May 1904.

69. In 1881 the birth-rate among the resident Indian population was 23.25 per 1000 and the death-rate 32.08 while in the 1908-1912 period they averaged 25.86 and 30.48 respectively.

70. The *Royal Gazette*, 23 Oct. 1869.

71. C.O. 384/165. Minute of Haynes Smith, 3 Feb. 1887.

72. H. Kirke, *Twenty Five Years in British Guiana* (London, 1898), pp.219-225.

73. The *Royal Gazette*, 31 Jan. 1854.

74. C.O. 384/165. Govt. Memorandum on the Bill to amend the law relating to Marriage, 18 Jan. 1886.

75. Kirke, pp. 241-2.

76. D.W.D. Comins, 'Note on Emigration from India to British Guiana, 1893', pp. 79-80.

77. The Doms were a tribal people who often performed the lowest offices such as carrying dead bodies and skeletons.

78. C.O. 384/144. Mitchell to Irving, 14 March 1883. See also T. Ramnarine, 'The Growth of the East Indian Community in British Guiana, 1880-1920' (D. Phil., Univ. of Sussex, 1977), pp. 198-99.

79. C.F. Andrews, *Indian Indentured Labour in Fiji* (Perth, 1918), p. 74

80. The *Argosy*, 26 April 1884.

81. *Daily Argosy*, 23 March & 24 April 1913.

82. C.O. 111/376. Scott to Kimberley, no. 100, 15 Aug. 1870; Duff, p. 320.

East Indian Women in the Caribbean:
Experience and Voice

Jeremy Poynting

Until recently, virtually everything written about Indian women in the Caribbean had been written by men. In so far as it is possible to synthesise a true history from such sources it appears to have been one of paradox. For instance, it is possible to believe that during the indenture period (1838-1917), Indian women in the Caribbean were both more free and less free than they had been in India. Male witnesses, whether Indian or non-Indian, sympathetic or unsympathetic, have tended to present images which are sharply polarised[1]. In European colonial writings she appears either as the demure, contented child-woman or as the exotic oriental seductress. As Indo-Caribbean women begin to explore their own history and experience, no doubt more integrated and fluid perspectives will emerge.

What this article attempts is no more than a preliminary survey of the sources which are available for gaining a picture of the Indo-Caribbean woman's experience. The main emphasis is on imaginative literature because, to date, it is there one finds the best (sometimes only) insights into that experience. The article has two sections: the first attempts a brief historical survey of the changes in the situation of Indo-Caribbean women; the last explores the emergence of imaginative writing by Indo-Caribbean women. Although Indian indentured immigration and settlement took place in Surinam, Martinique and Guadeloupe, to a lesser extent Jamaica and on a very small scale to some other islands, the article concentrates on Trinidad and Guyana, where the largest Indian populations in the Caribbean reside.

The Historical Experience

Undoubtedly, the experience of Indian women during the indenture period was one of multiple oppression: as an indentured worker in a system of quasi-servitude, as an Indian whose culture was despised as barbaric and heathen by all other sections of the population, and as a woman who suffered from the sexual depredations of the white overseer class and was restricted within the reconstituted 'Indian'[2] family structure. Yet it is also true that as wage earners under indenture some Indian women achieved a measure of independence, and even within the family it seems likely that women achieved some status in their role as the main preservers of Indian domestic culture (initially the principal means whereby Indians maintained their identity).

The reason for both the possibilities and the miseries of the Indian woman's experiences during the indenture period was her scarcity. Throughout the period the ratio of female to male immigrants always lagged well behind the ratio of 2:5 recommended by the immigration ordinances. In the early period of indenture in British Guiana (1851) it was as low as 11.3: 100, and even by 1891 the ratio in the resident population had risen only to 58:100.[3] In Trinidad in 1911 there was still only a ratio of 1000 women to 1354 men.[4] The planters regarded the importation of women as uneconomical, so the recruiters were never encouraged to try to meet the recommended ratios. Moreover, most of the Indian men who indented expected to return to India; as a result few married men were prepared to bring their wives. Both the nature of the women who came and the disproportion of the sexes had profound effects on the social life of the estates, the relationships of the sexes and the behaviour and experience of women. Rhoda Reddock has calculated that at least two-thirds of the women who indented were single.[5] Most of these were probably widows (forbidden to remarry), others were separated from their husbands, and a small number were prostitutes, though this category bulked large in the moralistic reports of the officials complaining of the difficulties of recruitment. In fact for many of the widowed or abandoned, indenture was probably seen as the only alternative to prostitution. There are good reasons then for suspecting a considerable independence of spirit amongst many of the women who came.

On the estates, because of their scarcity and because of their position as wage earners (though women on average earned only ⅔ of male wages), it is evident that some Indian women either went through a profound re-evaluation of their role or continued habits of independence brought from India. HVP Bronkhurst, a missionary in British Guiana noted:

> '...the Indian indentured woman in the colony feels that she is independent of her husband, as she has to earn her own living by

working in the field, and gets her weekly wages in her own hand. [6]

Bronkhurst also felt that this new spirit came from the woman's belief that she could 'change one lord and master with the greatest of ease.' Indeed, one Indian woman in Trinidad in the 1870s told Sarah Morton, a missionary:

> *When the last ship came in I took a Papa. I will keep him as long as he treats me well. If he does not treat me well I shall send him off at once.* [7]

There is also evidence that during the nineteenth century some Indian women maintained an occupational independence. Bronkhurst writes, for instance, of troupes of professional dancing girls and singers who earned a living by performing from house to house.

However, female independence was not unchallenged. Indian women paid a heavy price in beatings and in loss of life at the hands of men. As Bronkhurst noted, the male immigrant did not accept the increased independence of his wife but did 'everything at home to humble her.'[8] The most serious manifestation of male refusal to accept change in the role of women was the very high rate of wife-murder. In Trinidad, for instance, between 1859-1863 there were 27 wife-murders,[9] a ratio of 0.4 murders per thousand of the Indian population per year. (This would be equivalent to 24,000 wife-murders in a year in a population of 60 million like the UK's). As the ratio of the sexes improved, the rate of wife-murders fell. In British Guiana between 1894-1905 there were 29 recorded murders of Indian women, an average of 0.0196 per thousand per year.[10]

It is clear that towards the end of the indenture period the precarious independence of Indian women began to be curtailed. The planters became more concerned about marital stability on the estates because by then they wished for a settled Indian population which would reproduce the future labour supply without the costs of immigration. Managers began to exercise greater control over sexual relationships by, for instance, their power to transfer to another estate a man believed to be 'enticing' another man's wife. Some male immigrants also petitioned the Government in Trinidad for the right of a husband to prosecute an unfaithful wife and her partner.[11] The main reason for the 'restoration' of the position of women to one of subservience was the move from estate residence to village settlement. In Trinidad, from the 1870s onwards there was a rapid movement away, so that by 1891 54.7% of Indians were resident in towns, villages and small settlements. By 1921 there were virtually no Indians still resident on estates. This process permitted a partial reconstitution of traditional North Indian village culture. Whereas the conditions of indenture and estate residence made it impossible for the caste system, the joint family or traditional male-female role relations to function, in the villages traditional cultural institutions in an adapted form survived until the 1950s at least. Several aspects of this cultural and social reconstitution sharply affected women's lives. Some were withdrawn from estate wage-labour to unpaid labour on the lands which Indians began acquiring.[12] It is likely that the wives of some of the high-caste were returned to a state of domestic seclusion as fitting their husbands' status. Thirdly, because of the continuing scarcity of women, child-marriage became the norm. In the words of Charles Kingsley, 'the girls are practically sold by their fathers while yet children, often to wealthy men much older than they.'[13] Whether women attempted to resist this resubordination to patriarchy or welcomed the village settlements as a return to 'stability' is not known.

In Guyana, the movement towards village settlement began later and was much smaller. Even up to 1950, 43.7% of the Indian population remained resident on the estates. Although little detailed investigation has been carried out, there is some evidence to suggest that in the ex-estate villages in Guyana, the relationships of men and women were more equal, or at least more contested.

However, whether in village or estate, attitudes to women were such that when the Presbyterian Canadian Mission began to offer schooling to Indian children, such hindrances were placed in the way of female education that the effects have only just begun to disappear. In Trinidad in 1899, after thirty years of Canadian Mission schooling, girls comprised only 28% of total enrolment in the primary schools. This reflected only part of their educational disability since girls were much more likely to be kept at home to perform domestic chores and withdrawn from school early, as soon as their marriages were arranged.[14] Above the primary level inequalities sharpened. Although some secondary education for Indian boys began in 1883, it was not until 1912 that Naparima Girls High School was founded. V S Naipaul almost certainly gives an accurate portrayal of common Indian attitudfes to female education, right up to the 1930s at least, when, in *A House For Mr Biswas* (1961), Biswas hears his future bride's scholastic achievements outlined:

'... *She is a good child. A little bit of reading and writing even.*'

> *'A little bit of reading and writing ...' Mr Biswas echoed, trying to gain time.*
> *Seth, chewing, his right hand working dexteriously with roti and beans, made a dismissing gesture with his left hand.*
> *'Just a little bit. So much. Nothing to worry about. In two or three years she might even forget.'* (Fontana Ed. p.78)

Even when the Canadian Mission made specific attempts to attend to the education of Indian girls, their motives were chiefly to provide suitably domesticated and Christianised wives for the Indian teachers and catechists they were training. Basic literacy and numeracy were taught, but the emphasis was on housewifely pursuits.

The results of their neglect are predictable. Up to 1946 only 30% of Indian women in Trinidad were literate (against 50% for men) and amongst those over 45 only 10.6% were literate. In the census of 1931, only 4% of Indian women were listed as having professions, 72 as teachers (there were 368 male Indian teachers); about 13% were classified as self-employed shopkeepers, peasant farmers and other proprietors, but over 83% of all women in paid employment were domestic servants, general labourers or, the biggest group, agricultural labourers.[15] The *Indian Centenary Review* of 1945 was only able to include 16 women in its section of 223 biographies of persons in the professions or in business. (Kirpalani *et al,* pp. 131-169). All were Christians and most came from families which had attained professional status a generation before. Although one, Gladys Ramsaran, was a barrister, none could be described as being in public life. Voluntary social work appears to have been the one 'public' contribution non-professional Indian women were permitted to make. One woman included in the 'Who's Who', Amanda Nobbee, is described as a part-time writer of 'amusing articles on topical subjects' which appeared occasionally in the press, a collection of pieces called *English with Tears* (c. 1940), and some time later a collection of children's stories, *For Small Fry* (1957). Apart from the symbolic step of 'being' a writer, no great claims can be made for either the literary quality or the interest of this work.

In Guyana, Indian access to education lagged sharply behind that of Indians in Trinidad. Here the colonial government actively connived at denying Indian girls an education. One recommendation of the Swettenham Circular of 1904, which remained in force until 1933, was that no pressure should be placed on Indian parents who wished to keep their daughters in seclusion. In 1925 only 25% of the Indian children in primary schools were girls. Literacy rates were just as low as in Trinidad, through data from Guyana suggests that Indian women benefitted from the shift from the use of Indic languages to English. Whereas women comprised 30% of all Indians literate in English in 1931, they comprised only 16% of Indians literate in Indic languages. However, a truer index of Indian women's social status in Guyana can be gained from the voters register of 1947, the last year in which the franchise was limited by property and income qualifications. Indian women comprised 1.8% of all voters, 6% of all Indian voters and only 9.9% of all female voters.[16] Of the 1,082 Indian women entitled to vote there was an even smaller number who had begun to emerge from a traditional restricted role. Principally this group numbered the wives of the most westernised section of the Georgetown middle class. The major focus for the activities of this group was the British Guiana Dramatic Society, despite its name an exclusively Indian organisation. The BGDS looked both East and West. They performed plays, mainly by Tagore, which were staged in such a way as to celebrate the splendours of ancient India, but the themes included defence of the right of choice in marriage and acceptance of elements of westernisation. At their public concerts traditional dances and music rubbed shoulders with, for instances, Miss Nalini Singh's popularly received performances as 'a jive and blues singer'. It is evident that in all the BGDS's activities women participated fully.[17] At its centre was a strong-minded and cultivated woman, Alice Bhagwandai Singh, the wife of one of the leading politicians of the time, Dr J B Singh. Mrs Singh directed several of the plays, (the group functioned between 1929-1947) wrote several articles on cultural and social issues in journals such as *The Indian Opinion*, and was the founder in 1936 of the Balak Sahaita-Mandalee, a voluntary child-welfare society, a rather belated recognition by the Indian middle-class of the desperate poverty on the estates.[18] However, women like Mrs Singh took no part in political groups such as the British Guiana East Indian Association.

During the 1940s and 1950s there seems to have been only very gradual change in the position of East Indian women in Trinidad and Guyana. For the rural majority life changed scarcely at all. Girls were kept under surveillance once they had reached puberty and their marriages arranged, for about one third by the age of fourteen and for the majority before the age of nineteen. Women still very rarely owned any property, passed through the restriction of being the daughter-in-law (doolahin) in a strange household, and were obliged to show ritual respect to male kin.[19]

Two things began to change the position of Indian women in

Near Winiperu on the banks of the Essequibo, a typical local house with thatch roof replaced with corrugated iron

A typical local house in the villages of Guyana, made of wood and corrugated iron

Trinidad. Firstly there was a rapid expansion in the provision of schooling in both urban and rural Indian areas, the product very largely of the Indian community's own initiatives. The Hindu Maha Sabha, to a lesser extent the Arya Samaj and Islamic organisations, all built denominational schools during the 1950s. Attitudes to education, for both boys and girls, had changed sharply within the Indian commnunity as it attempted to catch up with other sections of the population.[20] Secondly, during the late 1960s and 1970s there has been rapid economic expansion in Trinidad, stimulated by the boom, now over, in oil prices. As a consequence, many semi-rural areas have become enmeshed in the cash economy and the explosion of consumerism which is deeply affecting many areas of Indian social and cultural life. One consequence is that there is a much greater acceptance of the contribution the Indian woman can make as a wage-earner to the family's participation in the consumer economy. However, not all parts of Trinidad have participated equally in the economic expansion, and there is evidence of a clear link between the level of an Indian settlement's participation in the cash economy and the extent to which women's roles have changed. For instance, Nevadomsky's re-investigation of the settlement of Felicity near the rapidly expanding town of Chaguanas (the 'Amity' of Klass's classic study of cultural retention in the 1950s in *East Indians in Trinidad* [1961]) shows very marked changes in the position of Indian women. His data indicates, for instance, that whilst only 17% of women over 35 had any choice in their husbands, 66% under 35 had; that although the average age for first marriage for women over 35 was 14, for those under 35 it was 17.5; that whilst a bride might live with her husband's family for a short time, 85% of married women under 40 were in their own houses less than three years after marriage and that in general, relationships between husbands and wives were becoming more equal, openly affectionate and sexually close.[21] Nevadomsky also asserts that as a consequence of the new career and wage opportunities, East Indian women were beginning to control their own fertility to an increased extent.[22] Whereas up to 1946 the fertility rate for Indian women in Trinidad as a whole had been nearly twice that of women of African descent for the age group 15-29, by 1970 the ratio had declined to 100/106 at age group 15-19 and to 100/131 at 25-29. However, Nevadomsky indicates that the degree of control women have over their lives varies sharply in terms of the socio-economic position of their families and their own success in the education system. A girl who showed the promise of attaining higher education

Reaping rice; the territory has a campaign to produce not only enough rice for the population but a surplus for export

and higher status occupation was likely to have much more scope in evading family pressures towards early marriage. This is confirmed by research carried out by Shamate Sieunarine in El Dorado in 1980 which showed that whilst employed Indian girls wanted free marital choice and later marriage, unemployed girls would still accept early, arranged marriage.[23] What must be noted is that the percentage of Indian girls with the qualifications which would take them into higher education is very small. There are no figures which give an ethnic breakdown, but for all girls in the 15-19 age group in Trinidad in 1970, only 9.2% achieved any 'O' levels at all and only 0.4% achieved 2 'A' levels; 78.7% left school without any qualifications.[24]

In those areas of Trinidad which have remained part of the rural economy, the position of women has changed far less. For instance, Judith Johnson's field work in Rampat Trace (carried out between 1968-1976 in the Debe/Penal area of South Trinidad) shows that whilst men have become much more involved in the wage-economy (particularly in the service industries) women's labour has become more important in the subsistence agricultural sector. Restricted to unwaged labour women's status has remained circumscribed. In Rampat Trace there are still extensive restrictions on adolescent girls and early, arranged marriages. Motherhood remains the main means whereby girls can attain any status and bring to an end the most submissive phase of her life as doolahin. Johnson notes that in general women are less healthy than men because girls are less well nourished than boys, and because women still have imcomplete control over their fertility. Contraception is widely available but not much used; instead abortions are widely practised. Johnson argued that this happens for two reasons which reveal much about the role of women. Firstly, many males are hostile to contraceptive methods which put women in control of their own sexuality; secondly, in a culture in which a women's main status is gained as a reproducer, abortions demonstrate a woman's continuing capacity for fertility.[25] Corroborative evidence for the continuing social and sexual restrictions on the lives of Indian women in rural communities in both Trinidad and Guyana are to be found in the persistence of 'matikor', particularly amongst older women, and the large-scale involvement of women in the Kali-Mai churches in Guyana. 'Matikor' is an all female ceremony which precedes the public stages of a wedding in which women drink, dance in sexually suggestive ways and sing 'gaari', extremely bawdy, ritually insultive songs.[26] During the state of possession in Kali-Mai worship women and girls quite frequently behave in highly uninhibited ways.[27] Both occasions may be seen as licenced expressions of revolt from norms which require the suppression of overt expressions of female sexuality.

Amongst the very small percentage of Indian girls who have achieved some level of higher education and occupational choice (a much smaller number in Guyana than in Trinidad), there are still obstacles of gender and ethnicity to face. As yet, the few who reach positions of status and power in business or the professions still warrant special features in Trinidad's glossy magazine for the new élite, *People*. For some of these, occupational achievement can still only be made outside of marriage,[28] both because of the degree of additional commitment a woman needs to succeed in a male oriented society and perhaps because even amongst university-educated men, some traditional role-expectations survive. As yet Indian women are almost wholly unrepresented in political life in either Trinidad or Guyana. In the Trinidadian elections of 1976 only 11% of all candidates were women, and only 4.4% were Indian women.

What is true of the position of women in the poorer rural areas of Trinidad has a more general applicability for Guyana. In a society which was always poorer (and is now on the verge of economic collapse) there has been no parallel to the stimulation of the semi-urban areas as occurred in Trinidad. In the past the access of Indians to non-agricultural employment was frustrated both by the absence of secondary educational facilities in the rural areas and by race discrimination in such Afro-Guyanese dominated areas as the civil service. Thus when the International Commission of Jurists investigated racial imbalances in the public services they found Indians seriously under-represented. The report recorded, but did not comment on, the even more dramatic under-representation of Indian women. For instance, at a time when Indians were 50% of the population, in 1965, Indian women comprised only 2.85% (395) of all employees and only 13.5% of female employees on the staffs of all the Government ministries. Even in teaching, Indian women were seriously under-represented, numbering only 12.7% of the whole teaching force and 26.8% of all women teachers.[29] Since 1964, Guyana has been ruled by a party which has manipulated the anti-Indian fears of its minority Afro-Guyanese supporters and wholly corrupted the electoral process to stay in power. Virtually all Guyanese suffer from the Government's mismanagement, corruption and oppressive rule; Indians who refuse to bow and scrape to the ruling party find themselves excluded from public employment or restricted to its lower levels. Indian women suffer both economically and sexually. Like most other Guyanese women their energies are consumed by the desperate daily struggles to find food and other basic domestic essentials. Indian women in Government employment also speak of coming under sexual pressure to obtain or retain their jobs. The Government controls 85% of the economy. It is impossible to quantify or independently verify such allegations,[30] but the sense of threat felt by many Indian women and their families is illustrated by the widespread Indian opposition to the introduction of the Guyana National Service in 1973. When GNS was made compulsory for both men and women wishing to enter higher education, it was seen by many Indians as an attempt to force racial integration, or rather the sexual integration of Indian girls. The fact that when the lists for compulsory induction were published at the University of Guyana they contained 53 Indo-Guyanese of the 63 persons listed, and that of the 25 women listed 90% were Indian, meant only one thing to the majority of Indians. Many Indian girls are reported to have dropped their university applications.[31] For those able to, escape to North America has been the main route out of these difficulties. For those unable to escape, the poor and unskilled majority, high unemployment has driven many women back into the home.

The outline of the historical experience and contemporary situation of Indo-Caribbean women given above is regrettably sketchy and impressionistic. With honourable exceptions lamentably little historical research or empirical investigation has been devoted to this topic. However, if the outline serves to show why it has taken so long for any Indo-Caribbean women's voice to emerge, it will have served its purpose.

Voice: Indo-Caribbean Women's Writing

The domestic, educational, occupational and social disadvantages suffered by Indo-Caribbean women are reason enough not to be surprised at the small quantity of imaginative writing they have produced. To date some forty individuals have contributed poems and stories to local journals; one collection of short stories and a dozen slim volumes of poetry have been published; as yet no novel has appeared. Much of the writing is undistinguished; many of the journal contributions are by adolescents who have subsequently gone silent. In addition to the more general reasons why people in the Caribbean (or anywhere) stop writing (lack of talent, lack of encouragement, lack of publishing outlets, lack of audience) there are clearly reasons more specific to women which are almost too obvious to mention. There are several male Indo-Caribbean writers who are enabled to write full-time because they are supported by their wives, but there are not, one suspects many males who look after their children to give their wives the same opportunity. Moreover, as is the case in societies where writers must publish their own work, it is not necessarily those with the least talent who keep silent. Not only is it often those who are more self-critical about their work who are less inclined to publish, but those without the material resources and those without the necessary self-confidence. One suspects that women feature disproportionately in the latter two categories. As yet there are, in my view, only three women who have achieved any real individuality of voice – the late Rajkumari Singh, Shana Yardan and Mahadai Das – though there are several others who, on the evidence of the small quantity of material they have published, display real potential.

If there is one over-arching concern in Indo-Caribbean women's writing, it is with human happiness and its denial by social injustice, religious bigotry, racism and sexism; and, to a far greater extent than in male writing, personal relationships are seen as central to that happiness or its absence. Although a good deal of writing on such personal themes belongs to the sentimental genre of women's magazine romance,[32] in dealing with such themes as the pain of unrequited love or the awakening of sexual feelings it can be seen as challenging the stereotype of the maternal and passive roles imposed on women in a patriarchal culture. In Leela Sukhu's collection, *Scattered Leaves* (1968), in the midst of much Mills-and-Boonish sentiment, there is an arresting description of the joy and horror of submission to the consuming power of love:

> *For a moment it seems like madness*
> *To see beauty in the gaping jaws of a reptile*
> *But oh! this feeling that runs in my blood*
> *Will send me like a child to a mother*
> *For the love of it*
> *Into the jaws of the monster.*[33]

The outstanding achievement in the exploration of personal feelings is to be found, though, in Shana Yardan's cycle of love poems, *This Listening of Eyes* (1976)[34] which portrays a tension between a feminine feeling of delight in the immersion of the whole personality in the minutiae of love's exchanges and a feminist awareness of the inequalities of power and the disparities of commitment between the man and the woman. In the making of these poems Shana Yardan also displays a rare, careful craftsmanship. Several poems explore a conflict between the pleasures of dependency and the urge to protect self-hood. The male is asked:

How can you walk into the garden of my life
And trample on the neatly laid beds of habit?
Or break the buds from struggling trees of thoughts....

but the woman has to admit that:

...in all learning I am untaught
Save in what you shall teach me.

What is desired is not submission, but equal joining:

Touch not nor break the buds that fragance lend
But graft them to that other self of mine
Which is you.

This poem illustrates how the effectiveness of the metaphors Yardan uses frequently depends less on their intrinsic originality that on the way they are developed logically within a coherent structure. Sometimes, though, images are more startling, as in the fourth poem in the sequence, in which the woman recognises that though she has given herself wholly, the main holds part of himself aloof:

So I play the age-old game with you
And run the gamut of cold safe intellect
While my soul shivers beside the unlit fire
Watching the tiger devour your bowels.

Here there is a metaphysical wit and intensity in these lines as she shifts the scene from the terminology of the 'modern' self-analytical lover, to a 'stone-age' scene of primitive emotions, by the play on the literal implications of 'age-old' and the link between the 'cold' intellect and the unlit fire which would have saved the man from his fears. She plays with the reader as well, for we are led to assume that what frightens the man is his fear of 'this primal thing'. It is not:

But rather the touch of soft returning fingers
Holding your hands but reaching for your dreams.

This theme of male-female tension is developed in later poems in the sequence where the woman divines that the male feels threatened by the naked exposure of her personality and attempts to reduce that threat by making her simply an object of sexual desire:

But you in your arrogance would fashion me
After the foolish delights of men
Fearful lest my utter nakedness
Causes you to discover the essence of my soul.

She wonders about the possibilities of shaking off involvement:

If you walk straight ahead
How far can you get?

but has to admit the imperative of:

The urgent call to walk the streets
Leading always to the abodes of men,
Houses with mysteries of their own.

and accepts that:

...one must endure the caterpillars
To be rewarded with butterflies.

The image is denser than might at first appear, not merely opposing the unpleasant and the beautiful, but the closed-up male and the possibility of his opening, and the earth-bound contacts of sex and the spiritial flowing together of the inner persons.

Only in a single poem by the Trinidadian, Niala Rambachan, 'Picture the Diablesse',[35] does one find any comparable attempt to go beyond romantic clichés. Rambachan's poem is a witty and ironic fable on the attitudes of men and women to female sexuality. At first it reads like a mocking telling of the old-old story of men who are tempted from their boring wives, 'white flour bag aprons covering our domestic bellies" by the diablesse (the she-devil with cloven hooves who lures men to their fate in forests), even though they have been warned by the 'straight, tough, leathery tongues' of their wives. The male is always tempted:

He had been expecting her all along
Has come on this path just for her...

but always manages to escape back to his domestic wife. However, the fable is not simply a satire on men who are tempted but frightened by the sexuality of women. Rambachan makes the diablesse more than a folklore demon, giving her the image of a woman pursued by her own sexual desire, ('Driven madly by that power and weakness'), which like her cloven feet is hidden 'under the frilled skirt' which she tears as she pursues the husband. Always she is left alone:

As she sadly closes the file on this victim
And starts preparing for the next prospect.

Then it becomes clear that the identities of domestic wife and diablesse are connected. The narrating wife speaks both of her 'dark skirt and white apron and closed face' and her inward 'obscene thought' as the errant husband returns; while the diablesse is pictured in the domestic task of mending her torn skirt,

In the dry daylight when the forest is no longer black
And she is no longer a myth to be feared.

The diablesse it becomes clear is the nightime sexuality of the domestic woman, whose threat the man runs from, though she senses 'the loss he experienced briefly.' But the diablesse is also 'our fear', women's fear of their own sexuality. The identity of the two female images is made clear in the ironic last two lines of the poem when the narrating voice, who speaks as one of the domestic wives, asks of the disappointed diablesse:

Does she then, maybe,
Sit down and write poetry?

In general though, writing specifically focussed on the position of Indian women has not notably extended the kind of treatments found in male fiction. Occasionally, indeed one finds regret for the loss of the traditional 'protected' role of women. Ann Marie Bissessar regrets the discarding of orhni and sari and asserts:

Young men were meant to be warriors
To protect their women and kin.[36]

More usually though the literacy focus is on the image of woman as victim: as the beaten wife (Diane Ramdass, 'The Drunkard')[37], the mother struggling against poverty (Veronica Raganoonan, 'Underprivileged')[38] or most popularly as the girl trapped or revolting against an arranged marriage. From Mary D'Kalloo's story, 'Doolarie'[39] written in 1948 up to Rajnie Ramlakhan's 'The Doolaha'[40] written in 1974, the theme has attracted several tellings,[41] often interwoven with protest against religious or racial bigotry. Of these stories only Rajnie Ramlakhan's could be described as even mildly feminist in perspective. Ramlakhan is also one of the first to attempt to dramatise the kind of conflicts experienced by the first generation of Hindu women with higher education. In her story, 'Flight',[42] the heroine is pressured on the one side by her parents to

marry a 'good Hindu husband' and on the other by her radical
Christian Indian boyfriend to abandon religion, family pieties and
convention. She wants to have a career, be socially committed and
involved in cultural activities, but she also wants children and within
the security of marriage. The boyfriend rebuffs her. At first she
contemplates suicide, but then sees that she must become truly
independent: 'From now on her life was to be hers and hers alone.'
However, she still hopes that one day the right man will come along.
The story is too brief to permit any real development of character or
exploration of the woman's feelings, but one suspects that it outlines
a theme which will be popular in future Indo-Caribbean women's
writing. In general though these stories of victimised women are
simply part of a wider repertoire of stock Caribbean social protest
themes, which though they relate to real social ills, have been
reduced to a formulaic clichéd literary response. Protest themes in
women's writing include indignant portraits of such oppressed figures
as the cane-worker, stories of poverty which drives to crime and,
more unusually, anti-war protest.[43]

With the exception of Shana Yardan, Rajkumari Singh and
Mahadai Das, few Indo-Caribbean women have dealt explicitly with
the theme of ethnic identity in their writing. It is no accident that all
three are Guyanese, the most self-analytical and, in the case of Singh
and Das, the most politically committed of all the writers discussed.

In 'Earth is Brown',[44] Shana Yardan explores her part Indian
ancestry, laments what has been lost, but indicates her own sense of
distance from that past. Even for her grandfather, India is only
memory, while his sons 'with their city faces' scorn his attempts to
hold on to old traditions. For Yardan herself even the physical
inheritance has become a liability in a Guyana dominated by the
Africans:

> *Oh grandfather, my grandfather,*
> *your dhoti is become a shroud*
> *your straight hair a curse*
> *in this land where*
> *rice no longer fills the belly*
> *or the empty placelessness*
> *of your soul.*

By contrast, both Rajkumari Singh and Mahadai Das, whose
work is considered separately below, embraced their Indo-
Guyanese identity much more positively.

For someone who has known Rajkumari Singh even briefly it is difficult to write dispassionately of her work. She was a warm, courageous, politically conscious woman, acutely alert to the wrongs of oppression, whether by one nation to another, one race to another or one sex to another. Though physically crippled by polio from infancy, hospitalised frequently, frequently in pain and her life ended prematurely by ill-health, she was a woman of great vitality and inner strength. During the last decade of her life, her strenuous involvement in public life would have taxed a far healthier person. Before that she had raised eight children and was invariably a surrogate cultural and artistic mother to younger writers and artists. Almost certainly she was more generous with her time to other people than was good for her own work, though that concern with people is what nourishes her work with honesty and feeling.

Her involvement with the arts, politics and the politics of culture was life-long. As a teenager in the 1940s she had been involved in the British Guiana Dramatic Society and she has been an articulate promoter of the Society's belief that Indians had a right and duty to maintain their cultural integrity. She wrote in 1945:

> We have experienced many attempts from without to absorb us as a distinct cultural group, and now more than ever, in our midst we find organised propaganda at work, aimed primarily to plunge us into the general melting pot towards a homogeneous culture...This we hate...[45]

During the 1950s she was inevitably heavily involved with her young family, though she managed in 1960 to publish her collection of short stories, *A Garland of Stories*. During the 1960s she became more involved in political activity in the Peoples Progressive Party, and in the mid 1960s she was made a member of the commission which investigated the dreadful racial savagery largely suffered by Indian women and girls during the Wismar disturbances of 1964. It was perhaps this experience which made her feel that racial understanding between Indians and Blacks was the most urgent cause in Guyanese politics. It was this feeling which lead her to make a well publicised split from the PPP, which she felt had become stuck in a sterile mould of opposition and ethnic chauvinism, and join the ruling People's National Congress, which appeared to have taken a lurch leftwards. She was aware that the PNC was an equally chauvinist organisation, but believed that unless Indians participated in national politics and culture, they, though a majority, would be reduced to total voicelessness in the country's affairs. In hindsight the decision to join the PNC must be seen as a mistake. Though she was sincere, for its part the PNC leadership was only interested in a cosmetic Indian presence in the party. Nevertheless, whilst she was involved with the PNC as a Captain in the newly formed Guyana National Service Cultural Division, there was a brief period of visibility for Indian artists and writers, which stimulated a small explosion of Indo-Guyanese writing. Rajkumari Singh was particularly involved with the formation of the Messenger Group[46] which was dedicated to bringing to public notice that 'Coolie art forms' were equally part of the Guyanese tradition. They put on several public shows and produced a few issues of their journal, *Heritage.*

Perhaps of Rajkumari Singh's own literary contribution it must be admitted that she lacked that ultimate gift with words to lift her poetry, drama and fiction to the truly memorable; yet she invariably had something interesting to say, always spoke with her own voice and generally communicated very effectively. Her work emerges out of a number of creative tensions: though intensely active in public affairs her poetry speaks of a deep need for spiritual withdrawal; though she was politically committed to the future and radical social change, her collection of short stories speaks of a longing for a static, pastoral, edenic past. She was always very consciously Guyanese, but equally concerned that the Indian material and cultural contribution to Guyana should not be overlooked.

The latter desire is expressed in several poems in her collection, *Days of the Sahib Are Over* (1971) and in a short play *Heritage* (c. 1973). *Heritage*[47] is more a colloquium than a play, but it airs frankly the differences between those Indians who advocated a boycott of all Government functions as a protest against the PNC's corruption of the electoral process and the discrimination against Indians in the public sector, and those like Mrs Singh who favoured participation. In poems such as 'Days of the Sahib Are Over,' and 'Per-Ajie' she reminds us of the Indian contribution to Guyanese history. The former is an Indo-Guyanese equivalent to the African's 'Massa Day Done'. She does not glorify the past under:

*the overlord whose hard, harsh discipline kept the brown
man cringing,*

> *crawling and grinning in sickening sycophancy.*

But she also reminds of the resistance and argues that writers must pass on a record of that past because:

> *...to know is vital, for the young, the unborn*
> *must never bow their heads believing*
> *theirs offered naught to the fight.*

And, as is so often the case in Guyana, much is coded in the poem. The third line implies that there is now a new sahib, the black middle-class, over the Indians:

> *Days of the Sahib*
> *are over*
> *or should be*
> *now that our land is free of the overlord's yoke.*[48]

However, she urges that this history be used to inspire rather than become trapped in the 'complexities of inferiority and hate', which she feared was the psychological basis of Afro-Guyanese politics. In 'Per-Ajie' Rajkumari Singh pays special homage to the steadfastness of Indian women, whose virtues she saw as central to the character of the Indo-Guyanese as a people 'bred to sacrifice and to achieve'. It is an important attempt to restore the Indo-Guyanese woman to the stage of history, but unfortunately the attempt to create a dignified language of tribute results in a poem which is archaically stilted. Nevertheless, Per-Ajie is strongly defined:

> *Per-Ajie*
>
> *I can see*
> *How in stature*
> *Thou didst grow*
> *Shoulders up*
> *Head held high*
> *The challenge*
> *In thine eye.* (p.15)

Proud though she was of her Indian heritage, Rajkumari Singh was never uncritical. Above all she believed that Indians should see themselves as Guyanese. In her fable 'Karma and the Kaietur'[49] tragedy occurs because of the dual loyalties of the Indian youth who returns to India to care for his aged mother, and because of the girl's lack of faith in her lover's return. Indians have to learn to stop

looking backwards, and other Guyanese must learn patience until the
need has gone. In other stories she deals with suffering caused by an
arranged marriage ('Sakina, I Love You Still')[50], caste prejudice
('Sardar Birbal Singh')[51] and Indian racial prejudices ('Hoof Beats
After Midnight'[52], and 'Juman Maraj'[53].) In her play, *The Sound Of
Her Bells* (c.1974)[54] she explores in Tagorean style the theme of
religious intolerance as Baba, a pious, zealous and priggish Hindu
pundit refuses to allow a professional dancer, Nirmala, to perform in
front of a statue of Lord Shiva in his temple. He protests that she is a
'consummate prostitute' and that her presence will desecrate the
temple grounds. One of the devotees, the liberal and sympathetic
Krishna, asserts that temples are for sinners and attacks Baba's
hypocrisy for taking money from those for whom he performs pujas.
Baba storms out of the temple but inevitably he returns to watch
Nirmala dance. Against his will he is moved and begins to question
his previous attitudes. However, Mrs Singh then rather blurs the case
she is making against male prejudices. Although she suggests rather
hesitantly that the sexuality implicit in Nirmala's dance is a legitimate
vehicle for her act of worship (Nirmala admits to Baba that, 'I do
satisfy my biological urging by means of the dance.') She then weeps
contritely for her sexually adventurous past. However, in 'No More
Kitchree For The Groom,' she speaks without any hesitancy of the
male-centredness of Indian culture, protesting the custom of giving
the son-in-law a dish of kitchree, which he will only begin to eat when
the bride's family has given him sufficient gifts:

> *as though, treasured maiden daughter*
> *was snatched from brothel*
> *to bag a husband.* [55]

By the mid 1970s Mrs Singh was moving towards a livelier,
more demotic diction.

There was also a more personal, private side to Rajkumari
Singh's work. Here her poetry speaks of an intense loneliness
and pain which sought at times for peace in bodily dissolution
and spiritual withdrawal. In a very early poem, 'Alone' she
compares the solitary soul to:

> *The pregnant paddy-sheaves*
> *Waiting to be threshed*
> *Waiting to lay down precious grains of rice*
> *To be relieved of the burden of bearing them.* (p.6)

The two urges – for action and achievement and detachment and dissolution – are bound always to remain in tension. There is symbolic resolution in the figure of Shiva, dancing god of creation and dissolution, whose devotee Rajkumari Singh declares herself in the opening poem of her collection, but as the poem 'Stealing Across the Poignant Silence' suggests, they were tensions which, in life, could only be acknowledged but not overcome. Listening to the conch calling worshippers to prayer, she feels a restless yearning:

For harmony with what is
To scatter from the sphere
The cacophony of men
Clamouring for rights
That mocks the sermon of yesteryear.

The sermons, however, speak with two voices: the other-wordly sage:

Spurning the dues
Of Action
Striving instead for perfection.

and the practical, achievement-oriented Indo-Guyanese:

Inspiring with edicts
That teach of doing
Before having... (p.9)

Though there are undoubted inadequacies of technique in Rajkumari Singh's work, she wrote out a complex perception of the world around her, was concerned with exploring the situation of the Indian woman in the Caribbean without allowing herself to become restricted to either ethnic or a gender ghetto, and achieved a distinctive voice. For that, as well as for what she made of her life, her memory should be honoured.

One of the younger former members of the Messenger group, Mahadai Das, has followed Rajkumari Singh in fusing Indo-Guyanese, feminist and radical nationalist perspectives in her work. Unlike other women's writing in the 'protest' tradition, Mahadai Das's work derives from a genuinely revolutionary framework, is distinguished by the originality of its perceptions and by the constant attempts to refine the form of its expression.

Her earliest poems are those of a sensitive adolescent, about
loneliness and disappointed love but written with a gothic excess of
image and delight in words which mark them out from the usual.[56]
Whilst these poems are full of undigested literary influences, she was
soon afterwards exploring the potential of demotic creolese in poems
such as 'Chile Is Who You Fooling', a sharp satire on empty-belly
pretensions and 'Me and Melda', a lively portrayal of an offended
woman about to do battle with a rival:

> *Yuh can bet de frack yuh gat on*
> *De portals a she ais*
> *wide open*
> *An de blood runnin red-man thru she brains...*
> *...Aye girl*
> *She gan tear out she hair*
> *And dig out she eye*
> *When she done...dat bitch*
> *She ain' gan good fuh no man.* [57]

Between 1973-75 Mahadai Das, along with other members of the
Messenger group, joined the Cultural Division of Guyana National
Service. She remained with G.N.S. long after others had left, an
idealistic revolutionary whose enthusiasm and hopes are to be found
in her first published collection, *I Want To Be A Poetess of My People*
(1976, 1977).[58] In this period one feels that she was not always well
served by those who supported and promoted her work. She was
regarded as a valuable ornament by the cultural establishment of the
ruling party, as an Indian, and a woman, and an exceptionally
photogenic one at that. She was flattered and the least meritorious
aspects of her work encouraged, and not given the kind of
constructive critisism which would have helped her to see what was
genuine in her work and what was not, which has now been left high
and dry by events and its own noisy sloganizing. Poems such as
'Militant', 'Akarra Did You Hear Us Marching', and 'He Leads The
People', have a naively exalted tone and are full of revolutionary
clichés. More interesting are the poems written in response to her
experiences of Kimbia, the G.N.S. camp in the Guyanese interior,
where there was an attempt to revive cotton production. In 'Look in
the Vision for the Smiles of the Harvest', Das displays an acute
sensitivity to the doubleness of experience, exploring the satisfactions
of taming wild nature whilst hinting that there is something
historically disquieting in the regimented production of acres of

cotton and suggesting that something has been violated in the destruction of the wilderness:

When the darkness falls around this Kimbia jungle
...like a cascade of tenderness
...like a mantle of love...
Hear the eerie cries of baboons of desolation driven into the
*   forest,*
Listen their whimpers of subjugation of lost dominance.

However, the poems in this collection which best represents Mahadai Das's gifts are those which explore her consciousness of the complex heritage of being Indo-Guyanese. As a child of a peasant family, she was sharply aware that the history of indenture and plantation labour had shaped her own evolution. She reviews that history in 'They Came In Ships,' a poem which achieves compression and impact through an allusive, montage construction, picking up scraps of her own researches, like the voice of Des Voeux:

I wrote the queen a letter
For the whimpering of the coolies
in their logies would not let me rest.

and making effective use of the simplest rhetorical devices such as repetition:

They came in fleets of ships
They came in droves
Like cattle
Brown like cattle
Eyes limpid like cattle

The poem also demonstrates a taste for verbal wit which becomes an increasingly important element in her later work. Referring to the complacent attitudes of the British Government investigators who came the colony in 1870 she puns neatly:

The Commissioners came
Capital spectacles with British frames.

If 'They Came In Ships' is weighted towards a picture of what was suffered, the next poem in the sequence, 'Cast Aside Reminiscent Foreheads of Desolation' (she had a weakness for lengthy titles at this stage) warns against becoming trapped in a prison of suffering, reminding Indians that there was creation too:

> *...you have helped build this land*
> *Brought forth, out of your womb a new industry*
> *of waving paddy leaves...*

Although in this collection Das is not immune to that sentimental abstraction, 'the people', she also portrays actual people rooted in their customary ways of looking at the world and their resistance to new ideas. In 'Your Bleeding Hands Grasp The Roots of Rice', she writes of a return to her parents, full of a sense of indebtedness to them for enabling her to have the education which has estranged her from them:

> *Your bleeding hands grasp the roots of rice*
> *in my fields*
> *And the seed of life you delved into the earth*
> *Has sprung up to mock me.*

By 1977-1978 Mahadai Das was writing a very different kind of poetry from the optimistic enthusiasms of *I Want To Be A Poetess Of My People.* She had seen the P.N.C. for what it was, a cynical party of the middle class which had fraudulently assumed the clothing of revolution to hang on to power. Perhaps alluding ironically to Jesus's parable of the impossibility of a father offering his son a stone when he has asked for bread, she writes:

> *Cold is my bread of stone.*
> *My bitter tea fouls*
> *Its inner course in the duodenum...*[59]

However, unlike many others, her disillusionment did not mean the abandonment of ideals and political activity. During the late 1970s she became active in the genuinely radical and multi-racial Working People's Alliance. However, after Walter Rodney's murder in 1980 and the killing of a number of other W.P.A. activists, she left Guyana for the United States where she still lives, though still deeply involved in Guyanese politics.

What is immediately noticeable about the poems in her second collection, *My Finer Steel Will Grow* (1982) is that they are both tighter in form and more controlled in diction and more imagined: metaphor rather than rhetorical statement carries the burden of meaning. They have an edge of passionate commitment, but there is also a new note of sometimes self-mocking detachment. They are poems of distress and anger which never lose hope. However, after the strident optimism of the poems in *I Want To Be A Poetess Of My People,* hope is seen from a newly chastened perception of human vulnerability. Working in a very disciplined way through two dominant metaphors, the images of warfare and the image of the body broken into separate inanimate parts, Das conveys very effectively a sense of how shattering defeat feels, how hostile the world:

> *How soon the cold rain, pellets*
> *shattering the thin grass.*
> *Shivering*
> *in my inadequate skin, I inside*
> *huddle pondering a sudden treason,*
> *a ransom that unprepares: a watch*
> *unconsidered.*
>
> *Unarmed against the sky, the earth*
> *bears barren limbs; inarticulate arms*
> *that hide origins. This heart*
> *is a handful of tissue I must coat*
> *in warmth before the guerilla air.* (p.6)

Even those who declare war on tyranny only come,

> *with our string of beads and our naked*
> *spears...with our shield of courage*
> *to reposess*
> *Our native waterfall.* (p.5)

Hope is found in a vision of cosmic justice, in solacing images of the inevitability of natural and seasonal change. Yet there is no thought that change comes through some miraculous divine intervention, but only through the workings of the individual and collective will in the political here-and now. In 'My Finer Steel Will Grow', it is out of the very humiliations of defeat and exile that new resolution is willed to come. The image of a hunted, outcast creature, a flea-ridden pot-hound, is used to describe the sense of inconsequence and placelessness of the defeated exile. The 'felled star' refers, of course, to Rodney's murder:

The felled star is like a dagger
Stuck deep in my heart. Anon. I am gone.
There is no place to rest
my accidental head.
It is a dog's life. Today there are no bones.

The flea-ridden creature is tormented by its humilations, its nature corrupted by rage and by fears of death:

my paws trace out this path
of death too often that I smell.

But in the process of this suffering a matamorphosis takes place:

...They [the fleas] pound
like a carpenter gone
beserk: hammering
rains the bullets
on my back.

Whilst the hammering arm,
in rhythmic falter flags,
my final steel will grow.

The shift in image from fleas to bullets to the hammering arm are perhaps awkward at a visual associational level, but there is a kind of metaphysical intensity. One suspects that Das is making deliberate use of echoes from Blake's poem, 'Tiger, Tiger', in the image of the hammering arm of the oppressor which is transforming the seedy pot-hound into a creature of 'fearful symmetry'. A similarly ironic use of literary allusion is made in the second part of the poem to suggest the enormity of the betrayal she has felt and perhaps mock her own former credulousness. Here the passage into exile is made wittily analogous to Paradise Lost, in the flight of a rebellious Lucifer from a corrupted heaven:

Ah yes! the government of heaven
has grown corrupt:
my passage to earth's eden
is laid with fire. (p.5)

On earth, Eden has been corrupted by the 'knotty schemes' of 'Spider' a neat amalgamation of the serpent in the garden and the Guyanese folk-perception of the political leader as the trickster spider, Anansi.

Not all the poems are equally successful. Sometimes Das seems unaware of the visual inappropriateness of the images she creates. For instance, in trying to find an image adequate to the evil of the murder of a priest, Father Darke, by Government thugs, she writes:

> *Like the bullfrog who croaks, they*
> *bare their teeth and prepare for the slaughter.*
> *While their fangs drip*
> *with the blood of priests and the aborted*
> *day;...* (p.7)

The image of some ludicrous horror film is unfortunately called up. However, such lapses are rare.

The other development illustrated by this collection is Mahadai Das's capacity to demonstrate that her political and personal concerns are aspects of the same experience, that the desire for a society which encourages human creativity within an environment of freedom is simply an expansion of what she seeks in personal relationships. In a long poem, untitled, in the collection, she explores the painful irony that it is the man's political despair which kills his capacity to respond to her, making him mimic the behaviour of the ruler protecting his boundaries from attack, and her take up the role of adversary to one she loves. She writes with a mature synthesis of understanding:

> *But only new time*
> *Can be your adequate mistress.*
> *The days are miserly, the hours*
> *Thin and vaporless, the new season a dream.* (p.13)

and assertion of her wound:

> *...your back*
> *a keel of stone bruising the red lake*
> *of my womb...* (p.11)

Again, she shows a new ability to work through the controlling framework of an extended metaphor which both shapes the poem and ironically describes the invasion of their relationship by political frustrations. He defends:

But I am learning your roster:
the bugle call at dawn,
your gate-shutting rites,
the changing of the guard.

While she plays the role of rebel:

I am the insurrection
your strong hand put down.

However, she cannot decide whether her guerilla struggle to resist his rejection is not more self-destructive than outright confrontation. The image of course also relates back to the world of political choices, between the heroic risks of staying and fighting, and the guerilla tactics of retreat, survival and exile:

...Had I stood
against the wall of my courage,
or had they fired at the dutiful
hour, it would have been
final.
I would have won
the case of my belief.
Instead, this
wretched sentence exiling me
to memory. (p.13)

The last in this short sequence of love poems, in seeking an image of love which is whole, uncomplicated and freely given, returns to an idyllic picture of East Indian peasant life. In the context of the collection as a whole the image is both touching and ironic. Touching because it admits a yearning for a simpler peasant life before the complications of knowledge and political involvement, and ironic because it is a world the poet knows she cannot return to, and a role for women she would reject:

Let us sling our pails
upon our arms' strong rods
and dance to the well.
Our men will still be sleeping
while we stoke the fire. The coals
will leap like joy in our hearts,
to flame. Our lords will wake

*to hot curries and fresh-baked
wheat.
And while it is still dark, they
will make their way to the fields.*

Mahadai Das is still a young woman and her work will undoubtedly continue to develop. Nevertheless, even at this stage it represents an important attempt to explore the sometimes conflicting commitments to being a political radical, being a woman and being an Indian in the Caribbean.

NOTES

1. For an extensive discussion of the image of Indo-Caribbean women in male Caribbean writing, see my article in *Journal of South Asian Literature* (University of Michegan, 1986).

2. The term 'Indian' is used with conscious imprecision to encompass the wide variation of culture and religious belief brought by indentured immigrants from colonial India to the Caribbean.

3. See Dwarka Nath, *A History of Indians in Guyana*, (London, 1970), p. 29, 143-145.

4. See Jack Harewood, *The Population of Trinidad and Tobago*, (London, 1975), p. 102.

5. See Rhoda Reddock, 'Indian Women and Indentureship in Trinidad & Tobago, 1845-1917: Freedom Denied', Paper presented to the Third Conference on East Indians in the Caribbean, UWI St Augustine, 1984.

6. *Among The Hindus and Creoles of British Guiana*, (London, 1888), pp. 145-146.

7. *John Morton of Trinidad, Journals, Letters and Papers*, (Toronto, 1916), p. 342.

8. *The Colony of British Guiana and Its Labouring Population*, (London, 1883), p. 252.

9. See D Wood, *Trinidad in Transition: The Years After Slavery*, (London, 1968), p. 154.

10. Figures compiled from *British Guiana Immigration Agent-General's Reports*. See also B Moore, 'Sex and Marriage Among Indian Immigrants in British Guiana During the 19th Century', Paper presented to the Third Conference on East Indians in the Caribbean.

11. See Reddock, *op cit*, p.37.

12. See Harewood, *op cit*, p. 137. Tables indicate that there was a large scale fall in the participation of East Indian women in gainful employment between 1921-1946.

13. *At last: A Christmas in the West Indies*, (London, 1878), p. 233.

14. See Angela Hamel-Smith, 'Primary Education and East Indian women in Trinidad 1900-1956', Paper presented to the Third Conference on East Indians in the Caribbean.

15. *The Indian Centenary Review*, Ed. Kirpalini *et al.* (Trinidad, 1945), pp. 53-55.

16. Nath, *op cit*, pp. 245-247.

17. I am indebted to the late Mrs Rajkumari Singh, Dr Hardutt Singh and to Mr Karna Singh (who is happily still alive) for this information.

18. See Peter Ruhomon, *History of the East Indian in British Guiana*, (Georgetown, 1947), pp. 244-245.

19. See M Klass, *East Indians in Trinidad: A Study of Cultural Persistence*, (New York, 1961), pp. 93-136; and A&J Niehoff, *East Indians in the West Indies*, (Milwaukee, 1960), pp. 101-110.

20. Niehoff, *op cit*, pp. 80-85. And see M Cross and A Schwartzbaum, 'Social Mobility in Secondary School Selections in Trinidad and Tobago,' *Social and Economic Studies*, 1969, pp. 189-207.

21. See J Nevadomsky, 'Abandoning the Retentionist Model: Family and Marriage Change Among the East Indians in Rural Trinidad', *International Journal of Sociology of the Family*, vol 10, 1980, pp. 181-198; and 'Wedding Rituals and Changing Women's Rights among The East Indians in Rural Trinidad', *Interntional Journal of Women's Studies*, vol 4, no 5, pp. 484-496.

22. See J Nevadomsky, 'Changing Conceptions of Family Regulation Among The Hindu East Indians in Rural Trinidad', *Anthropological Quarterly*, vol 55, no 4, 1982, pp. 189-198.

23. See S Sieunarine, 'The Social and Cultural Change in the East Indian Community of Eldorado in 1960-1980', Caribbean Studies Project, UWI.

24. See Harewood, *op cit*, pp. 120-121.

25. See Judith Johnson, 'The Changing Cultural Context of the Neo-Natal Period in an East Indian Rural Community in South Trinidad', Paper presented to the Second Conference on East Indians in the Caribbean, U.W.I. St Augustine, 1979.

26. See Kunti K Ramdat, 'Some Aspects of Indic Pejorative Usage Among Hindus in Guyana', Paper presented to the Third Conference on East Indians in the Caribbean.

27. Personal observation at Cane Grove Kali-Mai temple.

28. This is consistent with the findings of V Rubin and M Zavelloni's *We Wish To Be Looked Upon*, (New York), 1969, pp. 88-95, that East Indian girls were more likely than girls of any other ethnic group to see career and marriage as irreconcilable. See also F S Brathwaite and W R Aho, 'Race, Occupational Mobility and Career Aspirations Among Secondary School Teachers in Trinidad and Tobago', Paper presented to *East Indians in the Caribbean: A Symposium*, UWI St Augustine, 1975.

29. See *Report of the British Guiana Commission of Inquiry, Racial Problems in the Public Service*, 1965, pp. 49, 84, 87-93.

30. I make these comments on the basis of conversations with Guyanese both in and out of the country.

31. See Janet Jagan, *An Examination of National Service*, (Georgetown, 1976).

32. See for instance: Zorina B Ishmael, 'The Dead Past', *Chronicle Christmas Annual* 1958, (Georgetown), p.18; 'Back From The Dead', *Chronicle Christmas Annual* 1959, p.13; 'No Better Gift', *ibid*, p.19; Zorinah Shah, 'The Wind My Lover', *Corlit* vol 4, Dec 1974, p.27; B S Elaine Ali, 'Dreams', 'Hero of The Morning Glory', 'Heart', in *The New Wave*, Annandale, Guyana, 1974; Nirmala Shewcharan, *Beauty Lies Within and Other Poems*, Georgetown, 1978; and Lallita Narine, *The Illustration of Feelings*, Chaguanas, Trinidad, 1984.

33. Guyana, Sheik Sadeek, 1968, p.8.

34. Georgetown, NHAC 1976. Yardan's other work can be found in *Guyana Drums* (with S Douglas *et al*) Georgetown, 1972; *And Talking of Love Let Us* (with V Facey and L Cromwell) Linden, 1979; and in *Independence Ten*, ed A J Seymour, Guyana, 1976; and in *A Treasury of Guyanese poetry*, ed A J Seymour, Guyana, 1980.

35. *Antilia* (Trinidad) vol 1, no 1, 1983, pp. 41-42.

36. *The Indian Review*, vol 1, no 4, 1983, p. 10.

37. *Corlit*, no 2, April 1974, pp. 21, 39.

38. *Corlit*, vol 3, July 1974, p. 33.

39. *Trinidad Guardian*, 23 May 1948.

40. *Mukdar*, vol 1, no 2, 1975, pp. 36-38.

41. See for instance, Zorina Ishmael, 'And So Goodbye', *Chronicle Christmas Annual*, 1958, p. 37; and Darendra Persaud's play *Daughter's Dilemma*, Georgetown, typescript, 1963.

42. *The Indian Review*, vol 1, no 4, 1983, pp. 19-23.

43. See B S Elaine Ali, 'Portrait of Life', and Janet Jhondorie, 'Cane Cutter', in *The New Wave;*

Celia Dharanpaul, 'Bushrum', *Kaie,* no 8, 1971, pp. 51-55; and Patricia Persaud, 'Dog', *Chronicle Christmas Annual,* 1981, pp. 32-34.

44. *New Writing in The Caribbean,* ed A J Seymour, (Georgetown, 1972), pp. 113-114.

45. *The Dramag* (Georgetown) Special Christmas Number, Dec 1945.

46. The group included, amongst others, Mahadai Das, Rooplall Monar, Guska Kissoon, Gora Singh and Henry Muttoo.

47. Typescript, Georgetown, 1973. Rajkumari Singh's other plays include: *Roraima: A Radio Play, Hoofbeats At Midnight, The Sound of her Bells, A White Camellia and a Blue Star,* and *Bohemian Interlude.*

48. *Days of the Sahib Are Over,* (Georgetown, 1971), pp. 3-4.

49. *A Garland of Stories,* (Ilfracombe, A H Stockwell, 1960), pp. 31-39.

50. *ibid,* pp. 23-28.

51. *Kaie,* no 5, 1968, pp. 31-34.

52. *A Garland of Stories,* pp. 47-55.

53. *Heritage Two,* 1973, pp. 6-10.

54. Unpublished typescript, performed 1974.

55. Unpublished typescript, read at Messenger's Coolie Art Forms Show, 1973.

56. See for instance, 'There You Lie', *Heritage One,* Georgetown, 1973; 'Mystery of the Night', *Heritage Two,* Sept 1973; 'Haunted' 'A Long Wait', 'Change', *Kaie,* no 12, Oct 1975, pp. 107-109.

57. *Kaie,* no 12, pp. 114-116.

58. Guyana, national history and Arts Council, 1976; second enlarged edition, GNS Publishing, 1977.

59. 'My Bread of Stone', *A Treasury of Guyanese Poetry,* ed Seymour, 1980, pp. 130-131.

Indo-Caribbean Test Cricketers

Frank Birbalsingh

Cricket plays a special role in the historical, social and cultural development of the English-speaking Caribbean. It is not like hockey in Canada, baseball in the United States, or even cricket in England. In the English-speaking Caribbean, cricket does not merely stimulate delight or devotion; it is like the bull fight in Spain: a spectacle that can galvanize a people's spiritual resources, stimulate their national self-esteem, remind them of their place in the world. Defensive-minded people will think that this view of cricket demeans West-indians. On the contrary, it recognizes Westindian resistance to an oppressive colonial legacy; for it acknowledges test cricket as the first opportunity that Westindians had of demonstrating their abilities on the international scene. This is not to underplay the achievements of great Westindians such as Captain Cipriani, Hubert Nathaniel Crichlow, and Marcus Garvey[1] in advancing the social, political, and cultural development of the region. Nor does it suggest that West-indians can only demonstrate excellence in sport, anymore than it suggests that Spaniards can only fight bulls. The fact is that the performance of Westindian cricketers, since 1928, has achieved the widest recognition for territories such as Trinidad, Jamaica, Barbados, and Guyana, especially among ordinary people in the English-speaking world outside of the United States.

Representative Westindian Cricket teams began touring England since 1900, and in the early decades of this century, several English teams toured the Westindies; but official test matches were not played between the two 'countries' until 1928. In that year, a Westindian team played three test matches in England and lost all three. Between 1928 and 1950 Westindies played altogether nine series of test matches, mostly against England, but also against Australia and India. Not until 1950 did a Westindian test cricket team include an Indian player – Sonny Ramadhin of Trinidad. Since then a number of Indo-Westindians have played in test matches, notably Rohan Kanhai, Joe Solomon, and Alvin Kallicharan from Guyana.

The late Indian entry into Westindian test cricket has to be viewed against the social and political history of the area. This history consists mainly of changing relationships between a small group of ruling whites and the large majority of Afro-Westindians. Relationships are complicated by the presence of a group of brown people of mixed (chiefly European and African) blood. On top of this, there are smaller Asian groups, including the Indians, who form a majority of the population in Guyana and almost that in Trinidad. Discussion of Indo-Caribbean cricketers will be largely concerned with these two territories. In Guyana and Trinidad, and the English-speaking Caribbean as a whole, the dominance of Creoles is undisputed, during colonial times as well as after. (By 'Creole' is meant local whites, mixed-blood people and blacks.) Since the indenture system which brought Indians to the Caribbean only lasted from 1838 to 1917, Indians were latecomers to the society. Moreover, the original role of Indians as sugar plantation labourers or coolies would not have encouraged their participation in the leisure activities of a largely feudalistic, colonial society. Against this history it is easy to understand why it would be unlikely to expect any Indian representation in Westindian test cricket in 1928, and why it took more than two decades after that for Sonny Ramadhin to play for the Westindies.

Ramadhin was right-arm spin bowler, and he was selected in 1950 because of his performance in his first First Class match when he played for Trinidad against Jamaica and took eight wickets for 106 runs. He went on to take the most wickets (135) for the best average (14.58) on the English tour that followed. In the test matches of the tour he took 26 wickets, and with his 'spinning twin' Alfred Valentine of Jamaica, spearheaded the Westindian victory of 3 matches to 1.

The ensuing 1951/52 tour of Australia was disastrous for the Westindies: they lost 4 to 1. Ramadhin was relatively ineffective, although he did better on the New Zealand leg of the tour. In the 1952 series against India, his achievement was again modest – 13 wickets for an average of 36.15, although he was a match winner in the Barbados test, taking 5 wickets for 26 runs to give Westindies the only win in the five-match series. Ramadhin was in better form against England in 1953/54, when he took 23 wickets at 24.30 apiece, the next highest wicket takers being Frank King and Denis Atkinson with 8 each. He did not shine against Australia in 1955, but had won outstanding success taking 6 for 23 in the first test against New Zealand at Auckland in 1956. Then came the tour of England in 1957, when Ramadhin opened brilliantly in the first test with 7 for 49.

In their second innings of that match, May and Cowdrey put on 411 for England's 4th wicket, and practically destroyed Ramadhin's test career. His 774 balls in the game are the most ever delivered by a bowler in a test match. Although he played in subsequent series, and not without success, as in the 1959/60 series against England when he took 17 wickets, Ramadhin did not dominate again as he did in his pre-1957 days. He played in 43 test matches throughout his career and took 158 wickets at 28.96 apiece.

Ramadhin last represented the Westindies in the 1960-61 series against Australia, during which his place was taken by Lance Gibbs. Gibbs and Ramadhin are, without doubt, the greatest off-spin bowlers produced by the Westindies, and their careers invite comparison. Gibbs had the longer career – 79 tests for 309 wickets. He was also quite different from Ramadhin, who was much shorter, wore his sleeves buttoned to the wrist, and ran briskly up to the wicket delivering the ball with an unusually fast action for a slow bowler. His action resembled that of the left-arm English spinner D L Underwood, who also was quite fast for a slow bowler. Ramadhin used bounce less than the wiry, long-fingered Gibbs with his slow, hopping run up and Laker-like delivery. Gibbs's premeditation was evident in his deliberate, long stride, marked body swing, concentrated delivery and anxious follow through. In contrast, Ramadhin seemed to run, deliver and follow through, all in one quick, casual motion. No doubt this all-in-one action had something to do with his success. It helped to camouflage his grip on the ball and create the sense of mystery which Ramadhin presented to many batsmen.

An essential aspect of Ramadhin's mystery was his ability to bowl a leg-break with his normal (off-break) action. This made him difficult to 'read.' Jim Laker, one of the great English spin bowlers, says that when he and Len Hutton were once batting against Ramadhin in the 1950s, the illustrious Yorkshireman could make neither head nor tail of the bowling.[2] This was at a time when Hutton was at the height of his career. Cowdrey also has written:

> *I watched Cyril Washbrook score a hundred in the Test match at Lords and it was clear at the end as it had been at the beginning, that he could not read the spin.*[3]

This was the second test in 1950, when Westindies beat England, in England, for the first time. A calypso was composed to celebrate the victory:

Yardley [the English captain] tried his best,
But Goddard [the Westindian captain] won the test,
With those little pals of mine,
Ramadhin and Valentine.[4]

There must have been very few Westindians at the time who didn't
know the whole calypso by heart, and there cannot have been many
cricket fans the world over who did not regard the 'spin twins'
Ramadhin and Valentine with wonder if not awe. Without detracting
from Valentine's considerable skill as a left-arm spin bowler in his
own right, it is probably true that some of this success may have been
due to Ramadhin's mystery. It may be just a cricket legend, but some
people believe that batsmen were so frustrated by their inability to
'read' Ramadhin that they lashed out wildly, and Valentine, bowling
from the other end, stood to gain from this.

But it would be quite wrong to attribute Ramadhin's success
entirely to his mystery. His control of length, direction and flight
could be rigorous and unflagging. In the notorious First Test against
England in 1957, Ramadhin's figures in the second innings were 98
overs for 179 runs, in spite of the record-breaking partnership by May
and Cowdrey. On perfectly good wickets he could dismiss batsmen
through a combination of accurate length, unerring direction and
crafty variations of flight. In 1954, in the Bourda Test, he dismissed
the English opening batsman Willie Watson with just such a
combination. Ramadhin's orthodox off break dropped slightly
outside the left hander's leg stump and turned across his wicket,
rising to sufficient height to nip the bail off the off stump. Watson
played what he believed was a sage, defensive stroke, leaning well
forward to smother any turn or spin. There seemed no room for the
ball to get past him. But he was beaten by the flight. Imagine his
consternation when he was bowled! His face registered a suspicion of
mystery, as if the delivery had somehow confounded scientific laws in
physics and dynamics to evade his bat.

Ramadhin was clearly in the front rank of spin bowlers of his time.
His 158 test wickets was a landmark in Westindian cricket in 1961.
His main flaw seems to have been one of temperament. He did not
have much success against Australia. This may have been because he
could not withstand aggression from batsmen who used their feet.
Laker makes this point, and even says that the Australian batsman
Keith Miller would taunt Ramadhin before an innings in an effort to
cow his spirit.[5] For all that, Laker places Ramadhin third in his

ranking of spin bowlers of the 1950s, behind only Athol Rowan and Tom Goddard. Ramadhin was embittered by his experience at Edgbaston in 1957, when May and Cowdrey were allowed to use their pads defensively against him without playing a stroke. If the lbw rule now in force had been in effect then, Ramadhin's career might have lasted longer.

The 1957 English tour, which may be said to have ended Ramadhin's career, was the beginning of Kanhai's. It was a dismal tour and Westindies lost 3:0, with 2 matches drawn. In ten test innings, Kanhai could only muster 206 runs for an average of 22.88. It was a gruelling initiation made worse by the fact that Kanhai opened the batting and kept wicket in the first three matches. Yet he had top-scored twice, which proved that the promise he had shown in the preceding inter-colonial series was very much alive. In the Pakistan tour of Westindies during 1958, Kanhai did not excel, although he made 96 in one innings. It was not until the Westindian tour of India and Pakistan in 1958/59 that Kanhai's promise was really fulfilled. In 8 innings against India, he made 538 runs with 256 as his highest score. He followed this with an innings of 217 against Pakistan, and by the time England toured Westindies in 1959/60, the English players knew that the Kanhai they would encounter would be quite different from the fledgling batsman who could not make even one score of 50 in 10 test innings two years before.

This time Kanhai scored 325 runs for an average of 40.62. Again, as so often with Kanhai, the runs are less important than his manner of scoring. His batting in the second innings of the second test in Port of Spain revealed characteristic qualities of his approach to cricket. Westindies faced a total of 520 to win. On the last day of the match, they had reached a score of 188 for the loss of their five best batsmen. Of the accredited batsmen, only Kanhai remained in partnership with his captain Gerry Alexander. Although Alexander was a useful middle-order batsman, at midway between lunch and tea a West Indian victory was beyond contemplation. But three hours of stout defiance might earn an honourable draw. It is typical of Kanhai that with his own score in the late 80s, he suddenly launched into fast bowler Freddie Trueman, and hit him for 16 runs in a single over. Defiance through aggression! Soon after Kanhai was out for 110. The last Westindian hope went with him and England won by 256 runs. One can accuse Kanhai of rashness or irresponsibility. On the other hand, one can say that he had saved Westindian pride through direct, head-on confrontation with the enemy.

The innings in Port of Spain in 1960 is of crucial significance to Kanhai's career. It showed that he was unwilling to curb his naturally aggressive approach, and many commentators have observed that it has often curtailed potentially long innings of his. Far from regarding this approach as a flaw, however, it must be accepted as essential to Kanhai's character and personality, and regarded as his special contribution to the art of batsmanship. This art, for Kanhai, consists of daring, invention, pugnacity and flamboyance. Nothing illustrates this more vividly than the falling hook, a stroke which is now regarded as Kanhai's invention, and his own unique trademark. It was seen in the Port of Spain innings of 110 when he hit the spinner David Allen for a six and a four in one over. E W Swanton commented, 'I will swear that on each occasion the force of the blow caused Kanhai to leave the ground with both feet.'[6] Swanton captures the right mixture of awestruck wonder and genuine delight which Kanhai evoked with this particular stroke, even in its early stages, before he perfected it into a spectacle that crowds eagerly waited to see whenever he strode to the crease. The stroke invariably produced a boundary, with Kanhai left lying across the pitch flat on his back, his bat held above his chest, and his head raised to follow the direction of the ball. The bold innovativeness of the stroke represents the bold and almost recklessly innovative strokeplay that is to be found in Kanhai's batting as a whole.

The next four series in which Kanhai played – against Australia in 1960/61, India in 1961/62, England in 1963, and Australia again in 1964 – form the peak of his career as a test cricketer. In these series, Kanhai's aggregate scores were as follows: 503, 495, 497, 462. Never before of since was he able to achieve similar scores in consecutive matches. We may consult Richie Benaud, the Australian captain, for an authoritative opinion on Kanhai's achievement and reputation at this period, during the first half of the 1960s:

> *When Westindies came to Australia there was something of a battle between Sobers and Kanhai to decide the world's best batsman, and it says much for Kanhai that, batting alone, I thought he just shaded Sobers in that series [1960-61].*[7]

This opinion has the authority of someone who played as a bowler against Kanhai. Benaud further reports that one of the chief preoccupations of his teammates before and after each test match during 1960/61 was 'whether or not it was possible to keep Kanhai quiet.'[8] To instil such respect, not to say fear, in bowlers such as Alan Davidson, Ian Mechkiff, Ken Mackay, Lindsay Kline and Richie Benaud speaks for itself.

After 1965, Kanhai continued to play regularly for the Westindies, although recurring knee trouble caused him to miss several matches. There were some good tours and many brilliant innings, until his test career ended in 1974. By that time he had completed 79 test matches and scored 6227 runs for an average of 47.53. At the time only Sobers among Westindian batsmen had scored more runs. There is no doubt that Sobers was the better accumulator of larger scores. Yet a close look at Kanhai's figures shows that in addition to his 15 test centuries, he has 28 half-centuries to his credit. These figures confirm what has already been suggested: that Kanhai had been set for a big score many times, when his innings was abruptly curtailed. This happens to all batsmen, but it seems to have afflicted Kanhai an unusual number of times, and can only be explained by the quicksilver daring of his temperament, his insatiable audacity and an irrepressible susceptibility to provide an unhampered display of force and style. Like all great rather than good batsmen, he could punish the good ball as well as the bad. But great and equally pugnacious batsmen like Sobers and Bradman have huge scores to their credit. They could improvise as dexterously as Kanhai; but they also showed judicious restraint and a discipline which seemed to go against the grain with Kanhai.

Kanhai's genius was of a different order from the brilliance certainly of Bradman. It is best elucidated by C L R James, who speculates on the so-called craziness of Kanhai's batting. James writes, 'That could be the Greek Dionysious, the satyric passion for the expression of the natural man bursting through the acquired restraints of disciplined necessity.'[9] Jamesian hyperbole is probably the best thing to capture the full excitement and intense, nerve-tingling pleasure produced by Kanhai's batting. His wicket was always at risk, and you could not watch him without having your heart in your mouth. James singles out a particular innings of 170 which Kanhai made at a festival match against an English team at Edgbaston in 1964. The next morning, English journalists compared Kanhai to Bradman. But James disagreed:

They were wrong. Kanhai had found his way into regions Bradman never knew. It was not only the technical skills and strategic generalship that made the innings the most noteworthy I have seen. There was more to it, to be seen as well as felt.

*Bradman was a ruthless executioner of bowlers. All through this
demanding innings Kanhai grinned with a grin that could be seen
a mile away.*[10]

One can claim that Kanhai's batting was an expression of hard-won
freedom by a collective Westindian personality, restrained for
centuries by slavery, indenture and colonialism, but breaking out, at
last, to annouce itself to the world with unfettered zest and
enthusiasm. If this claim seems extravagant or far fetched, it is as
plausible an analysis of Kanhai's batting as any other. According to
James, Kanhai had attained freedom 'to create not only "a house for
Mr Biswas," a house like other houses, but to sail the seas that open
out to the East Indian who no longer has to prove himself to anybody
but himself.'[11] These lines are given special emphasis in James's essay
and confirm the link between Kanhai's batting and his East Indian
heritage of oppression through indenture in the Caribbean.

If there is any truth in James's analysis, we should see something of
the liberating quality of Kanhai's batting in all great Westindian
batsmen, from George Headley to Vivian Richards. Sir Neville
Cardus, perhaps the finest of all professional writers on cricket, sees
in the Westindian players 'natural instinct combined with acquired
technical sophistications' to produce 'an echo of the calypso.' No
doubt Cardus betrays an element of metropolitan rhapsodizing over
the naturalness of exotic Caribbean behaviour. But the unique
excitement and appeal of Caribbean players is acknowledged by
cricket crowds in all parts of the world, and there is no better
explanation than seeing it as a reaction to the oppression of slavery
and colonialism in the Caribbean. Cardus's view should be taken
seriously:

*But of all the delights Westindies cricket has showered on us, the
galvanism of Constantine, the quiet mastery of Headley, the
tripartite genius and stroke-play of Worrell, Weekes and Walcott,
the enchanted improvisations of Ramadhin and Valentine, none
has excited and delighted me, sent me so eagerly on the tip-toe of
expectation, as Kanhai, upright or flat on his back.*[12]

Cardus remembers Kanhai's hook. He must also have had in mind
(as did James in his easy) the innings of 77 which Kanhai made
against England in the Oval Test of 1963; for it is even more typical
than the 110 made in Port of Spain in 1960. Westindies needed 255

runs to win in their second innings at the beginning of the final day of the Oval Test. The openers Hunte and Rodriguez put on 78 before Rodriguez was out. Kanhai came in, and in 90 minutes scored 77 runs off 103 balls, hitting 10 fours and one six. When he was out at 191 for two, a Westindian victory was assured. Such devastation wreaked on bowlers like Statham, Shackleton and Lock cannot have been completely uncontrolled.

That Kanhai should be the main focus in this study of Indo-Caribbean test cricketers is entirely fair. In addition to his batting, he was a superb fielder in almost any position. Most of all, he became captain of the Westindies team after Sobers, and led them in three series – against Australia in 1972/73, and twice against England, in 1973 and 1974. Kanhai took over the captaincy at a time when morale was low, and the team had not won a series for four years. When his team beat England at Lords in 1973, by an innings and 226 runs, Kanhai's success as a captain was beyond dispute. This success continued into 1974 when Kanhai was again captain during the English tour of the Westindies. With the help of superb batting, particularly by Lawrence Rowe, he held England to a one-all draw in the five-match series. With his varied contributions as fieldman, wicket keeper, batsman and captain, Kanhai is undoubtedly the most celebrated Indo-Westindian who has represented Westindies in test cricket.

Joe Solomon is an exact contemporary of Kanhai's, a right-handed middle-order batsman and a useful leg-spin change bowler. He has played in 27 test against all the major cricketing countries, except New Zealand. In his first test series against India in 1958/59, he scored 351 runs and headed the average with 117. Sobers followed with an average of 92.83, Butcher with 69.42, and Kanhai with 67.25. But Solomon was never again able to equal his performance in this series. He settled down instead as a batsman who could be relied upon to hold up a sagging middle order. This he did many times, most notably in the extraordinary tied test at Brisbane in 1960. Solomon had neither the daring aggression nor the sparkling fluency of Kanhai. He was given to subtle deflections rather than full-blooded drives in front of the wicket. The square cut was was probably his most productive stroke. But in the tied test at Brisbane, he distinguished himself in a way that would leave his name forever in the record books. Not only did he score innings of 65 and 47, confirming his stout, unfussy reliability: he also achieved two crucial run outs that transformed that match into the memorable event it has become. In the run out that ended the match, Solomon had only one stump to aim at from his position at square leg. It would be uncharitable to attribute this feat entirely to luck. Solomon deserves credit for the coolness of nerve and the steady concentration which were essential aspects of his style and conduct.

The sedateness of Solomon was not to be found in the left-handed Alvin Kallicharan. Kallicharan, in fact, has been called 'the left-handed Kanhai' because of the forceful, aggressive style of his batting. In his first series – against New Zealand in the Westindies in 1972 – Kallicharan played three innings, averaging 109.5 and totalling 219 runs that included two centuries. Perhaps his home territory, loyal and familiar crowds, and the relatively moderate strength of the opposition contributed to this spectacular initiation. But it was no fluke. In subsequent series against England, Australia, India, Pakistan and New Zealand, Kallicharan continued to score heavily and consistently, even if he did not attain such an average again.

Kallicharan's career was curiously affected in the late seventies when Kerry Packer, the Australian financier, paid cricketers to take part in World Series matches that were quite separate from the regular cycle of test matches. Test players from most countries joined Packer amidst bitter conflict and controversy. Consequently, the Australian team that toured the Westindies were at full strength for the first two matches, then their most experienced players also joined Packer, and Kallicharan found himself captain of an equally inexperienced Westindian team. His own aggregate of 408 runs in the five matches for an average of 51 is distinguished enough. When combined with the strain of captaincy, it becomes even more distinguished. His 126 on the final day of the final test illustrates this. Westindies needed 269 to win, and by mid-afternoon had reached 88 for five. It took pluck and leadership, as well as batsmanship, for Kallicharan to keep the Australians at bay until close to the end, although he had only tail enders to support him.

Kallicharan's career reached its peak in 1978-79 when he was made captain for the full Westindian tour of India and Sri Lanka. So far as Indo-Caribbean cricket is concerned, this tour was most significant: both the captain and the manager – Joe Solomon – were Indian. This was a considerable advance from 1950 when Ramadhin was the sole Indian representative on the Westindian team that toured England. One has to remember, however, that this situation was produced by the Packer affair and the absence of the better-known Westindian players who were engaged in World Series cricket. When the Packer affair died down, the stars returned to the team and Lloyd resumed the captaincy. In the interim, Kallicharan had been captain for nine matches and had played a leading role in one of the most dramatic chapters in the history of Westindian cricket.

Kallicharan continued his distinguished career as a batsman with the reconstituted Westindian team. He toured Australia and New Zealand in 1979-80, then England in 1980, and Pakistan in 1980-81. In each case, he was one of the main Westindian run-getters. He was therefore at the height of his powers when he was banned from the Westindian team because he had played cricket in South Africa. His test career thus came to an abrupt end after he had played in 66 test matches and scored 4399 runs, including 12 centuries, for an average of 44.43. After the ban, Kallicharan continued to play English county cricket, representing Warwickshire, as Kanhai had done before him. But Westindies had lost a dashing batsman who would be remembered for courage and attacking power such as he demonstrated in the Prudential World Cup match against Australia in 1975, when he hooked Dennis Lillee repeatedly to the boundary.

Another banned player was Faoud Bacchus, who represented Westindies in 19 test matches and scored 782 runs for an average of 26.06. His finest achievement was a score of 250 against India at Kanpur in 1974. Bacchus was also frequently singled out for his alert and athletic fielding in a variety of positions. Sewdatt Shivnarine also played in test matches, 8 in all, for an aggregate of 379 runs and an average of 29.15. Ranjie Nanan played in only one test match, against Pakistan in 1979, when he took 4 wickets for 91 runs. One of the most notable of the Indo-Westindians who began playing test cricket in the 1970s was Raphick Jumadeen, a right-arm spin bowler who appeared in 12 matches and took 29 wickets at 39.34 apiece. Other Indo-Westindians who played test cricket are Nyron Asgarali, Ivan Madray, Inshan Ali, Imtiaz Ali, C K Singh, and L Baichan. The achievements of these 'minor' players do not measure up either in quality or consistency to those of Ramadhin, Kanhai, Solomon, and Kallicharan.

The achievement of all these players is remarkable when we consider that well after World War Two, most Indo-Westindians still lived largely in rural areas where they did not enjoy the social, educational and cultural advantages of many creole sections of the population. It was this fact, no doubt, that prompted the British Guiana Sugar Producers' Association to appoint Clyde Walcott as a cricket organiser, in the mid-1950s, to encourage sporting activities among the (mainly Indian) workers on the sugar estates. Walcott's influence was positive, and in time, other Indo-Westindian cricketers, apart from Kanhai and Solomon who started in the 1950s, began to emerge from the sugar estates of Guyana. This is the social-historical context within which we must evaluate Ramadhin's achievement in becoming one of the great slow bowlers of the post-war era,[13] Solomon's solid contributions to Westindian success, and Kallicharan's reputation as an outstanding attacking batsman on the international scene. This is also the context that most fully reflects the magnitude of Kanhai's achievement in securing a place for himself among the finest batsmen the world has seen.

The achievements presented here of one section of the Caribbean community are not intended either to advocate or sanction division within this community. Because Indo-Westindians represent a minority group within the English-speaking Caribbean, their performance in cricket, as in other fields, tends to be neglected. This account may have the merit of trying to redeem that neglect by filling a few more details into the larger historical record of Westindian test cricket. I have emphasized that cricket is not merely a game in the Westindies. The performance of Indo-Caribbean test cricketers exemplifies this as eloquently as the charged dynamism of Constantine, the tremendous fire power of Weekes, Worrell and Walcott, and the miraculous versatility of Garfield Sobers. Far from being divisive, this account asserts the Caribbeanness of players who have successfully broken out from the shared colonial oppression of slavery / indenture to express an impulse for freedom that is universal.

NOTES

1. Cipriani (Trinidad), Crichlow (Guyana), and Garvey (Jamaica) were leaders who, between the two World Wars did much to advance the cause of West Indian freedom and independence.

2. J Laker, *Spinning Round the World* (London, 1959), p.131.

3. C Cowdrey, *The Incomparable Game* (Newton Abbot, 1971), p.55.

4. The composer and singer was Lord Kitchener.

5. *Spinning Round the World*, p.209.

6. E W Swanton, *West Indies Revisited* (London, 1960), p.124.

7. R Benaud, *Willow Patterns* (London, 1970), p.112.

8. *Ibid.*, p.116.

9. C L R James, 'Kanhai: A Study in Confidence', *At the Rendezvous of Victory* (London, 1984), p.169.

10. *Ibid.*, p.170.

11. *Ibid.*

12. N Cardus, 'The Caribbean Flavour', *A Fourth Innings with Cardus* (London, 1981), pp.116-117.

13. Ramadhin's career originated in similar circumstances. He was noticed in the countryside by an oil company official who admired his bowling and facilitated his entry into first-class cricket.

David Dabydeen

Coolie Odyssey

(for Ma,d. 1985)

Now that peasantry is in vogue,
Poetry bubbles from peat bogs,
People strain for the old folk's fatal gobs
Coughed up in grates North or North East
'Tween bouts o' living dialect,
It should be time to hymn your own wreck,
Your house the source of ancient song:
Dry coconut shells cackling in the fireside
Smoking up our children's eyes and lungs,
Plantains spitting oil from a clay pot,
Thick sugary black tea gulped down.

The calves hustle to suck,
Bawling on their rope but are beaten back
Until the cow is milked.
Frantic children call to be fed.
Roopram the Idiot goes to graze his father's goats backdam
Dreaming that the twig he chews so viciously in his mouth
Is not a twig.

In a winter of England's scorn
We huddle together memories, hoard them from
The opulence of our masters.

You were always back home, forever
As canefield and whiplash, unchanging
As the tombstones in the old Dutch plot
Which the boys used for wickets playing ball.

Over here Harilall who regularly dodged his duties at the marketstall
To spin bowl for us in the style of Ramadhin
And afterwards took his beating from you heroically
In the style of England losing
Is now known as the local Paki
Doing slow trade in his Balham cornershop.
Is it because his heart is not in business

But in the tumble of wickets long ago
To the roar of wayward boys?
Or is it because he spends too much time
Being chirpy with his customers, greeting
The tight-wrapped pensioners stalking the snow
With tropical smile, jolly small chat, credit.
They like Harilall, these muted claws of Empire,
They feel privileged by his grinning service,
They hear steelband in his voice
And the freeness of the sea.
The sun beams from his teeth.

Heaped up beside you Old Dabydeen
Who on Albion Estate clean dawn
Washed obsessively by the canal bank,
Spread flowers on the snake-infested water,
Fed the gods the food that Chandra cooked,
Bathed his tongue of the creole
Babbled by low-caste infected coolies.
His Hindi chants terrorized the watertoads
Flopping to the protection of the bush.
He called upon Lord Krishna to preserve
The virginity of his daughters
From the Negroes,
Prayed that the white man would honour
The end-of-season bonus to Poonai
The canecutter, his strong, only son:
Chandra's womb being cursed by deities
Like the blasted land
Unconquerable jungle or weed
That dragged the might of years from a man.
Chandra like a deaf-mute moved about the house
To his command,
A fearful bride barely come-of-age
Year upon year swelling with female child.
Guilt clenched her mouth
Smothered the cry of bursting apart:
Wrapped hurriedly in a bundle of midwife's cloth
The burden was removed to her mother's safekeeping.
He stamped and cursed and beat until he turned old
With the labour of chopping tree, minding cow, building fence

And the expense of his daughters' dowries.
Dreaming of India
He drank rum
Till he dropped dead
And was buried to the singing of Scottish Presbyterian hymns
And a hell-fire sermon from a pop-eyed bawling catechist,
By Poonai, lately baptised, like half of the village.

Ever so old,
Dabydeen's wife,
Hobbling her way to fowl-pen,
Cussing low, chewing her cud, and lapsed in dream,
Sprinkling rice from her shrivelled hand.
Ever so old and bountiful,
Past where Dabydeen lazed in his mudgrave,
Idle as usual in the sun,
Who would dip his hand in a bowl of dhall and rice –
Nasty man, squelching and swallowing like a low-caste sow –
The bitch dead now!

The first boat chugged to the muddy port
Of King George's Town. Coolies come to rest
In El Dorado,
Their faces and best saries black with soot.
The men smelt of saltwater mixed with rum.
The odyssey was plank between river and land,
Mere yards but months of plotting
In the packed bowel of a white man's boat
The years of promise, years of expanse.
At first the gleam of the green land and the white folk and the
    Negroes,
The earth streaked with colour like a toucan's beak,
Kiskidees flame across a fortunate sky,
Canefields ripening in the sun
Wait to be gathered in armfuls of gold.

I have come back late and missed the funeral.
You will understand the connections were difficult.
Three airplanes boarded and many changes
Of machines and landscapes like reincarnations
To bring me to this library of graves,

This small clearing of scrubland.
There are no headstones, epitaphs, dates.
The ancestors curl and dry to scrolls of parchment.
They lie like texts
Waiting to be written by the children
For whom they hacked and ploughed and saved
To send to faraway schools.
Is foolishness fill your head.
Me dead.
Dog-bone and dry-well
Got no story to tell.
Just how me born stupid is so me gone.
Still we persist before the grave
Seeking fables.
We plunder for the maps of El Dorado
To make bountiful our minds in an England
Starved of gold.

Albion villages sleeps, hacked
Out between bush and spiteful lip of river.
Folk that know bone
Fatten themselves on dreams
For the survival of days.
Mosquitoes sing at a nipple of blood.
A green-eyed moon watches
The rheumatic agony of houses crutched up on stilts
Pecked about by huge beaks of wind,
That bear the scars of ancient storms.
Crappeau clear their throats in hideous serenade,
Candleflies burst into suicidal flame.
In a green night with promise of rain
You die.

We mark your memory in songs
Fleshed in the emptiness of folk,
Poems that scrape bowl and bone
In English basements far from home,
Or confess the lust of beasts
In rare conceits
To congregations of the educated
Sipping wine, attentive between courses –
See the applause fluttering from their white hands
Like so many messy table napkins.

A contemporary line drawing from an historical photograph of East Indian indentured labourers disembarking at Port Georgetown, Guyana. Circa early 20th century

David Dabydeen

Coolie Mother

Jasmattie live in bruk –
Down hut big like Bata shoe-box,
Beat clothes, weed yard, chop wood, feed fowl
For this body and that body and every blasted body,
Fetch water, all day fetch water like if the whole –
Whole slow-flowing Canje river God create
Just for *she* one own bucket.

Till she foot-bottom crack and she hand cut-up
And curse swarm from she mouth like red-ants
And she cough blood on the ground but mash it in:
Because Jasmattie heart hard, she mind set hard

To hustle save she one-one slow penny
Because one-one dutty make dam cross the Canje
And she son Harilall *got* to go school in Georgetown,
Must wear clean starch pants, or they go laugh at he,
Strap leather on he foot, and he *must* read book,
Learn talk proper, take exam, go to England university,
Not turn out like he rum-sucker chamar dadee.

David Dabydeen

Coolie Son
(The Toilet Attendant Writes Home)

Taana boy, how you do?
How Shanti stay? And Sukhoo?
Mosquito still a-bite all-you?
Juncha dead true-true?
Mala bruk-foot set?
Food deh foh eat yet?

England nice, snow and dem ting,
A land dey say fit for a king,
Iceapple plenty on de tree and bird a-sing –
Is de beginning of what dey call 'The Spring'.

And I eating enough for all a-we
And reading book bad bad.

But is what make Matam wife fall sick
And Sonnel cow suck dry wid tick?

Soon, I go turn lawya or dacta,
But just now, passage money run out
So I tek lil wuk –
I is a Deputy Sanitary Inspecta,
Big-big office boy! Tie round me neck!
Brand new uniform, one big bunch keys!
If Ma can see me now how she go please....

David Dabydeen

London Taxi Driver

From Tooting, where I picked him up, to Waterloo,
He honked, swerved, swore,
Paused at the twin-packed buttocks of High Street Wives,
Jerked forward again,
Unwound the window as we sped along,
Hawked and spat.

The talk was mostly solitary,
Of the new single, of missing the pools by bleeding two,
Of some sweet bitch in some soap serial,
How he'd like to mount and stuff her lipsticked mouth,
His eyes suddenly dreamy with designs –
Nearly missing a light he slammed the car stop,
Snatched the hand-brake up.
Wheel throbbed in hand, engine giddy with anticipation.
As we toured the slums of Lambeth the meter ticked greedily.

He has come far and paid much for the journey
From some village in Berbice where mule carts laze
And stumble over broken paths,
Past the women with buckets on their heads puffed
With ghee and pregnancy,
Past the men slowly bent over earth, shovelling,
Past the clutch of mud huts jostling for the shade,
Their Hindu flags of folk defiant rituals
That provoked the Imperial swords of Christendom
Discoloured, hang their heads and rot
On bamboo pikes:
Now he knows more the drama of amber red and green,
Mutinees against double-yellow lines,
His aggression is horned like ancient clarions,
He grunts rebellion
In back seat discount sex
With the night's last whore.

Mahadai Das

Bleeding Hands

Silently, I move in a vision of lost happiness
In a world forgotten:
Old woman
where you sit, feet plaited day by backbreaking day,
your bulging waist weighed by coppers in apron-pockets,
Do you know I have changed?

Old man
With your dry coconuts, each as another,
each day, each year like other years –
Don't you sense evolvement, misty-slow, painful –
new death.

A climb, fruitless step by stony step, to a barren star.

You sell your picky-picky chickens.
You weigh them on broken scales.
Don't you know, as you touch those scales –
one buys – one dies.

In your backyard, fertile, brown,
your fingers knead soil for my flat belly, and,
brown wrinkles multiply, one by one,
round your sunken sockets
for my stomach.

My shoes stand on a wasteland
while your twisting toes squeeze in a frenzy of squelching mud
which bears you life:
your bleeding hands grasp roots of rice
In my fields,
and the seed of life you delved into the earth
has sprung up to mock me.

Mahadai Das

They Came In Ships

They came in ships.

From across the seas, they came.
Britain, colonising India, transporting her chains
from Chota Nagpur and the Ganges Plain.

Westwards came the Whitby,
The Hesperus,
the Island-bound Fatel Rozack.

Wooden missions of imperialist design.
Human victims of her Majesty's victory.

They came in fleets.
They came in droves
like cattle
brown like cattle,
eyes limpid, like cattle.

Some came with dreams of milk-and-honey riches,
fleeing famine and death:
dancing girls,
Rajput soldiers, determined, tall,
escaping penalty of pride.
Stolen wives, afraid and despondent,
crossing black waters,
Brahmin, Chammar, alike,
hearts brimful of hope.

I saw them dying at streetcorners, alone, hungry
for a crumb of British bread,
and a healing hand's mighty touch.

I recall my grandfather's haunting gaze;
my eye sweeps over history
to my children, unborn
I recall the piracy of innocence,
light snuffed like a candle in their eyes.

I alone today am alive.
I remember logies, barrackrooms, ranges,
nigga-yards. My grandmother worked in the field.
Honourable mention.

Creole gang, child labour.
Second prize.
I recall Lallabhagie, Leonora's strong children,
and Enmore, bitter, determined.

Remember one-third quota, coolie woman.
Was your blood spilled so I might reject my history –
forget tears among the paddy leaves.

At the horizon's edge, I hear
voices crying in the wind. Cuffy shouting:
'Remember 1763!' – John Smith – 'If I am
a man of God, let me join with suffering.'
Akkarra – 'I too had a vision.'

Des Voeux cried,
'I wrote the queen a letter,
for the whimpering of coolies in logies
would not let me rest.'
The cry of coolies echoed round the land.
They came, in droves, at his office door
beseeching him to ease their yoke.

Crosby struck in rage against planters,
in vain. Stripped of rights, he heard
the cry of coolies continue.

Commissioners came,
capital spectacles in British frames
consulting managers about costs of immigration.
The commissioners left, fifty-dollar bounty remained.
Dreams of a cow and endless calves,
and endless reality in chains.

Mahadai Das

Beast

In Gibraltor Straits,
pirates in search of El Dorado,
masked and machete-bearing,
kidnapped me.
Holding me to ransom,
they took my jewels and my secrets
and dismembered me.

The reckoning lasted for years.
Limbs and parts eventually grew:
a new nose, arms skilful and stronger,
sight after the gutted pits could bear a leaf.
It took centuries.

In the caves where they kept me,
a strange beast grew.
With his skin of glistening jewels
and his deadly tongue,
even I was afraid of him.

In the dark Ajanta caves of my breast
ever since he has stayed,
with his measure of venom,
his exact poison and scintillating glitter.
At a certain hour, I almost love him.

Arnold Itwaru

From 'Shattered Songs'

dead, gone. something in me is dead, is gone. something
dies in its own growth, and those i knew are all gone
somewhere. if ever you should see my father do not tell him
i hardly remember what he looks like, tell him i did
not mean to leave like this. if ever you should see my
mother tell her i went on this journey and fell in, do not tell
her she cannot reach me nor i her, and if by chance perhaps
you see *her,* tell her this, tell her i remember her kindness,
i remember her kindness.

Arnold Itwaru

From 'Shattered Songs'

i remember smoke under blazing skies,
fields, beaches where skeletons eat the sand,
my father struck down his rented house, mother
buried out there somewhere, blizzards of bodies,
strangled cries by the fence where the cat
haunted the boundaries of the morning. i remember,
yet
like smoke, like smoke,
i float, i flow from dream to dream.
the child i thought i had left haunts me:
crying, wailing, smothered in silence he will
not be consoled and i am nearly 40,
floating,
still running,
kicking, screaming,
i who have tried to mend fences,
to fix my roof, to nail things down,
who now move in silence, whose songs are shattered

Arnold Itwaru

We have Survived

fresh water pain
whose illusion i am
an indentured present i want
and do not want
and have become
and have not

a delirium of remembered branches
across the woodsmoke dreaming dusk
across flights by air and land and water
dark voice in the labourings
of the morning's fall into night

middle-passaged
passing
beneath the colouring of desire
in the enemy's eye
a scatter of worlds and broken wishes
in Shiva's unending dance

uprooted
we have survived
the piercing morning
we have survived
death in the backdams and hovels of hope
we have survived
we are the surviving
we who know the snake's fangs
the tide's and the seasons' treachery
the boot the fist the spit of the British Empire

we have survived the breakage of speech
language which formulates us
in its curse

our men are proud: they bear handsomely
the garments of their imprisonment

our women awaken desire
cosmeticized and clothed in the imaginings
of their exploiter

a parade of painted voices
in the lachrimatories of mirrors and silences
in the Other's echo and call
the forgotten dead struck down in life
the lamentations in the villages and firesides
the weed-grown places of burial and hope
we have survived

indenture lives in dates and distances
not in the antic dance we dance
speech which speaks our death
in postures of greed and denial,
pain which strikes in the striking of each stricken hour

where is he, the gentle one
taken to the fields
who never returned?
where is she, milk on my tongue
who wept and toiled
and is no more?

and this child this youth
whose gleaming eyes i adore
whose speech i dread,
how will you fare in the labryinths
which lengthen and lengthen in their unopening?

Cyril Dabydeen

The Country

Take the country in us
as much as we are

Breathing through silences
the uprooted air

Buttressed:
another crossing –
this I shall tell again
turning with the wheel
        our encompassed selves

At a wave length
the continent's drift
I learn to live in essences
my landscape's time
on firm ground

        – unsettled
breathings
anew

Cyril Dabydeen

Atlantic Song

Hands beat against water
hands beat a rhythm against waves

hands are hardly wet in water
they sweat – oil of body and skin

pores, pores
against crystal water

etchings of waves
register the crossing

entering the hothouse
domain next –

   they raise
machetes in a virulent sun
assault upon history

pauper thin echoes
loss and separation

words criss-crossing
galley after galley

Cyril Dabydeen

Offsprings

I am far away. Meanwhile
sisters and nieces
have ways of getting fat.
I return home after three
years.
    I notice a few strange
    ones around, holding on
    to frocks, skirts.
I take them up in my arms.
Mothers remind them never to forget.
Always remember him.
Some storehouse of affection perhaps.
They do not understand.
    I will return again
    after another three years
    expecting more strange faces.
I take a few pictures this time.
Occasionally will look at them.
Show friends once in a while.
Alone now, I mull over events –
thinking, with what expression
shall they greet me, how shall
I perform next?

Cyril Dabydeen

We Are The Country

Heart's throb
goes beyond words
goes beyond the sea's wild limit

I watch the torrid
shape of the world
from this distance
heart aflame
imagining
a watery respite
blood beating still

we are one
with the sea
and land
enduring all

locked in
pulsating
saved
from withdrawal

land again –
we are the country
inhabiting us
while we breathe.

Cyril Dabydeen

Village

The village is a sprawled waste
where an old woman with gnarled hands
sweeps the floor under the house

Her grandson squints at the sun
collecting cobwebs from the remnants
of her ramshackle heart

Here the vagrants daily conspire
to capture the moon and hold her ransom
to beckon the sun into oblivion

& the old woman sensing this
mutters a warning – fearing
the fate of the incorrigible young

She wonders about him collecting
jewels for his dungheap
outshining the stars
setting his heart ablaze

& she dreams of a darkening
time when they will both
be watching the fugitives
on the run

Mother of Us All

Cyril Dabydeen

There was a shrillness about Auntie that often echoed throughout our house. Sometime she would stamp her feet and rage even more than my mother. The latter was the quiet type, but they were both of a kind in strange ways which took my long growing up to find out.

Auntie could really scold – there was none like her in the village. We talked about this, sometimes in hushed tones, but always with dread; and when she scolded we ran as far away from her as we could. But I was growing older each day, and recalcitrant stirrings began to awaken in me. Auntie sensed this; she knew now that I'd wait for her to appear close by, and she knew that I'd suddenly spring away as she drew within arm's reach. I trusted my two legs to carry me away from her. Auntie shouted after me, "I will get you! Wait an' see!"

From a safe distance I laughed. Auntie reddened considerably. I knew she'd go to my mother; I knew exactly what she'd say.

"See that son of yours...see how he jeers!" My mother should remain quiet, thinking.

"He needs a good scolding," said Auntie. "You should... you really should scold him!" Her voice would peter out into an incoherent stammer. My mother's lips twitched; and finally she'd say, "Maybe you should leave him alone. We were just like them... growin' up too..." My mother's ways baffled Auntie as they did me sometimes.

I guess the heat made us behave the way we did. In the tropics it's always hot, sometimes unbearably so. Sometimes I'd look at magazines with people skiing down ice-slopes from high hills and mountains. How I'd long to be one of them, wearing heavy, yet attractive clothes that were like costumes. I'd dream about this at night: in the darkness I was white, the whiteness of wool about me; everywhere, even as I squandered my time day-dreaming as well.

My mother would come up to me, quietly, unexpectedly, saying: "You must behave."

"But I do behave."

"Your Auntie... you must have respect."

"I always have respect."

Resigned, my mother walked away. Once more I imagined hurtling

down an ice-capped mountain at tremendous speed as I was
propelled by a fierce, uncomprehending force that glinted like the
sun on the tips of the ice everywhere. At home the same sun was
bearing down on me, making me dizzy. I saw Auntie passing by,
looking at me with a slight grimace: she always carried a grimace.
"You," she began, "wait an' see." I laughed. Auntie scowled
heavily. "Yes, wait an' see!" she muttered more loudly now.

The other children – nieces and nephews (two were my brothers) –
heard this. They began to mutter in a chorus, "Wait an' see" in
further admonishment.

I laughed hilariously. They laughed too. Auntie, from a distance,
scowled again, her teeth glinting white in the sun. My mother, still in
her shadow, waited, pondering, dreamy, her eyelids making quick
butterfly wings against the looming eucalyptus shrub surrounding our
house. A lone hisbiscus flower as large as a vase hung pendulant. I
breathed heavily as a mild wind blew. From across the Atlantic, the
heavenly trade-winds tempered the heat. Everyone breathed heavily,
in unison, like an organised accompaniment. Auntie smiled. My
mother's face dimpled and cracked: she remained emotionless. I felt
she was experiencing our thrill, our delight. Deep stoicism was her
way of coping with the world, her way of understanding. Only I knew
this now – and when I thought about ice-slopes, about coming down
with dive bomber speed, I'd think about her, watching me from afar,
and smiling, praising – being hearty. "You've done it! Done it!"

Our family remained like this for years. Auntie became mottled
along her ears and forehead. My mother forged on with inside
grimaces, inside pain. We watched their suffering. In storms, Auntie
howled like a baboon and grimaced with the thunder and lighting that
criss-crossed our village. Her mouth opened and closed, dripping
with fulsome rain. I listened to the constant pitter patter at nights as
the raindrops pounded on the galvanized zinc topped roof of our
ramshackle house. I waited for ice-slopes to intermingle in the mind:
everything white, white. Then it was sun again, and I meandered on
in the squelchy mud which caked around my feet. I re-entered the
house, furtive.

Auntie's admonishing glare.

"Go an' clean your feet!"

I obeyed.

My mother, looking out from the window, mirrored the horizon in
her eyes. She watched me wiping my feet. Then she looked away at
the trees. I remembered my father jumping down from a guava tree,

and lashing out at her in his fitful rage – he like a magician, himself a trick, appearing and disappearing in her life when least expected.

I waved to my mother.

She hardly waved back. Only signs of mechanical breathing.

And in her eyes, the words – "You must behave...!"

The other children followed me; I was the eldest. They took orders one moment. Another, they jeered and howled. They flew through windows and doors in temper – tantrums. We were real pests, and Auntie was always there, ready to intimidate, often succeeding.

The older I grew the more I watched the relationship between my mother and Auntie. Maybe, the latter, more than my mother, wanted us to grow up well behaved children.

But we were full of energy – we didn't want to be contained. We continued to clamber through windows and hurl through doors. We continued to jeer and create havoc in the interchanging seasons of sun and rain in the tropics, in the prodigal display of thunder and lighting in our lives.

Yet in the dead of night our fears were livid: there were palpable ghosts everywhere. Sometimes fears of reptiles, anacondas in particular that could secretly coil under our beds and wait to uncoil in dreams. Lizards, too, their transparent limbs scrawling patterns against the window panes, haunting us.

We'd cover our faces with blankets, we'd open our eyes in the dark and whisper our fears.

Auntie in the next room would knock against the wall. We'd think it was the devil coming alive. This was Auntie scolding. We knew she wanted to frighten us, and we imagined her a sorceress.

Suddenly another methodic thudding against the wall close to our beds.

Who?

We'd wait with bated breath. Was it really Auntie? Doubt assailed us. We held our breath. We felt defenceles, trapped by the dark. We kept hoping that the thudding wouldn't continue. But it did. Thud-thud-thud.

We looked at each other with fear in our faces; we cringed and drew the blankets closer to our eyes. We breathed more heavily – we could hear each other's fears. As the eldest, I felt now was the time to show leadership, courage. But I also felt fear: the eerie dark was alive with unnatural sounds.

A faint, funereal howl. Was Auntie really playing such a trick on us?

"It's nothing," I'd whisper to the others huddling around me, my voice weakening. "It's just her..."

But the others were panicking. One was crying, another sniffling. "It's her... it's her...!" My sudden impatience. I caught myself trembling.

We'd wait still, we'd be quiet, and remain sombre. Auntie would know that she was having an effect on us for our deadly silence was what she wanted, a sign we were scared. And, lying awake, or half asleep, we'd be thinking of a heavy shadow with intimidating strides stepping out among us; and with fear we kept waiting for the worst in our lives. Sleep saved us from the continuing assault of our imagination.

Auntie's face in glee. She turned around in the kitchen. My mother stood stationary before the earthen fireside, putting in wood chopped in two-foot long pieces from time to time. We remained huddled in a corner.

"So you're behaving now," Auntie began.

No answer.

My mother looked steadfastly at the fire which began to rage fiercely. Her face was etched in livid colours. Auntie continued to smile.

"So you're behaving,"she repeated in the midst of the glare which appeared to envelop the kitchen where we sometimes gathered for meals.

Auntie looked pleased.

My mother turned around once, then immediately looked into the fire again, moving closer and putting another log into it.

I also looked at the fire; the glare had faces. I saw the face of my father appearing and disappearing. Now he was the one who was scowling, grimacing. My mother continued poking the fire, violently – almost in a frenzy. I saw the tense ribbed veins on her hand.

Then my stomach growled. One of my nephews felt the same stirrings. He looked at me with a forced smile. The others noticed and began smiling too despite the fear of the previous night on the faces.

Auntie came closer to me. "So you're still the same eh?" She was scolding again, but without her usual grimace. She too was mild, her voice almost a whisper. My mother turned around once more; the fire immediately appeared to die down. She handed us plates with flat bread, the customary fare. We ate quickly while they both looked at us with satisfied grins.

My mother said to Auntie, "It's good that they eat."

Auntie mumbled a response, her own silence.

My mother added, "You see, they must be strong."

Auntie – quickly – "An' they must behave."

I looked at each of them from time to time, chewing slowly. They looked at us with appraising eyes. Then my mother's smile. Auntie smiled too. They were both looking at me and I felt fully grown at that moment; somehow I felt nourished by their words and attention. I swallowed quickly. The other nieces and nephews, looking at us, also swallowed quickly.

I nodded, an understanding of myself. My mother turned once more to the fire. Auntie blinked; in the darkness of her face, in the brownness of her skin, I briefly noticed my own paleness. As I looked at her, and in my mother's turn around once more, I sensed blood rapidly coursing through my body. Individual bones became rigid against my flesh. I became aware of my intensely beating heart: I wondered about my occasional frenzy and the frenzy of all the others. And I imagined my father and mother also in frenzy. Again I swallowed. This time, gulping down, my throat was a knot, I coughed.

Auntie began laughing.

All the others began laughing too.

Only my mother, against the brightening fire once again, stood rigidly, immobilely, her eyes livid, but expressionless, looking at me. And in her I could see my true self: I understood that deep inside me I nurtured a passion which I couldn't fully articulate, which lay hidden beneath my skin, coursing through my blood, subsisting in every crevice of my flesh and bones.

Cent and Jill

Rooplall Monar

Every time Christmas season approaching me does always remember one particular Friday gone back when me was a small boy going to estate two-storey white, red and colour pay-office.

This Friday self, last day befo' school shut for the Christmas season, been fall one year after they crown Elizabeth Queen in England and since then we had was to chant "God save the Queen" every morning instead of "God save the King", and then after we praying "O Lord grant this day our daily bread", we singing "Rule Britannia, rule the waves, Britons never shall be slaves..."

Me tell you, is every manjack singing hymns and Christmas carols while Headmaster Williams swaying he cane on the stage with he eyes close as though he conducting one music choir. And don't talk how the chorus does raise high as though it want rip out the rusty roof zinc which does rattle whenever hard breeze blow, while Smallie and Bertie in the back bench does mimic Headmaster, when Teacher Johnson attention focus on stage. And don't talk how Smallie and Bertie voice rusty and hoarse; true, it sounding like when you rubbing old rusty tin on concrete. And them picknie in fourth standard can't laugh or mock else is baker-dozen if Teacher Johnson only see, or baker-dozen and kneel-down if Headmaster Willams see.

Too beside, you can't report that Smallie and Bertie does mock Headmaster during hymn-singing, else if you ain't gat Saltfish or Rommel fo friend, prepare to take blows afternoon time from Smallie and Bertie if them a get one benching from Headmaster or Teacher Johnson. So pardna, though Smallie and Bertie and myself thick like konky, still me too does stifle me laugh in me throat like coal soon as Smallie and Bertie voice start to roar like rusty zinc.

Well, the week befo' the Friday reach, them picknie inside light-light, as though they could fly like bird, specially when them mind flash on them fancy sweetie and cent and jill which they does scramble-up in Big Manager yard on that last Friday afternoon befo' school close, just like when dog does fight among fo food which been a throw to them from verendah-top, while the Missie giggling.

And once them picknie getting sweetie and cent and jill, they ain't care bout the bruise-up and kick-up and push-down they does get during the scrambling. Some time fight does break-out, but is all in the fun once Big Manager Missie and them other manager Missie throwing sweetie and cent and jill.

Happen so the Friday reach. Soon as picknie reach in school yard, so is hustling and bustling. Some big boys start bet among themself which one among them gon collect the most sweetie and cent and jill. But two years now, Smallie and Bertie does always win the bet. True, they does collect more not only because them is ruffian but them is real bully. So them boys can't make the side. So the bet does only take place among Soto, Sonaboy and them pinnie-winnie boys like Dunkoo and Teeth.

This time them girl like Biban, Finey and Joan done know that, even if they ain't scramble fo sweetie and cent and jill, they gon still get. You see them boys been like them, and Saltfish and Smallie does always tease them girl, saying how they t'ick and luscious like flower, and that when them girl grow big, Saltfish and Smallie gon marry them, soon as they join the estate mule-gang. You see, in them days the estate was the world and them young boy ambition was to work in estate. Well, whenever them girl smile back, Saltfish and Smallie does believe all to Gawd them girl in love with them, and this belief does turn Saltfish and Smallie crazy fo scramble up sweetie and cent and jill, never mind the bruise-up and kick-up.

Morning time now, soon as Headmaster Williams ride-in school yard, every picknie come quiet, and about two minute after, school call-in, bang bang bang... and all them picknie line up according to they class while teacher counting them head to head with tamarind rod. Then Headmaster signal from the platform and all ahwe picknie start march in school like soldier, going to we respective class. When headmaster ring bell, cling cling cling, school come quiet instantly; even if one pin been drop down you could hear.

"Now children, you are going to the Administrative Manager's yard to sing carols and be given sweets, and I want you to behave accordingly." Headmaster talk on stage while he swaying he cane as though he preparing to bench some picknie. This time he eye straight in fourth standard back bench. And don't talk how Smallie and Bertie getting cold-sweat. They know Headmaster watching at them. Every teacher and school picknie know Smallie and Bertie is mischiefman, out of school or in school self. But don't matter how much time Headmaster warn or bench Smallie and Bertie, it make no difference. True, like badness is in they blood. And even all the licks they getting from the ole man self with soke-rope couldn't beat out the badness.

Well, when Headmaster done speechify, teacher start roll-call. After that, Headmaster silence the school, cling, cling, cling, pick-up he cane, close he eye and start: "Now sing after me..." and is carol after carol singing while Headmaster leading and directing as though he one lost blindman. Meanwhile Teacher Johnson and Urmilla eye like cat on them picknie. Even if you ain't want sing self, yuh bound fo do. And don't matter how yuh try fo show you face serious, it still breaking in smile, while you one hand done hold you belly fo keep down the laugh soon as Smallie and Bertie voice join in the chorus.

But this time Smallie and Bertie face more serious than you one, while they eye moving from Headmaster, who monkeying like ballet-dancer on stage, to them girls who watching Teacher Urmilla and wishing they could talk Englishify and red they lip like she.

After carol singing, Headmaster stop and open he eye as though he come out from one trance, then he wipe he face with one white hankerchief, smile, and say: "Good, children." All ahwe feel like one heavy load drop off we head, and some ahwe smile. But the moment we attempt to sit down, Headmaster say: "Now, come on, children, after me, 'London bridge is falling down, falling down, falling down...Rule Britannia, Rule the waves, Britons never shall be slaves...'"

We gnashing we teeth like when you crushing rockstone, while sweat bungle-up all under we armpits and between we toes. Meanwhile Teacher Urmilla and Johnson fanning theyself with exercise book as though they feel hot, and they face turn sour like lime when Headmaster eye surveying them picknie, but every time Headmaster watch them, the face break in one smile like when creek water ripple.

By the time we finish singing "God Save the Queen", eleven o'clock reach, and don't talk how them picknie vex, never mind they imagining the sweetie and cent and jill. Well after school call-in one o'clock time, every picknie face brim with expectation. After Headmaster done announce that school gon re-open such an such a date after the Christmas holiday, and after he done send home them small picknie between lil ABC and third standard, he shout from the stage, "Get ready to marsh to the Administrative Manager's yard", as though we is a pack of mule and must jump to attention any time Headmaster roar, just like how he and Teacher Urmilla and Johnson does jump to attention whenever Father-Manager enter school, and we had to stand up and say, "Good day, sir," as though Father-Manager is Gawd and ahwe is the servant. But in today school, me children say all them mimicry and slavish attitude cut out since this country get freedom.

Well, bout three minute after headmaster and teacher fix we in two row inside school yard, where the sun ready to kill you with hotness, me hear the sugar factory going chuk chuk chuk... and see the thick-thick black and blue smoke coming out the chimney and sailing over canefield side. And was heat to kill fo sure when we step on the red-brick road which curve like snake and end up in Big Manager yard. You see during them days we didn't have shoes and sacks like today school childredn. Eh-eh, we was barefoot, so every time we foot drop on the brick which hot-hot, we feel like cane-stump boring we foot-bottom or baboon pimpla chuk chukking it.

This time them picknie craning they head fo see if Big Manager Missie and other Missie on the verandah when they enter Big Manager yard, which look like one different world. Eh-eh, if you see them nice-nice flower and pave-in drive-way, and the grass mown level as though you could sleep on it, while Ismael and Routie, the gardener, bending low and tending the flower plant as though them flower plant is egg. Most time them old and feeble and shaking like leaf when they walking, but soon as cookie Mabel shout at them as though she is Big Manager Missie, Ismael and Routie come to life, though you could hear they bone going crack-crack just like dry bamboo in hot sun.

"Order, children," Headmaster shout while Teacher Johnson and Urmilla placing we in row again. This time you in riddle for know where Teacher Johnson and Urmilla summon up all this vigour, and moving like athlete when they know them Missie watching them.

And pardna, me could remember when them white Missie been look like fairy whenever they smile while they furee-furee hair been look like when fowl does set. And they lip red like cherry and they look real tender, but me ain't know how they been go look if they been wukking like me daddy and mumma in backdam just fo three-four dollar when week up.

Well, every time ahwe done sing one carol, them Missie up in the verandah clapping, while ahwe who stand-up on the lawn like soldier serious wonder fo know what good them Missie been do in they previous life for live in so big house now with nice yard, servant, and na have to sweat in backdam through rain or sun even if they sick like ahwe parents...

This time the hot sun dripping we body with sweat while Headmaster, Teacher Johnson and Urmilla wiping they face steady-

steady. By time we done sing the British national anthem and chant "Long Live the Queen", we feel as though we strength left we body, but when we think bout the sweetie and cent and jill, we inside come lively.

After Headmaster deliver one short speech, everybody shout "Hip hip, hurray..." then them two manager Missie start throw down handful sweetie and cent and jill while they giggling as though we is dog or carrion crow who gat fo fight fo the cent and jill and sweetie. And you should see the scrambling and fall-down and bruise-up while fancy fancy sweetie and cent and jill dropping down like rain and them manager Missie giggling and ahwe school picknie scrambling as though cent and jill is ahwe life.

This time Smallie and Saltfish like hog, True-true, if you see how they scrambling and fulling-up they pocket and butting who in they way, eh-eh, you been think was bachanaal. "Hip hip hurray...", sweetie and cent and jill dropping down like rain from them Missie hand while them picknie behaving as though they want kill each other and them Missie giggling just like how in them picture them Roman uses to giggle and shout hurrah hurrah while them slave and gladiator killing each other in the arena.

When me na able fo scramble fo more sweetie and cent and jill, me stand one side and watch the spectacle. And then it dawn on me true-true that the estate mule and oxen receiving better treatment and care and food than the sugar worker them, who punishing generation after generation, night and day, to make sure sugar profitable, and believe is they duty as the pandit and immam does say.

And too beside, is ahwe parents sweat does fatten the Manager and Missie and they treating we worst then mule. True, water been settle in me eye and me been wander for know what wrong thing ahwe parents been done fo suffer so much, and what good thing them Manager and Missie been do fo live king-life?

And when me na able fo bear the spectacle no more, me slip out and tell myself that Gawd gat favourite among people, but whenever ahwe parents eye-open it gon be one different story, and they might see Queen and kiss-me-ass Manager and Missie in different light. And if me didn't plunge in the canal by the Turn fo cool-off me passion, me been go explode like bomb.

Massala Maraj

Rooplall Monar

Was donkey years gone back. Maraj uses to wuk in the sugar estate spray-gang, which mean himself and them other men uses to spray the young sugarcane which does get worm and scaapian and ting. And the work bin going lil good for Maraj but back a he mind he always saying that he is a brahmin and backdam wuk na so prappa for he caste. But he can't ask Big Manager for another wuk.

You see, is the third transfer he get. First he uses to cut cane for years, then he was a farkman and then a watchman, but none a de wuk bin a suit am. But now Maraj want one other wuk, and fo weeks he thinking, thinking, how he gon approach Big Manager, and what excuse he gon tell him, so he could get one different wuk next week.

Then one Wednesday night what you think happen? Eh-eh, this Maraj jump-out he sleep as though he get one bad dream. But is not true. Is the wuk problem he just solve. Then he drop back pon de bed and talk in he mind: "Big Manja wife like coolie dal-purri an massala fow-curry with good pepper an onion an garlic, he-he, me gon talk with Big Manja fo get me one next wuk. Ha-Ha boy, yuh tink Maraj down here? memba me one smark brahmin...memba?"

And before them sugar worker can open they eye the second time to watch the sun on Sunday morning, Maraj, looking like one real pundit in he white dhoti and kurta, done find heself in Big Manager yard calling for Big Manager Missie long time.

This time you can't stap you mout' from wata. True-true, the massala fowl-curry and dal-purri smelling so high that even them deadman in the estate hospital mortuary could wake up too.

When Big Manager Missie taste Maraj dal-purri and massala fowl-curry she nearly bite off piece of she finger. Good thing Maraj tell she: "Tek yuh time Missie. Don't rush the brush. Is every week Maraj bringing dal-purri an massala fowl-curry fo yuh." Otherwise, Missie been turn dumb just like Jackoo who prappa peep them girls while they bathing in Overbridge canal, but he couldn't talk.

But the dal-purri and massala fowl-curry been too delicious so Missie couldn't control she tongue. Minutes after she tell Maraj that she never taste dal-purri and massala fowl-curry so delicious since she and she husband come on this plantation. Then she offer Maraj money, but Maraj fold he two hand in front like he one pundit, and say that he more than glad Missie please with the food, and that alone value more than money.

Afterward is every Sunday morning Maraj does hop-and-drop in the Senior Staff Compound like one second manager. And not one overseer dare question he, because they know he going straight to Big Manager Missie. Too beside, Maraj singing Hindi bhajan sweet-sweet like honey.

This time the massala fowl-curry and dal-purri want stifle you nose. Is smelling real high while you mouth want to water and you tongue going cha cha cha. Sometimes them overseer who playing games in the mess-hall na bin able a control they tongue, and is then they does offer Maraj money for he dal-purri and massala fowl-curry. But Maraj telling them straight in they face that it prepare special for Big Manager Missie.

True-true, Maraj ain't care one raas who vex or please. He know them overseer can't do he nothing because they know he come one of Big Manager Missie special.

Meanwhile, Maraj feeling nice-nice that even when he bathing by the wood-ghat by the black water canal late in the afternoon he singing Hindi bhajan sweet-sweet like sugar. True-true, you gon think is a service you hearing in one Hindu temple. And nearly every night when neighbour going to bed they hearing Maraj singing bhajan after bhajan, and they feeling so nice that even they don't know when they eye come heavy with sleep.

This time Maraj thinking for over three week how to tell Big Manager he want one nex wuk. Sometime when he brain run hot, and it can't think anymore, he does curse in he mind. But on this Sunday morning while he going to Big Manager Missie with the dal-purri and massala fowl-curry wrap up in lotus leaf, he face look bright and he skin smelling sweet as though he bathe in attar. And soon as them overseer spot he in the senior staff compound, he singing bhajan: "Govinda jayah jayah Gopala jayah jayah... Radha O maniwaree Radha O jai jai..."

When he see Big Manager Missie in the yard tending the flower plant, dress in short pant and jersey, he fold he hand and say: "Ram ram, Missie." Then he give she the dal-purri and massala fowl-curry. When he and Missie done chit-chat he clear he throat and say: "Missie, yuh know me getting ole, and me tink me na able with backdam wuk. Tell Manja fo get one next wuk an Shree Ram Bhagwan gon bless yuh..."

Eh-eh pardna, what you think happen? Maraj dal-purri and

massala fowl-curry do the trick. And now you can't talk too hard with Maraj at all. True-true, you gat to think twice, else you lose you wuk. Remember now Maraj wukking in Big Manager house, and in the Senior Staff Compound as carpenter because he been tell Big Manager that he know the wuk good.

And some days when he ain't got plenty work he preparing dal-purri and massala fowl-curry right in Big Manager kitchen. And anytime Big Manager invite he big friends them from Georgetown, or from them other sugar estate, is Maraj dal-purri and massala fowl-curry they knacking down after they take them scotch. And is every week Big Manager friends coming, and guess what is bringing them. Eh-eh, is Maraj dal-purri and massala fowl-curry.

But they got one saying: never trust one brahmin too much, otherwise he make you run pauper. And is true-true, Gaad, because Maraj is no exception. What you think happening? Maraj hand come 'fast' and Big Manager ain't know one damn thing. Pardna is every afternoon Maraj tiefing nail and putty. But he smart, he ain't tiefing plenty so you could suspect. Eh-eh, he using he common sense. Then one afternoon he take home varnish and sandpaper. This cause he wife to get mad.

"But Maraj," she tell he, "suppose Big Manja cook or de sweeper see yuh an tell Big Manja, what yuh gone tell Manja? Yuh ain't get lil shame. Nuh make yuh eye big. Tief, but nuh tief plenty fo get ketch."

"Chut," Maraj say. "You chupid woman. How cooky an sweepa see me, when me put putty in me saucepan an cover it with two-three biscuit. An me put lil-bit lil-bit nail in me langoti, an varnish in me green water bottle, an say me tekking home nice cool ice-water for me Marajin drink? Chupid woman, yuh. Think Maraj na gat sense? Maraj is smart brahmin."

Now Maraj logie come like one hardware shop. Anybody who want nail or putty or varnish going straight to Maraj. And Maraj selling the stuff far cheaper than them shopkeeper. And everybody believe Maraj getting them stuff from estate for lil-an-nothing. You see, they know that Maraj is the Senior Staff Compound carpenter, and too beside, he and Big Manager Missie thick-thick like conky.

This time Maraj tiefing like ass and like everybody blind like bat. And you got to be real smart to catch Maraj. But they always say Moon does run until daylight catch it, and is true story. Eh-eh pardna, Maraj push he hand too far, and it get burn.

What you think he did? One bright afternoon, after he made certain Big Manager cook and the sweeper and the Missie engaged elsewhere, he drag-out two timber log from Big Manager backyard and push them in the canal, which run aside Big Manager yard. About half-past four he send home he working clothes after he done change into one floursack langoti. When he made sure all obstacle clear he jump in the canal with one long rope. Then he stoop down and strap the two log together with one end of the rope and tie round he waist with the other end. And Maraj damn-well know greenheart don't float, so he know he safe. But the problem come when Maraj ready to pull them log. Don't matter how much he trying, them log ain't moving according to Maraj method. After Maraj loose six-seven curse, he decide to do something else.

You ever see people shying for patwau fish in one muddy trench? How they ducking in the water to pick up mud, then they raise-up and shy the mud in front dem as dem a walk? And if they spot bubble where the mud drop, they ducking and feeling for fish? Well is just so Maraj pulling them timber: schipp shy...schipp shy, schipp... and you who walking on the red-brick road gon believe all to Gaad this Maraj shying for fish, so you won't worry to watch he the second time.

And while Maraj going schipp shy, schipp shy... he talking in he mind how he is smart brahmin. Sometime he smiling by heself. And you who seeing he, gon believe Maraj tearing ass with patwau, and might want cuss-up yourself just because you ain't shying fo fish.

Well, when Maraj reach by the turn, not far from he logie, he want drop dead. If you been cut he, not one drop blood you been go find in he pinnie-winnie bony body. Yes, soon as he raise he head, he and Big Manager eye turn four. True, was Big Manager and Buddy John standing on the red brick road, running parallel with the canal Maraj inside.

"Afternoon, boss," Maraj tell Big Manager, and acting like he still feeling fo fish.

"Good afternoon, Maraj," Big Manager answer, but he serious just like when cow bruk rope. Then he say: "Maraj, I want to see you right away. Come out the canal. I am waiting."

Soon as Maraj hear that he breath want cut, and like he get belly-wuk. This time big-big sweat dropping down he face; all de time he fumbling in the water as them sweat dropping blop, blop...

"What happen, Maraj? Come out of the canal. I am waiting for you."

Maraj like he get one shock. He jump out of the canal blashai like one bush-dog, with one end of the rope still wrap-round he waist, while the next end leading to them log in the canal. And pardna, if you been there you been go buss-down with one prappa laugh. Maraj langoti been drop down, and all he private and pinnie-winnie behind showing. When Big Manager see that he eye brighten up, then he shake he head and say: "You are a thief, Maraj. The sweeper was right. She did see you pulling two logs from my yard."

Eh-eh pardna, Maraj think he dead sametime. You see Big Manager was like Gaad in the estate, and whatever he say is law. Well, Maraj start beg now: "Ow boss, ow boss."

"Come and see me tomorrow morning in my office," Big Manager tell Maraj, Then he and Buddy John, the estate ranger, left.

When Maraj reach and tell he wife, she want get mad. She start cuss he up-an-down, up-an-down until Maraj get damn vex, and dash down one prappa slap pon she. She shut she mouth sametime and sulk in one corner. As to Maraj, he cussing Big Manager sweeper all the cuss he know.

Next morning Maraj look ole an bruk-up. Is whole night he studying what Big Manager gon do wid he. In the office he begging Big Manager like one picknie; still Big Manager send he back to the backdam.

Now two-three weeks pass, and Big Manager Missie feeling like she tongue miss something. And don't matter who she get to prepare dal-purri and massala fowl-curry, it can't beat the Maraj taste. Even Big Manager feeling the same way, but he ain't telling the Missie.

After another two week, big Manager Missie can't bear it na more. She tongue does water when she mind flash at Maraj. And like the massala fowl-curry still lingering in she nose. Then she brain rocking like a see-saw because Big Manager birthday is next Friday, and she desire if Big Manager could enjoy one proper dal-purri and massala fowl-curry for lunch.

One bright afternoon she send call for Maraj when Big Manager gone out, and she and Maraj chit-chat awhile. After that Maraj glad like ass. True-true, morning and afternoon when he bathing in the canal he singing Hindi bhajan. But this time he singing rapturously with he eye close, as though he mind focus at Shree Krishna Bhagwan.

Bam... Day for Big Manager birthday reach. Nine o'clock in the morning, where you think Maraj was? Eh-eh, right inside Big Manager office waiting on he. And what you think Maraj have? Is dal-purri on massala fowl-curry wrap up in lotus leaf.

Soon as Big Manager come in he office, Maraj don't hesitate. He give Big Manager the parcel and say this is fo he birthday. Big

Manager can't talk. The smell from the dal-purri and massala fowl-curry want stifle he nose. And when he did talk, he mouth watering. He compliment Maraj and say he gon reconsider he decision about Maraj transfer.

When Maraj left Big Manager office he singing bhajan like one saddhu until he reach he logie. When he see he marajin wife, he laugh and say: "Eh-eh, marajin. If me boy didn't know fo prepare dal-purri an massala fowl-curry, soontime me been go dead with backdam wuk. Is gat luck me father show me fo cook dal-purri an massala fowl-curry with plenty garlic an onion an spice an massala. Gal marajin, Maraj still one smart brahmin."

And next Monday morning, who you think you seeking in the Senior Staff Compound? Eh-eh, is Maraj self, and he back on the job as carpenter. After then Maraj turn one big thing in the estate. He start prepare dal-purri and massala fowl-curry fo all them whiteman and them Missie living in the compound. And is then people start call he Massala Maraj. And because he get some authority in the estate, and he living easy without sweating, he stop thief.

Diwali

Janice Shinebourne

This is a short extract from Janice Shinebourne's second novel 'The Last English Plantation' (Peepal Tree Press, 1987). The extract is the short, closing chapter of the novel.

The novel contains 16 chapters which describe two dramatic weeks in the life of a 12-year-old Indo-Chinese girl, June Lehall, in the year 1956, in British Guiana (which became Guyana in 1966). The novel is set on an isolated, remote sugar plantation. It portrays the beginning of the process of destablisation which the country underwent in the 1950s, a central feature of which was an anti-Indian propaganda war which climaxed in violent scenes at Wismar in 1964 and the downfall of the country's first Prime Minister, Cheddi Jagan.

The anti-Indian implications of that time are focussed intimately through its effects on June and her family. An important contrast is made in the novel between a situation on the plantation where the pressure of plantation life actually throws people of different races and cultures together in times of greatest need, and a contrasting situation in the extremely class conscious, urban setting ruled by a European elite where race and colour are the most readily available indices of class and status and it is more difficult if not impossible to cross racial and cultural boundaries. This same theme is echoed in the author's first novel 'Timepiece' where different races are portrayed participating in African funeral rites and Indian wedding rites, and where women of different races and cultures act as surrogate mothers to each other's children. There is a sense in both these novels of grief for a fleeting experience of unity which seemed to disappear from British Guiana after 1964, but there is also a sense in Janice Shinebourne's writing of a need to confront frankly the extreme racial and political crises in the lives of Guianese in the late 1950s and early 1960s. This is a theme which she continues to explore in her third novel 'Victory', which she is working on currently, a novel which spans the pre and post independence period: 1961-1974.

There are two parallel climaxes in 'The Last English Plantation'. They include a militaristic confrontation between striking workers and the combined forces of the occupying British army and the local police; coinciding with June's revolt against her mother's pressures to deny their Indian identity and gain entry for the family, through June's

education, into the new class-conscious Guianese middle class. June
escapes to her surrogate grandmother, a devout aged Hindu woman
who reassures her of the integrity of her self. The novel closes with the
following extract, entitled 'Diwali'.

June did not see Ralph again until Diwali. She had gone back to
school by then and was grappling with the learning of British history,
geography, and English language and literature, although the British
were beginning to leave the country and talk about the coming of the
Russians continued. She was becoming accustomed to the ritual of
bicycling away from Canefields every morning, accustomed to
journeying to New Amsterdam and returning to New Dam every
afternoon.

When she cycled to and from the village she was part of the
movement between town and country. It was a continual movement
of people which did not allow her to feel alone, a movement which
she knew now did have a beginning and end, a movement which the
journey was witness to day after day. If in the end she did not have to
remember the lessons which she learnt in the classroom day after day
she would be sure to remember the movement of people of which she
had been a part. The habit of memory of her daily journeys became
her own discipline, separate from her parents, from the school and
the politics of the country.

It was the darkest night of November which was always chosen for
Diwali, so that the symbolism of the lights was felt more intensely,
and the meaning of exile and return deepened. In the afternoon she
was allowed to visit Nani where the children gathered to make diyas
with mud gathered from the backdam, coconut oil and strings of
cotton. As they made the diyas and set them out to dry in the sun
Nani told the story of Ram's exile in the forest,. As she recited the
story it seemed to lift her to another plane and she rolled the legend
off her tongue like a visionary, conjuring the mythical scenes so that
the children felt they were hearing them for the first time: the myth of
Indian kings, queens, princesses, princes, and the Indian empires of
Koshala and Sri Lanka; the movement of royal deities between the
celestial and earthly, between exile and return, their confrontations
with humanity and nature (sadhus, an army of monkeys, messenger
birds, the monumental battle between Hanuman the monkey god and
Ravna the demon king of Sri Lanka). The myth absorbed the
humiliations of their plantation existence and for one day they swept

and cleaned their houses as if they were cleaning away their own exile and its injuries in preparation for pretending tonight that they were transformed exiles, bearing the lights to light their own way on their patch of earth, that Lakshmi the goddess of prosperity and good luck would visit them that night and bless every lighted house. They would wear their best clothes, buy new pots, pay off all their debts, and exchange sweetmeats in the streets.

On this Diwali Cyrus and Lucille borrowed Mitch's car and took June to see the Corentyne for the first time. The Corentyne strip of road was better than Canefields'. There were larger houses in the crowded villages and along barren stretches of road where cattle grazed on flat land owned by one of the few powerful local families whose large houses were set so deep back on the horizon they were miniatures suspended between the sky and the land. Rose Hall was the main town on the Corentyne, not a colonial town like New Amsterdam but a sugar estate town, the only one of its kind, Cyrus explained. There were few handmade diyas and they were overshadowed by the strings of electric bulbs which framed the facade of the shops and houses. They arrived in the town as the lights came on, and with them, the jukeboxes, and the squibs and small fireworks let off by gangs of young men gathered outside the shops.

When they returned to New Dam the lights lit their way back to Mitch's. The diyas glowed the more brightly in the great darkness. The hurricane lamps did not need to be lit tonight. The lights were especially thick on the ground, along the paths, the bridges, the public road, culverts, and in the parapets. Every dark spot was searched out and a light placed there; it created a glow on the earth itself which seemed to suspend the people as they went to and fro with bowls of sweetmeat, and suspend the houses too. The myth of exile was alive.

She joined the children on the paths, running from house to house to replace the oil and wicks, racing each other to keep the lights alive and prolong the night. When their parents began to call them indoors and the last diya was refilled June found herself on Nani's landing which looked out across the whole village, the canefields behind, all the paths before. The lights traced and filled the circle of the village, lights on the rooftops, landings, windows, stairs and in every yard, on the ground everywhere. On this one night of the year the darkness was completely banished from New Dam and the power of the lights gave a feeling of hope and happiness which she felt the more for the feelings of loss and the dramas of this year.

SELECTED BIBLIOGRAPHY

1. A.H. Adamson. *Sugar Without Slaves* (Yale University Press, 1972)

2. F. Ambursley and R. Cohen, eds., *Crisis in the Caribbean* (Heinemann, 1983)

3. Ashton Chase, *A History of Trade Unionism in Guyana 1900-1961* (New Guyana Co. Ltd., Georgetown, 1964)

4. Malcolm Cross, *The East Indians of Guyana and Trinidad* (Minority Rights Group No. 13, London, 1973)

5. I.M. Cumpston, *Indians Overseas in British Territories* (Oxford University Press, 1953)

6. Leo A. Despres, *Cultural Pluralism and Nationalist Politics in British Guiana* (Chicago, 1967)

7. John La Guerre, ed., *Calcutta to Caroni: The East Indians of Trinidad* (University of the West Indies, Trinidad, 1985)

8. Cheddi Jagan, *The West on Trial* (Michael Jospeh, 1966)

9. Morton Klass, *East Indians in Trinidad: A Study of Cultural Persistence* (Columbia University Press, 1971)

10. K.O. Laurence, *Immigration into the West Indies in the 19th Century* (Caribbean Universities Press, 1971)

11. David Lowenthal, *West Indian Societies* (Oxford University Press, 1972)

12. Y.K. Malik, *East Indians in Trinidad: A Study in Minority Politics* (Oxford University Press, 1971)

13. Dwarka Nath, *History of Indians in Guyana* (London, 1975)

14. David Nicholls, 'East Indians and Black Power in Trinidad', in *Race*, XII, 4, 1971

15. A & J Niehoff, *East Indians in the West Indies* (Milwaukee, 1960)

16. Peter Ruhomon, *History of the East Indians in British Guiana* (Georgetown, Guyana, 1947)

17. P. Saha, *The Emigrtion of Indian Labour 1834-1900* (Delhi, 1970)

18. High Tinker, *A New System of Slavery: The Export of Indian Labour Overseas 1880-1920* (Oxford University Press, 1974)

19. Donald Wood, *Trinidad in Transition* (Oxford University Press, 1968)

LIST OF CONTRIBUTORS

DAVID DABYDEEN, from Guyana, is lecturer in Caribbean Studies at the University of Warwick and Junior Research Fellow at Oxford University. He was educated at Cambridge and London Universities. His first book of poems, *Slave Song,* was awarded the 1984 Commonwealth Poetry Prize.

BRINSLEY SAMAROO, from Trinidad, took a BA and MA at Delhi University and obtained his Ph.D in History from London University. He has been teaching at the University of the Westindies since 1969 and was Head of the History Department between 1976-81. He is presently a Minister in the Office of the Prime Minister of Trinidad and Tobago, having served as leader of the Opposition in the Senate from 1981-86.

FRANK BIRBALSINGH teaches literature at York University, Canada and is author of several articles on Commonwealth Literature.

CYRIL DABYDEEN, from Guyana, is author of several volumes of poetry, short stories and novels. He lives in Canada where he is widely recognized as one of the leading Caribbean poets.

MAHADAI DAS is a graduate student at the University of Chicago. Her poems have appeared in Guyanese journals and anthologies.

SAHADEO DEBIPRASHAD and DOWLAT RAM BUDHRAM, formerly lecturers at the University of Guyana, now live in North America.

RAMESH DEOSARAN is Senior Lecturer in Sociology at the University of the Westindies and a Senator in the Parliament of Trinidad and Tobago.

KUSHA HARAKSINGH is Senior Lecturer in History at the University of the Westindies (Trinidad)

SANDEW HIRA, from Surinam, is presently researching Dutch colonial history in Holland where he now lives. He is the author of several articles on the Dutch Caribbean.

ARNOLD ITWARU teaches at York University, Canada. He is author of a collection of poems, *Shattered Songs,* (1982), and his poems and stories have appeared in several Canadian publications.

BASDEO MANGRU is a graduate of the University of Guyana where he was also a lecturer in History. He obtained his doctorate from London University and presently lives and works in the U.S.A.

ROOPLALL MONAR is a Guyanese poet and short story writer. His publications include *Backdam People* (stories) and *Koker* (poems), both published by the Peepal Tree press.

JEREMY POYNTING obtained his doctorate from the University of Kent for a pioneering dissertation on Indo-Caribbean literature. He is the founder of the Peepal Tree Press which specializes in Indo Caribbean writing. He is currently a Visiting Fellow at the University of Warwick, Centre for Caribbean Studies.

TYRON RAMNARINE lives and works in Kansas, U.S.A. He was previously lecturer in History at the University of Guyana.

SAM SELVON is one of the Caribbean's most distinguished novelists. He is Writer in Residence at the University of Calgary in Canada.

VERENE SHEPHERD, a graduate of the University of the Westindies, is doing a doctoral dissertation on Caribbean history at Cambridge University.

JANICE SHINEBOURNE, from Guyana, is a graduate of the University of Kent and author of two novels, both published by the Peepal Tree Press. She lives in England.

INDEX OF NAMES AND ORGANIZATIONS

A contemporary line drawing of a 'tadjah' from an historical postcard, Guyana, c 1906

Tadjah or Tazia was a Muslim festival which was celebrated in Guyana. It still survives in Trinidad, Surinam and to a lesser extent in Jamaica as the 'hosay' festival

Other titles by
Hansib Publishing

INDO-WESTINDIAN CRICKET
By Professor Frank Birbalsingh and
Clem Shiwcharan
ISBN: 1 870518 20 9 HB   PRICE: £7.95

THE SECOND SHIPWRECK:
INDO-CARIBBEAN LITERATURE
By Dr Jeremy Poynting
ISBN: 1 870518 15 2 PB   PRICE: £6.95

THE WEB OF TRADITION:
USES OF ALLUSION IN
V.S. NAIPAUL'S FICTION
By Dr John Thieme
ISBN: 1 870518 30 6 PB   PRICE: £6.95

BENEVOLENT NEUTRALITY:
INDIAN GOVERNMENT POLICY AND
LABOUR MIGRATION TO
BRITISH GUIANA 1854-1884
by Dr Basdeo Mangru
ISBN: 1 870518 10 1 HB   PRICE: £12.95

THE OPEN PRISON
By Angus Richmond
ISBN: 1 870518 25 X PB   PRICE: £4.95

COOLIE ODYSSEY
By Dr David Dabydeen
ISBN: 1 870518 01 2 PB   PRICE: £3.95

A READER'S GUIDE TO WESTINDIAN
AND BLACK BRITISH LITERATURE
By Dr David Dabydeen and
Dr Nana Wilson Tagoe
ISBN: 1 870518 35 7 PB   PRICE: £6.95

ESSAYS ON RACE, CULTURE
AND ENGLISH SOCIETY
By Dr Paul Rich
ISBN: 1 870518 40 3 PB   PRICE: £6.95

100 GREAT WESTINDIAN
TEST CRICKETERS
By Bridgette Lawrence and Reg Scarlett
ISBN: 1 870518 65 9 HB   PRICE: £10.95

BARRISTER FOR THE DEFENCE
By Rudy Narayan
ISBN: 09506664 2 4 PB   PRICE: £6.95

BOOK OF COMMONSENSE
Compiled by Neil Prendergast
PB   PRICE: £6.95

FROM WHERE I STAND
By Roy Sawh
ISBN: 0 9956664 9 1 PB   PRICE: £5.95

MY THOUGHTS, 2nd EDITION
By Pamela Ali
ISBN: 1 870518 06 3 PB   PRICE: £3.95

HOGARTH, WALPOLE AND
COMMERCIAL BRITAIN
By Dr David Dabydeen
ISBN: 1 870518 45 4 HB   PRICE: £15.95

THE GREAT MARCUS GARVEY
By Liz Mackie
ISBN: 1 870518 50 0 PB   PRICE: £4.95

THE CARIBBEAN: GUYANA,
TRINIDAD & TOBAGO,
BARBADOS, JAMAICA
By Steve Garner
ISBN: 1 870518 55 1 PB   PRICE: £6.95

GREAT FIGURES FROM THE
THIRD WORLD
By Liz Mackie and Steve Garner
ISBN: 1 870518 60 8 HB   PRICE: £11.95

SPEECHES BY ERROL BARROW
Edited by Yussuff Haniff
ISBN: 1 870518 70 5 HB   PRICE: £10.95

THIRD WORLD IMPACT
7th EDITION
Edited by Arif Ali
ISBN: 0 9506664 8 3 PB   PRICE: £9.95
ISBN: 0 9506664 8 3 HB   PRICE: £13.95

RASTA AND RESISTANCE
FROM MARCUS GARVEY TO
WALTER RODNEY
By Dr Horace Campbell
ISBN: 0 95066 645 5 PB   PRICE: £6.95
ISBN: 0 95066 645 5 HB   PRICE: £9.95